Slow Movies

Slow Movies

Countering the Cinema of Action

◆

IRA JAFFE

WALLFLOWER PRESS
LONDON & NEW YORK

A Wallflower Press Book
Published by
Columbia University Press
Publishers Since 1893
New York • Chichester, West Sussex
cup.columbia.edu

A complete CIP record is available from the Library of Congress

ISBN 978-0-231-16978-3 (cloth : alk. paper)
ISBN 978-0-231-16979-0 (pbk. : alk. paper)
ISBN 978-0-231-85063-6 (e-book)

Contents

In memory of Howard

Introduction

"We want a cinema that puts the brakes on, slows things down. What we have to start doing if we want to study film history and the aesthetics of film history is to look at how different filmmakers are taking this other path."

– David Bordwell, at a symposium in 2007 devoted to Béla Tarr's cinema[1]

"it is in stillness that one may be said to find true speed"

– Trinh T. Minh-ha, quoted in Karen Beckman and Jean Ma (eds), *Still Moving*[2]

Let me begin by citing one more comment relevant to this book's intent: "Slow Movies That Are Still Compelling", an *All Movie Talk* podcast in December 2006, noted that "many times the word 'slow' is used as a synonym for dull or boring, and certainly that is often an apt description, but we want to make a case for movies that work without speeding from one plot point to another". While the podcast's goals comported with the views of Bordwell and Trinh, its classification of two disparate films, *Tokyo Story* (Yasujiro Ozu, 1953) and *Raging Bull* (Martin Scorsese, 1980), as slow movies suggested that what is "slow", perhaps like what "works", is debatable. As I explore acclaimed slow movies made since 1984, the year of Jim Jarmusch's *Stranger Than Paradise*, my aim is to examine elements besides plot that make certain movies both slow and compelling – so compelling, in fact, as to warrant greater notice by the general public as well as by those who closely study film history and aesthetics. The approaches in recent slow movies to plot, character and emotion – and to stillness, motion, time and space – underscore aspects of contemporary existence rarely foregrounded in either popular or art films. These slow movies augment cinema's historic achievement in mirroring a wide range of humanity.

Movies of the last three decades that I am calling slow represent a style or disposition embraced by cinephiles around the world. Created by some of the finest film artists working today – in Argentina, China, Hungary, Iran, Portugal, Romania, Russia, Turkey and the United States – these movies have been hailed at Cannes, Berlin, Venice, Sao Paulo, Toronto, New York and other international film festivals as well as in the pages of leading film journals. Yet in the US and elsewhere, several of these movies and their directors remain largely unknown to the general public and even to many film students. While studies exist of individual directors of slow movies, some of whom, like Gus Van Sant, make "faster" films as well, no book has undertaken a critical examination of significant slow movies and their directors as a group. This study draws together several such movies and investigates their major artistic and philosophical interests. It explores what makes their form and content compelling as well as how they relate to slow films by earlier directors, including Ozu, Robert Bresson, Michelangelo Antonioni and Carl Theodor Dreyer, to which they are often compared. The study also touches on intersections of slow movies and writings by Gilles Deleuze, André Bazin, Bresson, Laura Mulvey and other analysts of film and culture.

The following directors and slow movies comprise the book's focus:

Jim Jarmusch (US): *Stranger Than Paradise* (1984) and *Dead Man* (1995)
Gus Van Sant (US): *Elephant* (2003)
Todd Haynes (US): *Safe* (1995)
Alexander Sokurov (Russia): *The Second Circle* (1990) and *Mother and Son* (1997)
Nuri Bilge Ceylan (Turkey): *Distant* (2002) and *Climates* (2006)
Cristi Puiu (Romania): *The Death of Mr. Lazarescu* (2005)
Cristian Mungiu (Romania): *4 Months, 3 Weeks and 2 Days* (2007)
Corneliu Porumboiu (Romania): *12:08 East of Bucharest* (2006)
Lisandro Alonso (Argentina): *Liverpool* (2008)
Pedro Costa (Portugal): *Ossos* (*Bones*) (1997)
Manoel de Oliveira (Portugal): *A Talking Picture* (2003)
Abbas Kiarostami (Iran): *Taste of Cherry* (1997) and *Five Dedicated to Ozu* (2003)
Jia Zhang-ke (China): *Still Life* (2006)
Béla Tarr (Hungary): *Werckmeister Harmonies* (2000) and *The Turin Horse* (2011)

To varying degrees, these movies are slow by virtue of their visual style, narrative structure and thematic content and the demeanour of their characters. With respect to visual style, the camera often remains unusually still in these films, and when it moves, as it does persistently in Béla Tarr's work, it generally moves quite slowly. Curtailed as well is physical motion *in front of* the camera. Furthermore, editing or cutting in slow movies tends to be infrequent, which inhibits spatio-temporal leaps and disruptions. Not only do long takes predominate, but long shots frequently prevail over close-ups. Consistent with these stylistic elements, which may distance and irritate the viewer, is the austere mise-en-scène: slow movies shun elaborate and dynamic decor, lighting and colour. Moreover, the main characters in these movies usually lack emotional, or at least expressive, range and mobility. Indeed, the characters' "flat", affect-less manner (a notion I draw from Fredric Jameson's analysis of postmodernism, even though slow movies often seem adamantly *pre*-modern) possibly sets these films apart from precursors such as Antonioni's *L'Avventura* (1960) and *Eclipse* (1962), both of which feature the highly emotive Monica Vitti, and Tarkovsky's *Stalker* (1980).[3] Further, a bit like slow-movie characters, the plot and dialogue in slow movies often gravitate towards stillness and death, and tend, in any case, to be minimal, indeterminate and unresolved. Complaints that "nothing is happening", prompted earlier in history by films directed by Antonioni, Andy Warhol and Chantal Akerman, paintings by Mark Rothko and Barnett Newman, and plays by Anton Chekhov and Samuel Beckett, arise anew regarding several of the slow movies explored in this book.

The cinematic traits sketched in the last paragraph bear on filmmaker and scholar Paul Schrader's study *Transcendental Style in Film: Ozu, Bresson, Dreyer* (1972), as when Schrader writes of a sense of privation and desolation conveyed in films by his three canonical directors partly as a result of constraints they impose on emotion, physical action, camera movement, cutting and mise-en-scène. In addition, however, Schrader often discerns in his transcendental films successful quests for spiritual grace, holiness and redemption such as rarely occur in contemporary slow movies, which tilt in a more secular and bleak direction. One would also hesitate to argue that in most contemporary slow movies worldly wisdom, if not spiritual grace, illumines the emptiness and desolation.

◆

"In all film there's the desire to capture the motion of life, to refuse immobility", says French filmmaker Agnès Varda,[4] and other filmmakers including Dziga Vertov have held similar views. Yet retarded motion and prolonged moments of stillness and emptiness distinguish contemporary slow movies. Such movies take place off the beaten track. Even when their locales are not entirely removed from urban commercial life, these movies depict an emotional and geographic sphere relatively free of the distractions Walter Benjamin, among others, found characteristic of pell-mell modernity. In such movies, furthermore, time assumes qualities famously described by Gilles Deleuze in *Cinema 2: The Time Image* and other writings. Especially since World War II, he argues, motion and action have yielded to time as cinema's predominant subject. Far more in the time-image than in the motion- or action-image, Deleuze finds spatiotemporal lacunae – "empty" or "deserted" spaces as well as "empty time" or the "halting of time"[5] – such as figure significantly in recent slow movies. In addition to spatiotemporal vacancy and arrest, the French philosopher points to the prominence of characters who, like those in slow movies in which "nothing happens", observe rather than act, are seers rather than agents.[6] In Deleuze's time-image cinema, then, time itself – no longer occluded by action, motion or emotion – becomes salient.

Deleuze refers to the time-image as the thinking image. Conceivably the empty time and space of slow movies open the way to a cinema of contemplation, a cinema congenial to Raymond Bellour's "pensive" or reflective spectator.[7] The physical stillness, emptiness and silence in slow movies may instigate, for instance, pensiveness about the non-existence that precedes and follows life, or about metaphysical emptiness in the human soul, a void at the root of human consciousness, such as Martin Esslin deems central to slow dramas of the Theatre of the Absurd by Beckett, Eugene Ionesco, Luigi Pirandello and others who have influenced directors of slow movies. Obviously laypeople as well as playwrights and filmmakers contemplate one void or another when life slows down. Asked why Hillary Clinton persisted in her quest for the Democratic Presidential nomination in 2008 even after the nomination appeared out of reach, an aide replied: "The psychology of it all is very complicated. I'm sure you don't want to slow down because once you do, you start to think about things."[8] Slow movies often provoke new thoughts, not all of which feel good. Nonetheless, in a dispatch from the 2008 Cannes Film Festival, film critic Manohla Dargis endorsed the counterweight to action cinema afforded by slow movies: "one [tendency, represented by *Indiana Jones and the Kingdom of the Crystal Skull*, directed by Steven Spielberg] keeps the volume turned up while the other [represented by *24 City*, directed by Jia Zhang-ke] employs a more modulated register; one fosters distraction while the other encourages contemplation."[9]

Obviously slow movies, like slow plays, neither enact Futurist manifestos exalting speed nor emulate cinematic blockbusters. But they do underscore fundamental features inherent in non-digital motion pictures, including stillness, emptiness and absence. Laura Mulvey stresses cinema's "essential stillness", "the halt and stillness inherent in the structure of celluloid itself", in *Death 24x a Second: Stillness and the Moving Image* (2007) and other writings.[10] Mulvey points out that life-like motion on the screen derives in celluloid cinema from still photographs that advance intermittently, stopping as often as starting within the motion-picture projector gate, just as initially imageless celluloid advances intermittently through the camera. Moreover, she indicates, still photographs as well as motion pictures betoken the *absence* in the here and now – along with the *presence* in the past – of the life and motion they depict. In *Time Passing: Modernity and Nostalgia* (2003), Sylviane Agacinski makes similar observations: "The [photographic] imprint touches us because it has been touched itself and because it speaks to us of presence and absence at the same time."[11] And Stanley Cavell draws attention in *The World Viewed* (1979) to "that specific simultaneity of presence and absence which only the cinema can satisfy".[12] Further, cinema's betokening of absence possibly prompts Agacinski to assert that "the time of waiting, of coming death, of death that is going to come, the cinema has made into one of its principal domains".[13] It seems appropriate, in any case, that absence, stillness, emptiness and death, which inhere both in motion pictures and everyday life, emerge now and again as explicit concerns of slow movies.

Indeed, these concerns may figure more prominently in slow movies to be explored in this book than in the films cited by Deleuze as exemplary of the time-image. When compared to the minimalist slow movies, a number of Deleuze's films seem fast-paced, dense, talky, showy, even spectacular. A major reason for the disparity is that his films often zealously depict memory, the past and inner life. *Citizen Kane* (Orson Welles, 1941), for instance, which Deleuze considers the greatest instance of the cinema of time, hinges on extensive flashbacks of Kane's life, and *Diary of a Country Priest* (Robert Bresson, 1950) relies on the priest's recital, in voice-over, of his innermost thoughts as well as on his dialogue with parishioners. Other formal aspects of these two films also distinguish them from recent slow movies: the frequent cuts or editing in *Diary of a Country Priest*, for example, and in *Citizen Kane* – interlaced with deep-focus, fixed-camera long takes – the rapid montages, lightning sound mixes and vaulting camera movements, as well as the very dramatic lighting, compositions and decor. Not only do recent slow movies seem more austere than *Citizen Kane* and *Diary of a Country Priest*, but the psychology of their characters seems more one-dimensional. Moreover, with exceptions such as *Elephant*, slow movies temporally diverge from Deleuze's time-image even as they bring it to mind. For their sparse narratives usually adhere to the present moment, to what D. N. Rodowick calls "chronological time", "time experienced as succession in the present", rather than to nonlinear, more complex time, wherein aspects of the real and the imaginary, and of past, present and future, commingle.[14] Such acrobatics of time and perspective yield in recent slow movies to a continuous stillness, silence, impassivity and emptiness in the present tense.

Global art-house cinema since World War II has generally been considered slow, of course. But slow movies addressed in this book share an extreme stringency that sets them apart from most recent art cinema as well as from Deleuze's exemplary films. Consider, for instance, Majid Majidi's *The Willow Tree* (Iran, 2005): while slow compared to Hollywood action fare or Chinese *wuxia* films,

Majidi's film is far too melodramatic and solicitous of the viewer's sympathy to qualify as a slow movie in the manner of another Iranian film, Kiarostami's *Taste of Cherry*, joint-winner of the Palme d'Or at Cannes in 1997. Something similar may be said of two contrasting Turkish films: *Bliss* (Abdullah Oguz, 2007), hailed by Stephen Holden as "visually intoxicating ... a landmark of contemporary Turkish cinema",[15] and Nuri Bilge Ceylan's more emotionally restrained and morally ambiguous *Distant*, winner of three major prizes at Cannes. One instance of emotional redundancy rather than restraint in *Bliss* occurs when the non-diegetic song "Is My Only Hope Lost in My Tears?" plays over the image of the heroine, a rape victim in flight from the village that has rejected her, as she presses her tearful face to the window of a speeding train. Filmgoers who have enjoyed *My Dinner with Andre* (Louis Malle, 1981), almost all of which depicts a conversation about life and art between two old friends who meet for dinner in a New York restaurant, rightly regard it as a slow film that works. Yet the verbal agility and cultural passion of these two individuals, a struggling playwright and an erstwhile theatre director, situate *My Dinner with Andre* outside the slow-movie realm, in which characters tend to be less than articulate, especially about art and emotion. In *The Diving Bell and the Butterfly* (Julian Schnabel, 2007), a sudden injury leaves the central character paralysed, yet if only because of the quick, ubiquitous editing and camera motion, the film is hardly slow. Nor do Theo Angelopoulos's stunning films such as *Ulysses' Gaze* (1995) and *Eternity and a Day* (2004) fit the slow-movie pattern proposed in this book. For while the Greek director employs long takes far more extensively than Schnabel does, his cinema's visual splendour and emotional intensity exceed slow-movie norms. More important, his rendering of human subjectivity, of his characters' recollections and imaginative wanderings, entails frequent departures from chronological time and external reality – twin mainstays of slow movies.

◆

As both the spectators of such movies and the fictive characters who appear in them sidestep the frenzy of modernity, a slow, perhaps mythical past is invoked and a future more contemplative than the present is envisioned. Jim Jarmusch seemed to allude to such aspirations in his description of the media environment in which he shot *Stranger Than Paradise*, his first major success as a filmmaker: "MTV was just starting ... with its barrage of images. [...] It seemed like filmmaking was starting to imitate advertising."[16] Rejecting this tendency, Jarmusch sought the purer time of contemporary slow movies, time undisturbed by advertising. Such "pre-advertising" time bears affinity to the natural "sense of time and rhythm of life" that Teshome Gabriel has encountered in Third World cinema.[17] It may also correspond to popular aspirations in economically advanced societies today, as observed by Agacinski in her daily life in Paris: "our contemporaries

dream ... of finally becoming available to time and not of being continually deprived of it".[18] Agacinski adds that Walter Benjamin on his cosmopolitan strolls
exemplified such openness and availability, including, she suggests, letting oneself
"be traversed by time [and] inhabited by the traces of a past that is not [one's]
own".[19] Even if the rather one-dimensional characters featured in contemporary
slow movies do not achieve such openness, these movies can help the viewer to do
so, as they probe what it means to be available, as well as vulnerable, to time.

Various art forms and activities in addition to slow movies address the contemporary dream "of finally becoming available to time". A museum designed
by Portuguese architect Alváro Siza drew the following praise in 2007 from architecture critic Nicolai Ouroussoff: "Ultimately the passageways are yet again
a way of drawing out the time spent in thought, allowing us to absorb more
fully what we have just experienced. In a way they are Mr. Siza's rejoinder to the
ruthless pace of global consumerism [and to] the psychic damage wrought by a
relentless barrage of marketing images."[20] Ouroussoff also cited Siza's own words
regarding the connection between time and thought: "The big thing for me is the
pressure to do everything very quickly. That is the problem with so much architecture. This speed is impossible. Some people think the computer is so quick, for
example. But the computer does not think for you, and the time it takes to think
does not change."[21]

Nor, perhaps, does the time it takes to feel. Dr Jessica L. Israel, chief of geri-
atrics and palliative medicine at a leading New Jersey medical centre, wrote in
the *New York Times* in 2008: "I learn to slow down, to feel the gravity of the
moment, the power of time."[22] Probably similar goals inspired the Slow Food
movement, which arose in the 1980s in Italy, the country where Italian Neorealist
cinema developed in the 1940s, to the delight of André Bazin and other cinephiles.
Both Bazin and, to a lesser extent, Deleuze hailed Neorealism as a slow cinema
in which time proceeded more naturally and continuously than in films from
Hollywood and elsewhere brimming with action and motion. Slow Food's focus
on local, natural foods to be enjoyed unhurriedly relates also to Slow Gardening's
call "for gardeners to relax, take their time and follow seasonal rhythms, instead
of doing everything at once – an urge that's especially prevalent in early spring".[23]
Similarly, Slow Medicine advocates less aggressive care for the elderly, supporting their comfort but otherwise letting nature take its course. Slow Design, Slow
Cities and Slow Life designate further efforts, like Slow Food, Slow Gardening
and Slow Medicine, to become more available to time.

Such purposes also inform the World Institute of Slowness, based in
Kristiansand, Norway, and in Austria the Society for the Deceleration of Time,
which once challenged Olympics organisers to award gold medals to athletes
who had the slowest times. There is also the Slow-Sex movement, headquartered
in the One Taste Urban Retreat Center in San Francisco, which stresses "orgasmic
meditation" or "deliberate orgasm". According to the *New York Times* in 2009,

the Center stages an early morning ritual in which possibly a dozen women, naked from the waist down and with eyes closed, are stroked by clothed male "research partners" who are not necessarily their romantic partners. "The idea, similar to Buddhist Tantric sex," reported the *Times*, "is to extend the sensory peak – and publicly share it – before 'going over,' as residents … call climaxing." The *Times* added that while "men are not touched by the women and do not climax", they claim to "experience a sense of energy and satiation". An early influence on the retreat's founder was a Buddhist friend who "had a practice in what he called 'contemplative sexuality'".[24]

If advocates of slowness lean in a political direction, it is probably to the left, given their critiques of globalisation and capitalism as well as of haste. Yet the political order is not ordinarily their salient and explicit concern as it is Agacinski's in her praise of what might be called slow time. She links slow time not just to thinking, or to pleasure and physical health, important though these things are, but principally to the survival of democracy, to what I would term "slow politics". For democracy's survival requires in her view the citizenry's commitment to take time – or as she says, "claim time, wrest time" – for the proper conduct of debates essential to democratic life. "Any public debate", she writes, "implies waiting periods, time lags, delays between speeches and responses".[25] But while public debate demands patience, waiting and tolerance of "the time that most actions require",[26] modern media generate contrary rhythms as they clamour for "the right to see and to know without limits and without delays".[27] Much as Jim Jarmusch has resisted MTV and filmmaking as advertising, Agacinski recommends "a rethinking of democracy that emphasizes", as her book's blurb states, "patience in the face of our current temporal frenzy".[28]

Jonathan Rosenbaum has written of Abbas Kiarostami's *Taste of Cherry*, "Few films are more attentive to the poignancy of time passing and the slow fading of daylight."[29] As in other slow movies, time in *Taste of Cherry* emerges as a subject in its own right, no longer subsidiary to action and motion; and its prominence, suggests Kiarostami, prompts the viewer to participate more creatively in the film. An admirer of Jim Jarmusch and other slow-movie makers, the Iranian filmmaker remarks, "I believe in a cinema which gives more possibilities and more time to its viewer [and which is] completed by the creative spirit of the viewer".[30] His summoning of the viewer's "creative spirit" perhaps bears on Agacinski's political agenda, for the filmgoer who has grown accustomed to "completing" films that offer "more possibilities and more time" may be readier than most to join Agacinski's quest for patient, creative engagement in democracy.

The aesthetic as well as political emphasis on the creative viewer raises an obvious question, however: who makes time nowadays to see slow movies that offer "more time" – and that win honours at international festivals such as Cannes, Berlin, Venice, Sao Paulo, Toronto, New York, and so on? When exhibited in commercial theatres, these slow movies are largely unattended (perhaps because they are usually free of the explicit sex and violence audiences decry but support at the box office). A. O. Scott's report "The Whole World Is Watching, Why Aren't Americans?" notes that audiences for slow movies, as for other international art cinema, have diminished in the United States. He opines that the US public neither knows nor cares about major film artists and the "creative [cinematic] ferment" around the globe. Further, not only the "mass public" appears either oblivious or indifferent, but also "the aesthetically adventurous, intellectually curious segment of the public that has historically been there for foreign films".[31] Presumably it was this adventurous audience that turned out in the US at the end of World War II to applaud foreign films later cited by Deleuze as exemplary in some ways of the time-image: Italian Neorealist films by Vittorio De Sica and Roberto Rossellini, for instance, and films by India's Satyajit Ray and Japan's Ozu. Similar enthusiasm greeted new films from Europe, Asia and Latin America towards the end of the 1950s and in the 1960s. Obviously contemporary slow movies, whether foreign or domestic, fail to meet criteria of speed and spectacle the predominately youthful US film audience has come to expect. Yet America cannot just be "about speed, hot, nasty, bad ass speed", as Ricky Bobby (Will Ferrell) in Adam McKay's NASCAR satire, *Talladega Nights* (2006), suggests is the case.[32] Nor is it desirable that most movies favoured by Americans boast the blockbuster dimensions cited by Manohla Dargis: "big stars, big stories, big productions, big screens ... big returns ... and all manner of cinematic awesomeness".[33]

There remains a further obstacle to the embrace of contemporary slow movies: even mature audiences prefer to avoid the understated emotional pain in this cinema. "America, as a social and political organization, is committed to a cheerful view of life", wrote Robert Warshow.[34] Possibly a similar commitment to optimism prevails in mass culture everywhere. Even if (or perhaps because) "the mass of men lead lives of quiet desperation", to quote Henry Thoreau,[35] apparent good cheer is mandatory. "Nobody seriously questions", said Warshow, "that it is the function of mass culture to maintain public morale, and certainly nobody in the mass audience objects to having his morale maintained".[36] Yet the mastery of form and the acuity of feeling that distinguish works of art, even when the subject matter is painful, have an uplifting rather than depressing effect on spectators alert to form and feeling. Such is the case with Picasso's *Guernica*, Munch's *The Scream* and Shakespeare's *Hamlet*, for instance, and to some extent Béla Tarr's *The Turin Horse*, Lisandro Alonso's *Liverpool* and Jia Zhang-ke's *Still Life*. Yet in such movies the viewer also confronts the frequent repression and indeterminacy of feeling, in contrast to the overtness of *Guernica*, *The Scream* and *Hamlet*. In other words, slow movies are hard to take not simply because they portray feelings contrary to optimism. Rather, they also inhibit the expression of such feelings, just as they restrict motion, action, dialogue and glitter. Slow movies thus bring to the fore cheerless aspects of existence that are likely to worsen if ignored, but drape them in stillness, blankness, emptiness and silence.

The sad truths and aesthetic stringency of recent slow movies possibly bring to mind Piet Mondrian's proposal, in response to World War I, that art be put on a diet. Perhaps his call for discipline resonates today as global society contends with poverty, illiteracy, strife, disease and ecological danger. Amid such struggles, the slow, frugal, deliberate movies explored in this book may yet find a larger, more appreciative audience.

◆

"Deadpan", my first chapter, concerns Jim Jarmusch's *Stranger Than Paradise* and *Dead Man* and Alexander Sokurov's *The Second Circle*. The main deadpan characters are a Hungarian immigrant (played by John Lurie) who resides in lower Manhattan in *Stranger Than Paradise*, an accountant (Johnny Depp) from Cleveland mortally wounded after going west for a job in *Dead Man*, and a young man (Pyotor Aleksandrov) who arrives in a remote Siberian village to bury his father in *The Second Circle*. The last two of these films focus on decay and dying, but all three depict physical and spiritual listlessness. The slow-movie tactics in these films yield a sense that emotion, and not simply motion, is retarded, suspended or repressed. Such lack of affect and mobility are marked by deadpan facial expressions, extended pauses, sparse dialogue, minimal plot, barren spaces, a static camera and unusually long takes.

Besides amplifying the weight of time, the resistance to action and emotion in these films suggests Robert Bresson's influence on both Jarmusch and Sokurov – an American and a Russian born two years apart early in the 1950s who have long admired the French director. Aesthetic preferences congenial to both filmmakers are stated throughout Bresson's *Notes on Cinematography*, as when he writes, "Against the tactics of speed, of noise, set tactics of slowness, of silence"[37] and "production of emotion determined by a resistance to emotion".[38] As if overstressed by such strictures, *The Second Circle* for a time becomes darkly comic, and *Dead Man* turns to grotesque violence.

The second chapter, "Stillness", addresses Gus Van Sant's *Elephant* and Sokurov's *Mother and Son*. As noted earlier, the appearance of life-like motion on the screen historically has ensued from the intermittent advance of still photographs through the motion-picture projector gate. *Elephant*'s rendering of the Columbine High School killings repeatedly depicts the taking and developing of still photographs; in addition, the movie portrays time and action as not simply advancing but also reoccurring or remaining eerily frozen, as in a photograph or celluloid frame. Commenting that Van Sant seems determined in *Elephant* "to keep things moving ... even while arresting that flow", J. Hoberman has suggested an alternate title: *Time Stands Still*.[39]

Sokurov's *Mother and Son* brings to mind another type of stillness – that of romantic and sublime landscape paintings by Caspar David Friedrich and others.

Lauren Sedofsky has remarked in *Artforum* that Sokurov's "paradigm is indeed painting",[40] while Andrew Sarris's review, "*Mother and Son*, a Still Life", observes that "Mr. Sokurov goes so far as to distort his images with the equivalents of brushstrokes and mirrored reflections. The two actors are not lacking in screen charisma but they are held in check to the point of forced immobility, as if posing for a lifelike picture."[41] Somewhat like the horror in *Elephant*, the depiction of both the mother dying in Sokurov's film and the love between her and her son (Gudrun Geyer and Alexei Ananishnov) evokes simultaneously the stillness of painting, the stillness inherent in motion pictures, and Roland Barthes's "immobility … at the very heart of the moving world".[42] Unnatural pauses in the son's movements in *Mother and Son* accentuate that in this painterly movie about dying, as in life and cinema generally, motion is not ceaseless. The stillness shadowing every movement finally prevails.

Chapter three, "Long Shot", concerns *Distant* and *Climates*, both of which were written as well as directed by Nuri Bilge Ceylan, born in Turkey in 1959. The chapter's title refers mainly to the psychological distance between Ceylan's characters, to their "Antonioniesque" difficulties in communicating, and consequently to the unlikelihood of their finding happiness. As Anna (Lea Massari) says of her relationship to Sandro (Gabriele Ferzetti) in *L'Avventura*, "You know, it's terrible to be far away from one another." Similarly, both *Distant*'s Mahmut (Muzaffer Özdemir), a commercial photographer, and *Climates*' Isa, a university instructor played by Ceylan himself, are regarded by most commentators, who see strong affinities between Ceylan's films and Antonioni's, as psychologically remote from themselves as well as from those they might love. In *New Turkish Cinema: Belonging, Identity and Memory*, Asuman Suner writes that Ceylan's characters are not only remote, confused and inarticulate, but lost and empty, practically dead. She sees them as typical of the "emptied" characters who inhabit Deleuze's time-image cinema,[43] characters described by Deleuze as "suffering less from the absence of another than from their absence from themselves [and] from the world".[44]

Like Suner in regard to Ceylan's characters, Deleuze saw Antonioni's as denizens of time-image cinema. Yet Ceylan's films clearly differ from Antonioni's – in their deployment of the camera, editing and sound, for instance, and in their rendering of emotion. Such differences point to the aesthetic distinctness both of Ceylan's cinema and of recent slow movies in general.

"Wait Time", the fourth chapter, addresses works by Cristi Puiu and Cristian Mungiu, Romanian filmmakers born at the start of the 1960s, and Todd Haynes, an American born at the end of the decade. The chapter draws inspiration from Martin Esslin's statement in *The Theatre of the Absurd* that the subject of Beckett's *Waiting for Godot* "is not Godot but waiting, the act of waiting as an essential and characteristic aspect of the human condition". He adds that "it is in the act of waiting that we experience the flow of *time* in its purest, most evident form. If we are active, we tend to forget the passage of time, we *pass* the time, but if we are merely passively waiting, we are confronted with the action of time itself."[45]

The films highlighted in this chapter – Puiu's *The Death of Mr. Lazarescu*, Mungiu's *4 Months, 3 Weeks and 2 Days* and Haynes' *Safe* – depict characters who do little but wait over long stretches of time. They await medical and other professional care for problems that could be life-threatening (and that in *The Death of Mr. Lazarescu* end in death). But the urgency of these problems most likely heightens rather than contradicts Esslin's description of our experience of time "in the act of waiting". Characters in the films by Puiu, Mungiu and Haynes cannot "forget the passage of time" as they endure physical and psychological pain. The alienating silence, indifference and delay they confront in seeking care make it no easier for them to "*pass* the time".

Chapter five, "Drift and Resistance", investigates the deliberative realism of Lisandro Alonso, born in Buenos Aires in 1975, and Pedro Costa, born in Lisbon in 1959. Although Costa was hailed as "the Samuel Beckett of cinema"[46] when a retrospective of his work opened at the Tate Modern in London in 2009, his *Ossos* – about a coterie of young slum dwellers – is more eventful and probably more melodramatic than Alonso's *Liverpool*, which concerns the long, solitary journey of a merchant sailor (Juan Fernández) to visit his aged mother. Both films, however, withhold information and actions that might amplify the spectator's understanding of what is happening. Both films "bear witness to the indeterminate",[47] according to Jean-François Lyotard the role of avant-garde art, and as is typical of slow movies. Time seems decidedly slow and empty in *Ossos* and *Liverpool* partly because these movies decline even to acknowledge, much less resolve, their mysteries.

Gus Van Sant has endorsed "drift" and "getting lost" as legitimate viewer re-actions to slow movies such as *Gerry* (2002), his film about two hikers who lose their way.[48] Similarly, Alonso has spoken of his pleasure in "leaving" films in which he is "very interested" (perhaps because they are indeterminate), then escaping for a time into his own world, or into those parts of his world evoked by the moving images he has just left, and finally returning to the film.[49] Like Kiarostami as well as Van Sant, Alonso hesitates to restrict or dictate the spec-tator's response to his films, preferring instead that his films be open to both drifting and multiple interpretations. While Alonso's characters have few options in life, one could say he wants spectators of his films to be free. Thus he brings to mind, in addition to other filmmakers, French philosopher Jacques Rancière, who rejects in *The Emancipated Spectator* the premise that "what the spectator *must see* is what the director *makes her* see", and advocates instead the "dissociation" of these two – of "cause and effect".[50] The film or performance, he writes, must be "the third thing that is owned by no one, whose meaning is owned by no one … excluding any uniform transmission, any identity of cause and effect".[51]

If mystery and indeterminacy free Alonso's spectator to drift, they help Costa resist the spectator, and such resistance the Portuguese filmmaker deems central to art. Not unlike Bresson, Sokurov, Alonso and others, Costa emphasises reticence and concealment. "Sometimes in the cinema it's just as important not to see, to hide, as it is to show", he argues. "The spectator can see a film if something on the screen resists him." For the spectator to "enter", there must first be "a door" saying "Don't come in."[52] Slow movies often resist and distance the spectator, and the films of Costa and Alonso are more opaque than most; but ultimately they do let the spectator in.

"Life-Drive, Death-Drive", the sixth chapter, examines dualisms of presence and absence and of life and death in slow movies by three celebrated filmmakers born some thirty years apart from each other – Manoel de Oliveira in 1908 in Portugal, Abbas Kiarostami in 1940 in Iran, and Jia Zhang-ke in 1970 in China. In Oliveira's *A Talking Picture*, a history professor and her daughter (Leonor Silveira and Filipa de Almeida) on a sea voyage to historic sites contemplate "the mists of time" that obscure the past. They reflect not only on the vanishing of the past and its unknowability, but also on how much of it has been devoted to war and killing. Then they fall victim to a terrorist attack that confirms this devotion. In Kiarostami's *Taste of Cherry*, the main character (Homayoun Ershadi) drives his car on the outskirts of Tehran, trying to find someone who will bury him if he commits suicide. But how serious is his death drive – does he really want to die, or perhaps just meet people? In a later film, *Five Dedicated to Ozu*, Kiarostami rehearses his own death as auteur by going to sleep after setting up his camera on an empty seashore.[53] Finally, in Jia's *Still Life*, a coal miner (Han Sanming) in search of his wife and daughter who have been missing for sixteen years, travels to a region where 2,000-year-old towns and their history are being destroyed to make way for a gigantic dam.

As mentioned earlier, Agacinski, Cavell and Mulvey address what Cavell terms the "simultaneity of presence and absence" inherent in motion pictures. The events shown in a movie belong to the past. They seem present but are absent. Cavell also addresses *our* absence at the movies. Being absent from the world we see on the screen and invisible to it may lead us to feel carefree in the movie theatre. Yet the feeling of being absent and invisible in the actual world (and of being unable to influence or participate in it) obviously may prove disturbing rather than liberating. Such is the grim condition of slow-movie characters such as *Still Life*'s coal miner and *Liverpool*'s merchant sailor, both of whom bring to mind Slavoj Zizek's individual "excluded from the civil order who can be killed with impunity"[54] Indeed, almost palpable in many slow movies is the lure or threat of killing and death; these films evoke a vision of humanity expressed by an early biographer of Freud: "Not only the life-drive is in them, but the *death-drive* as well."[55]

The final chapter, "Rebellion's Limits", investigates Béla Tarr's *Werckmeister Harmonies* and *The Turin Horse* as well as Corneliu Porumboiu's *12:08 East of*

Bucharest, three slow movies in which both individual and collective rebellion appear largely incoherent and futile. Porumboiu's comic film, winner of the Caméra d'Or for best first feature film at Cannes in 2006, depicts a local TV talk show in which citizens consider whether a small Romanian town, where the film takes place and Porumboiu was born in 1971, participated in the Romanian revolution of 1989 that drove communist dictator Nicolae Ceausescu from power. Also in question is whether the fall of communism greatly changed life in Romania. More difficult to determine than the answers to these questions are the location, time frame and precise nature of the events in Tarr's *Werckmeister Harmonies* and *The Turin Horse.* Why are the latter's main characters, who reside in a nameless wasteland, unable to abandon their home as they attempt to do after their well dries up, and what causes the expanding darkness that signals their deepening paralysis and the end of the world? What are the origins and actual facts of the offscreen destruction reported throughout *Werckmeister Harmonies,* engendering frightened calls for action and the ascension of a ruthless new regime unlikely to improve on the old?

Born in Hungary in 1955, one year before the abortive uprising against Soviet communist rule, Tarr tends to make films in which individuals and societies do not easily improve their lot. He condemns the use of stories in movies partly because they mislead viewers, he says, "into believing that something has happened [when] in fact, nothing really happens"[56] – nothing really upends the stagnancy of human life. Such pessimism informs various slow movies. *Nothing Happens,* the title of Ivone Margulies' study of *Jeanne Dielman, 23 quai du Commerce, 1080 Bruxelles* (1975) and other films by Chantal Akerman, alludes to this pessimistic attitude as well as to the frequent complaint that slow movies are plotless. The phrase in Margulies' title relates also to *Waiting for Godot* (first performed in 1953), which anticipated recent slow movies much as *Jeanne Dielman...* did twenty years later. "Nothing happens, nobody comes, nobody goes, it's awful", says one character in *Waiting for Godot,* which begins with Estragon's line, "Nothing to be done."[57]

Tarr avers that since nothing happens in his movies, "all that remains is time. This is probably the only thing that's still genuine."[58] Yet in his stringent cinema, as in other slow movies, not just time looms larger as action is displaced or diminished; cinematic form itself comes to the fore in a new way. A cut, camera move, slant of light, the texture of a wall, the posture of a character – all become more prominent, and afford the pensive spectator rare insight and pleasure. Hence the formal artistry of slow movies belies their indications of human incapacity, of nothing happening, of time as empty or dead.

Deadpan

Stranger Than Paradise, Dead Man and The Second Circle

"I want your face to be a blank sheet of paper. I want the writing to be done by everyone in the audience."

– Rouben Mamoulian, directing Greta Garbo in *Queen Christina*[1]

"Art is only where ... reticence exists."

– Alexander Sokurov[2]

The films of Jim Jarmusch and Alexander Sokurov, two fiercely independent film-makers born two years apart in the early 1950s, differ in various ways. Jarmusch's work tends to be more humorous, playful and ironic. Also, he consistently prefers to depict ordinary characters and actions. He has said he would rather "make a movie about a guy walking his dog than about the emperor of China",[3] and that he wants to highlight the "moments between what we think of as significant".[4] Sokurov, by contrast, has occasionally embraced significance rather than avoided it. The Russian's feature-length films have included, for instance, the "dictator trilogy" – semi-fictive studies of Hitler (*Moloch*, 1999), Lenin (*Taurus*, 2000) and Emperor Herohito (*The Sun*, 2005) – plus the celebrated *Russian Ark* (2002), a dreamlike meditation concerning more than two centuries of pomp and privilege in Russia (with some two thousand actors and actresses in St Petersburg's re-nowned Hermitage museum packed into a 96-minute Steadicam shot, reputedly the longest unbroken shot in film history).

Yet Sokurov has also focused, not entirely without humour, on humble and ordinary existence, as in *The Second Circle*, which portrays an impoverished young man's struggle to properly bury his father, whom he finds dead in the father's ruin of an apartment in a remote, moribund Siberian town. Even in depicting ordinary events, though, Sokurov differs from Jarmusch. For the insignificance of characters in *The Second Circle*, and the commonness of death itself, not to mention the sustained, darkly comic interaction between the young man and a female undertaker, do not prevent the film from conveying a distinct spirituality. In praising *The Second Circle*, critics including Susan Sontag, Stuart Klawans and David Sterritt have pointed to its spiritual and moral force, and such readings have been encouraged by Sokurov himself: "I was always driven by visual aesthetics, aesthetics which connected to the spirituality of man, and set certain morals."[5] *The Second Circle*'s "sobriety and ... sublimity" (to use Sterritt's words)[6] seem a world apart from the impishness of Jarmusch's *Stranger Than Paradise*, and distinct as well from *Dead Man*, which despite its spiritual intimations seems more rooted than *The Second Circle* in caricature and grotesqueness.

Nonetheless, besides a commitment to ordinary, unheroic characters and events, *Stranger Than Paradise*, *Dead Man* and *The Second Circle* share a minimalist, slow-movie aesthetic, evident in their slow pace and spare plot, their empty moments and spaces, their economy of words and gestures, and their resistance to what Jarmusch once termed "over-blown action scenes" and "overly dramatic scenes".[7] The restraint enacted in these films is manifest also in the minimally expressive faces of their main characters, who tend to be immobilised and depleted emotionally as well as physically. Indeed, these characters at times appear drained of emotion much as *The Second Circle*'s images appear drained of colour. Moreover, the blank expressions on these characters' faces may also bring to mind the blank, black leader that succeeds each scene in *Stranger Than Paradise* and the opaque whiteness of blizzards in Cleveland or Siberia that consumes whole frames in *Stranger Than Paradise* and *The Second Circle*.

Juan A. Suárez, in his valuable book on Jarmusch's films, has referred to *Stranger Than Paradise* as a film of "blank affect".[8] Other critics have used a similar term, "deadpan", to describe aspects of either *Stranger Than Paradise* or Jarmusch's entire oeuvre. Luc Sante, for example, has cited "deadpan dialogue"[9] in *Stranger Than Paradise*; J. J. Murphy has cited the film's "deadpan comic humor";[10] and Dennis Lim has written that Jarmusch has "made a specialty of the deadpan odyssey" throughout his career.[11] "Deadpan" seems relevant to *The Second Circle* and other slow movies as well, since in many of them emotion, rather than just physical motion, is curtailed or arrested.

Such deadpan elements call to mind another key resemblance between Jarmusch and Sokurov, which is the admiration they share for Robert Bresson, who in his filmmaking and writing strongly advocated emotional restraint. (Of the main character, Michel, in Bresson's *Pickpocket* (1959), James Quandt quips in his commentary for Criterion's DVD of the film, "No *deaderpan* has crossed the screen since Buster Keaton.") Formerly Nicholas Ray's graduate assistant at New York University, Jarmusch has spoken of his respect for "very formally pure films, films by Carl Theodor Dreyer or Bresson",[12] while Sokurov, who studied filmmaking with Andrei Tarkovsky, has stated that "Bresson created a cinema language as much as anyone has, including Eisenstein".[13]

The "language" created by Bresson relates to several key features of the slow-movie aesthetic that Jarmusch and Sokurov share in addition to the inclination to circumscribe emotion. Yet as noted in the introduction, Bresson's films, including *Pickpocket* as well as *Diary of a Country Priest*, can be surprisingly action-packed, though rarely violent, and fast-paced – Quandt observes that *Pickpocket*'s average shot length equals that in concurrent Hollywood films. Consequently Bresson's *Notes on Cinematography*, a book of maxims directed both to himself and to other filmmakers, may comprise a more reliable guide than his films to slow-movie values. Whether focusing on pace, motion, sound or emotion, Bresson's *Notes on Cinematography* advocate strict restraint and minimalism: "Production of emotion determined by a resistance to emotion." The pianist "does not slap emotion onto the keys. He waits for it."[14] The work of art must advance slowly, quietly: "Against the tactics of speed, of noise, set tactics of slowness, of silence."[15] "Be sure of having used to the full all that is communicated by immobility and silence."[16] "Build your film on white, on silence and on stillness."[17]

In addition to emotion, speed and noise, Bresson is wary of "drama", much as Jarmusch's films and Sokurov's *The Second Circle* resist "overly dramatic scenes". "The real is not dramatic", writes Bresson. "Drama will be born of a certain march of non-dramatic elements."[18] Reductions of both drama and emotion, he says, will result from choosing and training non-professional actors wisely. "Nine-tenths of our movements obey habit and automatism", he writes. "It is anti-nature to sub-ordinate them to will and to thought."[19] Consequently the best non-professional actors – or "models", as he calls them – would be those most capable under his direction of restraining or relinquishing will, thought and emotion, while allowing a combination of what he terms habit, automatism and mechanism to prevail: "Model. Reduce to the minimum the share his consciousness has."[20] "No intellectual or cerebral mechanism. Simply a mechanism."[21] "Model. Has become automatic, protected against any thought."[22] Further, Bresson's actor embodies or represents psychic enclosure: "Model. Closed, does not enter into communication with the outside world except unawares."[23] "Model. Withdrawn into himself. Of the little he lets escape, take only what suits you."[24] The model, in short, refrains from conventional acting: "It is not a matter of acting 'simple' or of acting 'inward' but of not acting at all."[25] And (in upper case for emphasis): "YOUR MODELS MUST NOT FEEL THAT THEY ARE DRAMATIC."[26]

Bresson's *Notes on Cinematography* anticipate slow-movie constraints regarding not just drama, acting, thought and emotion, but also the spoken word. "The things one can express with the hand, with the head, with the shoulders!", writes Bresson. "How many useless and encumbering words, then, disappear! What economy!"[27] *Pickpocket*, he aptly predicted before shooting this film in 1959, "will be a film of hands, of objects, of looks."[28] And Martin La Salle, who played *Pickpocket*'s central character, later remarked in Babette Mangolte's documentary *The Models of Pickpocket* (2003): "I think Bresson chose me because of these hands, these eyes, the intensity."[29]

Reflecting Bressonian doubt about the efficacy of the spoken word, Jarmusch states, "The language of acting is not primarily a spoken language ... You can read how people feel or where they're at emotionally without knowing what language they speak."[30] Thus he does not so much reject emotion as espouse non-verbal and perhaps universal routes to it. Bresson's approach turns out to be similar: he does not banish drama entirely, but insists that it emerge from "a certain march of non-dramatic elements"; nor does he ban the "production of emotion", provided it is "determined by a resistance to emotion". As filmmaker, Bresson strove to evoke in his models nearly dazed, mindless states of being such as he identified with "automatism" and "mechanism", and in order to achieve this goal he was prepared to put his models through forty takes or more of the simplest action, such as climbing a flight of stairs. Moreover, he would rarely tell his models just what lack or excess made another take necessary or what emotion he sought. Yet his *Notes on Cinematography* assure the reader that "from a mechanism ... emotion will be born".[31] Of note once again, then, is that while Bresson and Jarmusch share a resistance to the spoken word and a belief, more generally, in Bresson's maxim, "One does not create by adding, but by taking away",[32] these filmmakers allow for emotion and even seek it out. The path is stringent, however. For Bresson in particular, emotion attains maximal purity, naturalness and truth only by approximating blankness, silence and stillness. He writes, "It is the flattest and dullest parts that have in the end the most life."[33]

◆

Stranger Than Paradise consists of 67 one-shot scenes, by J. J. Murphy's count,[34] and each is succeeded by black leader. Were every shot action-packed, the "blackouts" might be considered necessary to slow things down or to allow the viewer time to think or take a breath. But in almost every shot the action, dialogue and motion are minimal, and the camera is largely stationary. Moreover, almost every shot incorporates, within its threadbare action, pauses in the form of silences, still moments and empty spaces. The blackouts not only constitute yet more radical pauses beyond the borders of each shot, but also add ballast or structure to the film. While the plot evolves unpredictably, the black leader returns consistently, at once joining and separating the one-shot scenes. The leader also lends momentum to the film: somewhat like the intermittent pauses of celluloid in a traditional motion-picture camera or projector gate, each blackout both halts the film and ushers it forward. Also notable, though, is that like the durations of scenes in *Stranger Than Paradise*, the lengths of the blackouts vary, complicating the film's rhythm though keeping its basic structure intact. Another complication is that some blackouts contain offscreen diegetic sounds such as footsteps, either carried over from the preceding shot or introducing the next. Consequently the blackouts are not entirely external to the film's plot.

Jarmusch has spoken of the blackouts in relation to *ma* – a Japanese term referring to the spaces between things; he has also likened the black pauses to "moments between what we think of as significant". As indicated earlier, such empty spaces and moments seem to him central to life, and therefore worth emphasising in his films. It occurred to Pauline Kael that Samuel Beckett's dramas reflect a similar attitude but that *Stranger Than Paradise* suffers in comparison: "Those blackouts have something of the effect of Beckett's pauses: they make us look more intently as Beckett makes us listen more intently – because we know we're in an artist's control. But Jarmusch's world of low-lifers in a wintry stupor is comic-strip Beckett." In Kael's view, *Stranger Than Paradise*'s world is enfeebled – lacking energy, seriousness and depth as well as control. She decries its "bombed-out listlessness" and lack of terror in the face of black spaces and of moments that portend immense voids. In this film, she says, "the desolation is a gag".[35]

The film opens in stillness and desolation. Its first image reveals the full figure of a woman (Eszter Balint) in a long, dark coat standing starkly still with her back to the camera near converging pools of water and mounds of dirt on a nondescript airfield. While the woman appears in the right foreground, an airplane sits parked a bit further back in the frame's left half, but pointing toward the upper right. In the remaining space – deep, grainy and slightly soft-focused – appears more land, water, blank sky and, at the horizon, dim outlines of buildings. Except for the woman's stolid back, no person appears in this empty space, this wasteland, which turns out to be a gateway (probably La Guardia Airport) to the cultural and financial splendour of New York City. Underscoring the image's predominate silence is the hum of an aircraft, which has begun prior to this opening shot over credits on a black screen announcing the film's title and author. An airplane emerging from screen right now flies absurdly close to the woman, and then passes over the parked plane out of frame. By this point the viewer notices the woman's head turning slightly to the left, apparently tracking the flying plane. Notable also is the woman's impassive youthfulness as she lifts her luggage from the ground and walks unhurriedly towards the lower left out of frame, whereupon the parked plane, still pointing in the opposite direction, starts inching up what now appears to be a runway. The long take then ends without the camera having budged, and additional credits appear on a black screen.

The plane moves at the end of this initial, desolate scene of minimal action as if cued by the woman's motion. But the absence of overt communication between her and the machine (or a pilot or other person within it) reflects somewhat amusingly the absence of human connection and communication throughout the shot. It is not even clear that the woman has emerged from either of the two planes that appear in this image. Nor is it certain that she has recently landed. For all we know, she may be a vagrant onlooker – or, as occurs at the end of *Stranger Than Paradise*, a person who has missed a plane or decided against boarding it. It's possible, of course, that the absence of footage showing the woman emerging from a plane, as well as the absence of other human life and activity, merely result from budgetary constraints. In any case, though, the sense of ambiguity and disconnection is perfectly in keeping with the rest of the film.

After the additional credits, which conclude with the sound of a telephone ringing, the second single-shot scene begins in an empty, shallow interior space dominated by a white wall, bare except for a small calendar posted near the top. The ringing phone rests in extreme soft focus in the lower left of the frame, near the bed, not far from the apartment door on the right. When Willie (John Lurie), yawning and looking carefree, comes through the door, sits on the bed and picks up the phone, the low-angle camera tilts up slightly, centring him in the frame so that he blocks our sight of the wall and calendar and fills the emptiness. But in the ensuing conversation with his aunt, Willie suggests other voids that are emotional as well as spatiotemporal. She has called to say that his cousin Eva, due to arrive in New York from Budapest, will stay with him for ten days rather than just overnight before going on to Cleveland. Insisting that his aunt speak in English, and that ten days with his "little cousin" will disrupt his "whole life", Willie stresses that he has not heard from Eva's branch of the family in ten years. Then he exclaims, "I don't even consider myself a part of the family. Do you understand?"

In fact there's little to disrupt in Willie's meagre life, since he is unemployed and loafs a lot. Certainly cooking does not occupy him, for as Eva will see, he relies on TV dinners, which he views as very American. Seeing himself as American, in fact, may be his chief pursuit, though it makes his life no less empty. His cousin's imminent visit perhaps threatens to disrupt his life by filling the emptiness and challenging the self-image he has fashioned. Eva may bridge the divide Willie has established between his past, his family and his native country, on the one hand, and his present as an American who disowns his origins on the other. She may disrupt his life by reconnecting it.

Hints of this possibility emerge in the subsequent four images as she walks towards Willie's apartment through his bare urban neighbourhood. Although a title announcing "The New World" appears within the blackout following the telephone conversation, the new one-shot scene is as divorced from newness, hope, speed and spectacle as the first two. Here in front of the decrepit wall of a building is a stretch of broken, sun-drenched sidewalk empty except for some trash until the young woman from the airfield steps into frame. Visible initially is her full figure, including her face, registering mild curiosity but little else. Then, as she continues walking and the camera remains static, only the lower half of her body is seen, briefly reinforcing a sense of her as physically and emotionally detached and mysterious. Next she stops walking, bends into frame, removes a cassette tape recorder from a shopping bag she carries along with her luggage, and turns on Screamin' Jay Hawkins singing "I Put a Spell on You". Resuming her walk, she exits the frame accompanied by the song, trailed by her long black shadow, and succeeded by another blackout.

In the next two scenes, each composed of one long take, she walks within deeper spaces that reveal more of the vacant urban environment – possibly Manhattan's Lower East Side. Like the airfield, and in contrast to Hawkins' fervid, erotic song that runs through the first of these shots, the streets and buildings look almost lifeless, and the shops and other businesses appear closed. Two lone male pedestrians stride past Eva in the first long take, while two or three other men loiter in the far distance. No person other than Eva appears in the second shot (except for an indistinct, ghostly couple, a pointillist mirage, in the background). A few parked cars and trucks appear in the first shot, but almost no vehicle is seen moving in either scene. Soft traffic noise replaces the song in the second shot, despite the absence of visible traffic. There is virtually no other sound in these scenes. Probably the only dynamic element, other than Hawkins' song, is the graffiti on a shuttered storefront: "U.S. OUT OF EVERYWHERE. YANKEE GO HOME."

Contrary to such anti-US sentiment, Willie implicitly affirms his enthusiasm for his adopted country at the start of the next scene, the film's sixth shot. As it begins, he lies fidgeting in bed in his usual getup, including his fedora and suspenders. Hearing a knock on the door, he rises and opens the door to the impassive woman whose slow advance we have been observing since the film's opening shot. Eva's reunion with Willie starts poorly. When she greets him by his Hungarian rather than American name, he retorts that he is no longer the person she refers to. He commands her to call him "Willie", and – as he told his aunt on the phone – to address him only in English. Although Eva accedes to his demand, harm has been done to Willie's strict sense of himself as American rather than Hungarian. For he has been obliged to answer to his original name, language and identity. Moreover, he must now live with a family member, and thus reconnect with his family, for at least ten days. When he tells Eva she is to stay with him that long, she at first looks dismayed. Yet she is spared his extreme sense of reversal or backtracking. Not having rejected, as he has, either the old world or the new, she can accept both worlds and allow their respective influences to intermingle as she readies herself for Cleveland, where she will reside with her aunt rather than exist utterly apart from her family.

Eva's projection of Screamin' Jay Hawkins' "I Put a Spell on You" onto the dead streets leading to Willie's apartment suggests that such mingling of old and new worlds has been underway prior to her arrival in America. It would seem she has not been in New York long enough for her enthusiasm for Hawkins to have developed here. More likely, Budapest was the place where she embraced diverse cultural products and influences, a process surely requiring, even as it fostered, openness and self-acceptance such as Willie lacks. Drawn to Hawkins in the old world, she returns him to the new, the place of his birth, and invokes him as an antidote to the aridity of Willie's neighbourhood. Though only implicitly, she will also employ the operatic, uninhibited Hawkins as a foil to what Kael would call Willie's listlessness, a condition almost certainly related to his denial of his past, his rejection of family, the old world, history and his original name. Critics have tended to overlook the importance in *Stranger Than Paradise* of Hawkins' voice. Thomas Elsaesser and Malte Hagener note, however, in "Cinema as Ear: Acoustics and Space" (a chapter in their recent *Film Theory: An Introduction Through the Senses*) that motion-picture sound is perhaps more three-dimensional, kinetic, enveloping and dynamic than the motion-picture image, which by contrast is considered flat and two-dimensional. Elsaesser and Hagener add that sound is deemed capable of giving "body, extension and shape to the (2-D) image".[36] One could say that Hawkins' voice in *Stranger Than Paradise* both lends three-dimensional dynamism to the image and suggests a mingling of worlds that Eva, despite her relatively deadpan manner, embraces and Willie rejects.

A few extra-diegetic facts may bear on Hawkins' surprisingly potent off-screen role in this film. Screamin' Jay was born in Cleveland, Eva's destination (only forty miles from Akron, where Jarmusch was born). Early in the 1980s, when *Stranger Than Paradise* was being made, Hawkins was relocating to New York City. He would appear (as a hotel clerk) in Jarmusch's *Mystery Train*, set in Memphis, in 1989. In 2000, he died in Paris. Thus he resided in two famous American cities where Eva is about to live, and journeyed by the end of his life to Europe, where Eva was born and raised. Hawkins himself was born in 1929, a child of the Great Depression as well as of an oppressed race. He won fame as a singer, musician, writer and performer, especially after he wrote and recorded "I Put a Spell on You" in 1956.

Thus Hawkins' singular energy and talent most likely brought him social and economic benefits consistent with the notion of America as a land of opportunity and upward mobility. Yet it seems doubtful that Eva invokes Hawkins primarily as evidence of American dynamism. Rather, he embodies a force even more universal and primitive. The emptiness, stillness and silence of the downtown streets on which Eva walks to Willie's apartment do not hold spiritual promise as such conditions might for Bresson; rather, their blankness seems inimical to life. As already indicated, Hawkins' unfettered singing and howling defy these lifeless conditions and challenge, as we will now see, Willie's fixity and self-enclosure.

A few days after Eva arrives in New York, Willie returns home to find her dancing happily, though alone and somewhat woodenly, to "I Put a Spell on

You". She plays the song again about a year later in the story, soon after she, Willie and Eddie (Richard Edson) set out for Florida in the same car Eddie borrowed so he and Willie could visit her in Cleveland. A short time in Cleveland's harsh wind and cold convinces Willie and Eddie to "rescue" Eva, as she puts it, by taking her to the sunshine state. At first the three of them, together in the front seat as they drive south, boast of their wisdom in escaping winter. But the next one-shot scene occurs at night rather than during the day, and now their exuberance gives way to Kael's "bombed-out listlessness". Eva sits in the back alone, while the two men in front look bored, weary, oblivious to her and to life itself. Exasperated, Eva turns to Hawkins to shatter the alienating silence.

Willie's disapproval of "I Put a Spell on You" is fierce and immediate, both when he returns home to find Hawkins' voice accompanying his dancing cousin in the kitchen and when she plays the song in the car bound for Florida. "Oh, that's awful ... It's horrible", he exclaims in the car. In the kitchen, he instantly turns the song off, exclaiming, "What the fuck is that? ... I really hate that kind of music." Eva's terse reply in each instance identifies the cause of his anger better than he does. Defending her choice of Hawkins in the kitchen, she coldly tells Willie, "He's a wild man, so bug off." And in the car she says, as if pressing the absent singer to her breast, "He's my main man."

Relevant to the impact of her ripostes is that when Willie returns to find her dancing in his kitchen to Hawkins' song, he has in hand a new dress for her. But when he presents it following their argument, she tells him it is ugly; later, though she wears it as she leaves his apartment to go to Cleveland, she removes it and discards it in a trash can on a nearby street in the night. This gift marks a big shift in Willie's attitude towards her: he has come to enjoy his cousin's company, even to smile at her and playfully look her in the eye; and he has become less guarded, more outgoing and generous. The gift may even signal that rather than wanting Eva to head for Cleveland and stop disrupting his life, Willie wants her to stay, even wants to be her main man (though he may be unaware of his desire, and social propriety may prohibit it). Thus Eva's rebuffs come when Willie is particularly vulnerable.

After observing and then greeting Eva at the trash can on his way to Willie's apartment, Eddie finds his friend bereft – "She's gone, man", says Willie. Eddie has called Eva "cute" in the past – in fact, he has admired her more openly than Willie has. Now he tells Willie he has seen her on the street, though when Willie asks if he approves of the dress, Eddie says nothing of her trashing it. Then the two buddies just sit and mope, each with a can of beer in hand. Rather than face Eddie, who looks towards him repeatedly, Willie stares stubbornly at the floor. Silent, sad, awkward, they sit absorbing the loss of Eva for perhaps fifty seconds, until the scene ends. So conclusive is this pause that an early version of *Stranger Than Paradise*, which Jarmusch circulated in order to raise funds to make the rest of the film, ended here. Without question one of the film's most significant pauses, it underscores the change in Willie's experience of Eva. Initially it was her arrival from Europe that threatened to disrupt his life. Now it is her departure that alarms him.

Her praise of Hawkins as "a wild man" most likely deepens for Willie the implications of her leaving. Provoked by Willie's angry silencing of Hawkins in the kitchen, Eva's defence of the singer may be taken to preclude her ever embracing Willie's rising desire for her – a desire all the more precious since Willie's desires and feelings are faint and few. Eva's defence of Hawkins, particularly as it is coupled with her dismissively telling Willie to "bug off", may imply that in her view Willie isn't nearly wild enough; that he lacks energy, passion and the capacity for wonder and abandon; that he is as narrow and rigid in spirit as he appears to be physically (though again, how much he consciously registers such implications remains unclear). In thrall to Hawkins' raw force, Eva does not mention the sexism implicit in his song. But alas Willie has sexist impulses too, while lacking wildness.

A question then arises, as it often does with major characters in slow movies, most of whom appear emotionally restricted, stalled or hemmed in: can Willie achieve anything like Screamin' Jay's dynamism? And, can Willie do so while remaining severed from his origins, his family, the old world? These questions implicitly arise, even before Eva utters a word to Willie, when he reacts defensively in the film's sixth shot to news that she is on her way from Budapest to his apartment. The same questions persist in the film's closing moments when Willie books an airline flight to Budapest, and then, without intending to, flies away. He buys the ticket only because he thinks Eva is on the plane and he means to stop her leaving. Confidently instructing Eddie to wait for him and Eva at the borrowed car parked some distance away, Willie walks off inside the terminal. The next shot finds Eddie standing by the car in a bare, nondescript space similar to that occupied by Eva at the film's start. Then an airplane sweeps over him and the car much as one flew past Eva in the film's opening shot. Concluding that Willie is aboard, Eddie bemoans his friend's fate as he gets in the car and drives out of frame: "Ah, Willie, I had a bad feeling … Damn … What the hell you gonna do in Budapest?" But if Willie is flying to Budapest, Eva is not. In the next shot, which concludes the film, she returns to the Florida motel room she has shared with Willie and Eddie, and sits silently alone prior to the film's final blackout. If Willie is on the plane as Eddie says, Eva has not told him to take it, and may not even know that he has. Nor has she advised him to return to his roots in order to embrace the full range of his life and spirit and thereby become more expansive and free. This conjunction, I have suggested, of his self-denial or self-repression and his disavowal of his identity and history has loomed throughout the film, in tandem with his expanding desire for Eva. Finally, to be with her, he seems willing to return to the old world he rejected. Through no conscious design of hers, yet very much because of her, he heads back home to Hungary.

◆

Not long after *Stranger Than Paradise* was released, Jarmusch described it as "a repressed film".[37] Indeed, minimalist if not repressive impulses influence its elliptical rendering of physical events as well as emotion. The end of the film, for instance, shows neither Willie's rush to catch the plane nor his reaction when he fails to find Eva on board. Also offscreen are significant earlier actions such as Eva stealing groceries and cigarettes and Willie and Eddie attending dog and horse races in Florida. Further, when Willie, Eva, Eddie and Eva's Cleveland suitor view a kung fu movie in a theatre, the movie is never shown – just vocal sounds of combat pummel the four viewers who sit unmoved and unmoving for a very long take. Screamin' Jay Hawkins, though a dynamic force in the film, also remains unseen. Besides being expensive, more onscreen action, motion, drama and emotion might have disrupted *Stranger Than Paradise*'s "formal purity". One aspect of this purity, the one-shot-per-scene rule, precludes reaction shots and close-ups that might underscore human emotion; also avoided are camera moves that might serve as dramatic cues or stress marks (an exception is the pan of empty space between the Florida motel room and Eva seated on a stone bench – after the men have gone to the races – which emphasises Eva's aloneness and disappointment). Throughout Jarmusch's career, critics more supportive than Kael have applauded his cinema's minimalism and restraint. Luc Sante has hailed *Stranger Than Paradise*'s "spare look",[38] for instance; Cathleen McGuigan has embraced the film as "so minimalist that watching it was a Zen experience"[39] (Jarmusch himself has described Buddhism as "a philosophy that speaks to me more clearly than others"[40]); and Juan A. Suárez has praised the "minimalist self-restraint and formal control" of Jarmusch's films.[41]

As noted, Suárez also values *Stranger Than Paradise*'s deadpan manner. He writes specifically of the characters' "blankness and inexpressiveness",[42] of their emotions as "muted" though "important", and of performances that "emphasize disengagement and blankness".[43] He also connects blankness to flatness: "rather than well-rounded 'individuality,'" he says, Jarmusch's characters "communicate 'presence': the temporality of bodies that wait, ponder (it's hard to know what), and get bored"; he finds in these characters and their circumstances "a transposition into film of the flatness and muffled expressiveness of minimalist performance and dance, where subjectivity is generally eschewed, performers are reduced to physical presence, and emotions are deflated through repetition, everyday gesture, and linguistic banality".[44] The blankness and flatness of character and emotion cited by Suárez also influence in his view the rendering of action and time in *Stranger Than Paradise*: "Most scenes are devoted to inaction"[45] and are filled with "dead time ... much of what happens on camera could be described as 'empty' moments during which characters bide their time".[46]

Quite apart from the blackouts following each shot, which Jarmusch termed "empty spaces ... needed" between scenes, space as well as time in *Stranger Than Paradise* seems blank, empty and flat. Suárez notes the film's "impersonal

landscapes" (aptly likening them to "the inert physical presence of the performers") and the "vacated quality in the city"[47] – meaning New York City in the
film's first segment, prior to the main characters' trips to Cleveland and Florida.
Suárez also remarks that when Eva, Willie and Eddie visit Lake Erie in Cleveland,
there's "nothing to see but a vast, frozen expanse among swirls of wind and
snow".[48] One might quibble over "vast ... expanse", for when the three friends,
standing at a railing, their backs to the camera, peer out at Lake Erie, the blank
whiteness they confront, which Eddie calls "beautiful", looks flat more than vast,
as it holds no visible hint of objects delineating depth or distance.

Such whiteness – flat, grainy, opaque – occurs repeatedly in *Stranger Than
Paradise*, not merely at Lake Erie. It hovers outside the windows of the Florida
motel room, and along the nearby sandy shore where the three travellers briefly
stroll. When Willie and Eddie return to the empty motel room from the horse race
after betting successfully on "Mighty Joy", Eddie exultantly opens the curtains in
order, he says, to "shed some light on the situation"; but the light within the room
remains as it was, while the world outside, veiled in white as previously, remains
barely perceptible through the windows. A similar whiteness fills the windows of
Willie's New York City apartment during the day, while at night the blankness of
those windows turns black. Thus, blacks and whites block sight of the surrounding world (whether urban buildings, water-craft or motel lawn chairs) and lend
a quality of dreary sameness and enclosure to locales throughout the film. When
Willie proposes they drive to Cleveland, he tells Eddie he wants to "see something
different". As reviewers have noted, though, shortly before they view Lake Erie
with Eva, Eddie informs Willie, "You know, it's funny. You come to some place
new, and everything looks just the same", to which Willie replies, "No kiddin',
Eddie."

◆

The Second Circle's initial image mirrors the blank, white blizzard at Lake Erie
in *Stranger Than Paradise*. But the isolate male figure (Pyotor Aleksandrov) observed in long shot walking through the snow in *The Second Circle* prior to
the film's opening credits appears more vulnerable than the shivering friends in
Stranger Than Paradise who face the lake together from the security of a pier with
a metal railing. Indeed, whereas these friends stand upright as they ponder the
storm, *The Second Circle*'s solitary pedestrian, after mysteriously looking back
and drawing his hands to his face, drops to his knees. Then the storm engulfs him
before he can stand. He vanishes into its whiteness, which itself is consumed in
the fadeout terminating the shot. The resultant sense of loss and emptiness, of a
passage into nothingness, seems more arbitrary and extreme than anything of the
sort in *Stranger Than Paradise*.

Although *The Second Circle*'s isolate figure probably evokes stronger emotion in the audience than *Stranger Than Paradise* ever does, in the opening scene

no close-up of his face appears which might divulge his feelings directly and intimately. Indeed, in Kino's 2006 release, no close-up occurs during *The Second Circle*'s first seven minutes. Nor are words spoken that might reveal the man's thoughts and feelings more precisely than the images do. Instead, the viewer tends to infer or read emotion into this character. Even when the long shot of him dropping to his knees indicates an emotional as well as physical faltering, the exact nature of his feelings and concerns remains sufficiently obscure to prompt the audience to project emotion onto him.

"Mighty Joy" seems an incongruous name for a race horse or any other living being in *Stranger Than Paradise*, since the characters in that "repressed" film seem constitutionally incapable of having mighty experiences and feelings. Even Eva as she dances to Screamin' Jay's song, or declares him to be her main man, seems relatively contained. *The Second Circle*'s man in the snow, though, is perhaps more complicated. From the moment he confronts his dead father in the scene following the opening credits, it is hard to doubt he has strong feelings. Further, he remains obsessed with the corpse throughout the film, and tears occasionally graze his lean, tense face; he also breathes and swallows fretfully; his head turns nervously; his eyes close in weary distress; and he kneels or crouches several times, apparently weighed down by sorrow. But even at such moments his face usually remains surprisingly impassive, and no word escapes his lips. Not unlike Bresson's model, he seems withdrawn into himself, caught in a web that restricts visual and verbal expressions of feeling. Although Stuart Klawans describes *The Second Circle* as not only "harrowing in its simplicity" but also "devastating in its emotional power",[49] emotion in this film frequently seems more ambiguous and deeply buried than in *Stranger Than Paradise*. Despite the grief attributed to the son and the moral and spiritual force ascribed to the film as a whole, *The Second Circle* is often notable for its blank, affect-less manner as well as its slow pace, sparse plot, dead moments and empty spaces.

Perhaps a way to understand the film's dualism of intense emotion and blank affect is to regard the son's terse, impassive manner as itself expressive of his grief. Yet a desolate young man likely would mourn more volubly and openly than *The Second Circle*'s son does. The suffering central character (Cornelio Wall) in *Silent Light* (Carlos Reygadas, 2007), for instance, having been unfaithful to his wife, at times looks rigidly vacant as he reflects silently on the wrong he has done. But at other moments he breaks down, weeping and shaking convulsively. The demeanour of *The Second Circle*'s son changes similarly just once. When he is physically attacked by a gaggle of passengers in a bus, his face grows contorted, his teeth are bared, and his mouth opens wide, as if emitting a scream. But no scream or other loud noise is audible during this attack; we hear only low, vague scuffling and breathing. Also peculiar is that several passengers in this claustrophobic scene seem either not to notice the attack or not to care. Moreover, the scene is followed by one that begins with the son asleep. Hence the bus episode featuring the son's unusual expressiveness can initially be regarded as a dream or nightmare, though later the son refers to it as a real event in which he was robbed. In any case, at no other point in the film, including the son's slapstick struggle with the undertaker (Nadezhda Rodnova) as the two convey the father's corpse into the coffin and out of the apartment, does such wildness or loss of control supplant the fixed, clamped-down expression on his face. As indicated above, however, the fact that he remains for the most part deadpan, a figure of blank affect, incites the audience's empathy and its capacity to project emotion.

The notion of an active audience relates not merely to slow, minimalist films like *The Second Circle*, of course. In directing Greta Garbo in *Queen Christina* (1933), for example, Rouben Mamoulian reportedly told her, "I want your face to be a blank sheet of paper. I want the writing to be done by everyone in the audience."[50] Relevant as well is Lev Kuleshov's legendary experiment using images of the actor Ivan Mozhukin at the dawn of Soviet revolutionary cinema. In this exercise, one of several highlighting the centrality of editing in the filmmaking process, Kuleshov juxtaposed an image of Mozhukin looking blank or neutral to shots of a baby, a bowl of hot soup, and a dead body in a coffin. Test audiences then praised the actor's performance – his joyful response to the baby, his hunger for the soup, and his grief over the deceased. In other words, the experiment related not simply to editing but to perceptions of emotion in the cinema. Since Mozhukin's face was in fact expressionless, the feelings ascribed to him were absent from the screen. Yet these were feelings – towards the baby, the soup and the dead body – that viewers were expecting and hence projected onto the screen.

Similarly, the audience expecting the son in *The Second Circle* to mourn may project grief onto his blankness, lack or deficiency. The audience also may project the spirituality often attributed to *The Second Circle*, though here the incitement is somewhat different: the undertaker and other professionals responsible for arranging the funeral and for preparing the father's body for burial at times seem profane rather than just spiritually neutral or empty. Death for them has become all too commercial and routine. Perhaps more than the son's blank or ambiguous affect, their impiety provokes *The Second Circle*'s audience to project spiritual value. It remains to consider other factors related to the film's form and content that are likely to influence the audience's expectations and reactions.

One aspect of *The Second Circle*'s slowness is that its plot does not move from good fortune to bad, or vice versa. Rather, it both begins and ends in images of emptiness and dissolution: the blank snowstorm prior to the opening credits that seems to absorb the son, and the closing image of the father's empty room after the son has hurled bedding and other of his father's belongings into an immense fire in the night. Following the son's deed, but before the film cuts to the empty room, a slow-drifting mix of smoke, mist and clouds engulfs the son, erasing him from view much as the snowstorm does in the opening image.

There are further instances in which *The Second Circle* draws the son towards nothingness and death. Besides being absorbed by snow and smoke, he is consumed by the film medium itself. Shortly after he arrives at his father's apartment, he helps a mortuary worker carry his father's body outdoors at night to wash it in the snow. As the son kneels on the cold ground, his hands press the snow into his father's chest, groin, thighs and legs. Next the son stands, looks down towards his father, and from side to side. Then he turns away from his father and the camera, whereupon the camera tracks slowly down his back. But as the camera continues down his legs, an optical effect whites them out, and then, a moment later, consumes the rest of the image. One reviewer has referred to the white-out as "a visual signal of palpable emotional force".[51] But whose emotion is being signalled? The son's? The director's? Or might the white-out betoken the response of the active audience, blanching at the son's ordeal?

Another optical effect claims the son during a deep-focus long take that finds him at the edge of the apartment's vestibule outside his father's bedroom, where three mortuary workers further prepare the corpse for burial. In the foreground, the son alternately stares through the bedroom entrance at the activity in the background and faces away from it. Earlier in the shot, as the workers knocked on the door, the camera slowly descended from high above the son to the level of his body next to a sink. As work on the corpse proceeded, a dissolve interrupted the long take, excising a few moments in the cosmetic treatment of the corpse but otherwise leaving the shot's content and composition unchanged. Then a male visitor entered, quickly hugged the son, and left. It is immediately following this visitor's departure that the peculiar optical moment occurs. Whereas the preceding dissolve in this scene encompassed the entire image, now the son alone fades out, into the vestibule's blackness, while all else including the bedroom activity and characters remains intact and continuous. The son does reappear, following a modest camera descent and pan. But the overall effect remains disorienting because the son re-enters along a wall on screen left rather than from the right, where he had stood before. In any case, the film again has demonstrated his vulnerability to cinematic manipulation as well as to natural circumstances. The father's death and the disposition of his body are crucial concerns throughout the film, starting with the first shot following the credits. Equally important, though, is whether the son can remain viable as well as visible.

His responsibility for his father's body draws him not just closer to death, but also, one might argue, *into* death. It's unlikely that he and his father were emotionally close while his father was alive. One reviewer has suggested that the two were estranged.[52] Certainly as he makes arrangements for his father's funeral the son has little to say about him and nothing to say about their relationship. Yet as he painstakingly applies snow to his father's body in the night early in *The Second Circle*, he seems to grow bonded to his father in death, and so he remains for the rest of the film. Moreover, in intimately touching and scrutinising his dead father, the son possibly notes a keen resemblance between the corpse and himself. Indeed, the emaciated, desiccated dead man seems almost a sad caricature of the lean, rigid younger man. It is the resemblance to the father as well as their sudden physical intimacy that may help explain the son's upset when he awakes, in the scene following the physical attack on the bus, to discover he has been sleeping beside his father in his father's bed. The son darts up, startled and agitated.

Later in *The Second Circle*, following the deep-focus scene in which he fades out of the image while watching mortuary technicians work on his father's face and body, the son takes a mattress from a closet. He is asleep on this mattress a few feet from his father's bed at the start of a yet later scene that underscores the resemblance as well as the intimacy between the two figures. After shaking his head free of sleep, the son advances fully clothed from the mattress to his father's bed, lowers the cover from his father's face, and opens his father's eyes. The dead face in close-up now looks surprisingly youthful and unworn and closely resembles the son's face. Indeed, it almost certainly is the son's face (or a slightly distorted mask or mannequin of it).[53] A long shot of the young man standing still by the bed succeeds this image. Then a second close-up of the dead face appears. Here it is more brightly lit, except for its forehead shrouded in darkness. The camera, posted a bit higher than in the first close-up, and angled towards the subject's right side rather than below the chin, here takes in more of the face, which appears older and more worn than before, fleshier and more stubbly, and, especially around the shadow-laden eyes, more lined and creased. Also, perhaps due to rouge applied by the mortuary technicians, the face looks less pale, or ruddier than previously. This close-up lasts much longer than the first, and the greater duration causes the corpse's blank, open-eyed gaze to become all the more arresting. Further, for most of the shot the camera moves very slowly over the face – as slowly as it moves over most things in this film of exceptionally slow camera movements. Moreover, during this movement some of the darkness or shadow initially cloaking just the forehead slowly wends its way downward. The shadow's passage, in tandem with that of the camera as it alters the face's angle in the frame, lends an eerie, barely perceptible motion, a life-like presence, to this face. One might say that the living son's replacement of the dead father in the first close-up has endowed the dead with life. Or one could stress that the son in the first close-up was not alive, in which case the living son has seen himself dead.

One critic has described *The Second Circle* as a "love story between a man and his father's corpse".[54] More broadly, the film posits and explores an extreme intimacy between life and death. Sokurov has argued that "the purpose of art is to prepare man for the fact of death. Art gives us many chances to rehearse events of this nature", he adds; "art is like a coach".[55] Yet Sokurov's statement does not get at the interpenetration of life and death in *The Second Circle* as effectively as Nancy Ramsey's comment in the *New York Times* does. In *The Second Circle*, she says, "death as a natural part of life is inverted: life seems a part of death".[56]

Perhaps equally to the point, in *The Second Circle* the two are intertwined.

As already indicated, *The Second Circle* returns repeatedly to images of the father's corpse and to questions, both implicit and explicit, of what shall be done with it. Shall it be burned or buried? How shall it be washed and dressed? May its eyes be opened? For how long shall it remain in the apartment? How is it most properly lifted into the coffin, lowered down the stairs, manoeuvred out the door? Any film centred as this one is on questions surrounding an old man's starkly immobile carcass is bound to have its slow moments. The son's restricted movements, in addition to his fixity of expression, amplify this slowness. Even when the young man travels to the outpatient clinic to request the death certificate, he seems largely static, for he remains in the same position in the right half of the frame for the entire journey (which is rendered in a single long take). Similarly, as the son vanishes into the smoke at the end of the film, into the snowstorm prior to the credits, or into the whiteness of an optical effect after he washes his father with snow, he is stationary rather than in motion. In other words, he does not stride into emptiness; it simply overtakes him. At other times, too, he remains relatively still, whether standing, sitting or crouching.

The frequency of the son's crouching and kneeling – as he peers solitarily at the corpse, for example, and either observes or turns away while others such as the undertaker and mortuary workers prepare the corpse for burial – further establishes him as inert and disempowered. In crouching, moreover, he occasionally assumes a fetal pose underscoring his incapacity. His persistent questions about what is going on and what he should be doing also bespeak his trauma. He appears to be immobilised not solely by his father's death but also by his ignorance of burial routines and of the town and people amongst whom his father died. When the mortuary assistant, who arrives after the departure of the ambulance medics, covers the corpse's feet and then its face, the son anxiously asks, "What are you doing?" And when the assistant starts to lift the corpse, the son asks, "Where are you going?" Previously the son was equally anxious as he asked the medics for a death certificate and then for directions to the outpatient clinic where they informed him he could acquire it. Once at the clinic, he plaintively asks, "Why is the clinic so empty today?" When the clinic doctor refers adoringly to Lenin as "Ilyich", the bewildered son asks, "Which Ilyich?" It remains for the doctor's child-like assistant, who may be her progeny, to assure the son that things will turn out all right.

During most of the film, the son encounters rebukes rather than assurances. In response to his question about a death certificate, for example, a medic tells him he should have placed his father in a hospital – "everything would have been simpler then". It is the hefty undertaker, though, who rebukes the son most profusely. He provokes her partly with his incessant queries: Why must documents be prepared in order for his father to be buried? Which documents are required? Whose passport must be provided – his own or his father's? Why must the corpse be dressed in a cap and socks – and in slippers rather than shoes? A breaking point occurs when, at the end of strained negotiations between him and the undertaker over funeral costs, he finds his wallet empty, and concludes he was robbed on the bus. The exasperated undertaker, who must address several more deaths that day, departs as the son fumbles with his wallet and searches his father's closet for money to pay her.

The relationship between the son and the undertaker further deteriorates when she returns at an unexpected moment several scenes later. The son has opened his dead father's eyes, as described above, and the two unnerving close-ups of the corpse's face have ensued. The second close-up has been followed by an image of the bowed son peering woefully at the father in the dark. It's here that the film cuts to a very different shot – brighter than the one it replaces, in sharper focus, and taken from a lower angle – in which the angry undertaker appears to tower over the space occupied by the son in the prior shot and to look down on him. Presumably he looks up from this lower, offscreen space to confront her glare rather than his father's as she hurls her gloves and then her pocketbook at him and demands he bring her the coffin. Although the son pledges to reimburse her for the coffin, her anger persists as she issues more orders. Then she and the son add a few items to the corpse's attire and to the bedding in the coffin and manoeuvre the coffin containing the corpse out of the apartment, through tight doorways, and down a steep and narrow staircase. The entire process, starting with the undertaker's reappearance, which interrupts the son's gaze at his father, consumes more than 14 minutes (or nearly 17 per cent) of the film's running time; and at every step the truculent undertaker fires commands at the son and hurls epithets like "idiot" and "asshole".

Her endless instructions are rudimentary and repetitive, as if directed to a witless child: "Go get it." "Put it down." "Take this thing. Take it." "Put it there. Like this." "Pillow. Cover. Go get them." "Come here. I said come here … Don't you understand? Stand here." "Put them on. Hurry up." "Give me a blanket. There. Spread it, please." "Cover him. Get the pillow." "Do I have to get it myself?" "Lift him up. Lift him." "Don't be afraid. It's your father." "Get the flowers." "Faster." "Come here." "Stand here." "Are you going to move or not?" "Move up. There. In front." "Lift him up." "Turn around." "Lift him. You're tipping him. Turn around." "Lift it higher. Lift higher. Higher." "Bring it back. Bring it back." The flustered son tries to comply, but he has trouble finding things and moving as quickly as she requires. Rather than take the time to search for socks for the corpse, the son hastily removes his own. As already noted, he also questions the need for some items, such as slippers for the corpse, which the undertaker explains are required by law. Then the son asks, "Aren't people always buried in shoes?", to which she replies, "What a smart-ass. I can tell you have a lot of funeral experience." He does not, of course; as elsewhere in the film, he is unknowing and subservient, unable to make a move without directives from an expert, who in this case humiliates him.

Yet as several reviewers have noted, this lengthy scene following the stillness and silence of the son's scrutiny of his father's face offers surprising comic relief, almost suspending the weight of death while depicting the father's departure in his coffin from the apartment. Various factors account for the comedy. For one, the imperious undertaker poses amusing contradictions. Despite what she calls her extensive "funeral experience", for instance, she fears touching the dead; yet she disallows such squeamishness in the son, stressing with less than perfect logic that the corpse is his own father. In addition, as she does not trust herself to accurately measure the corpse's height – a task essential to deciding on the size of the coffin – she casually assigns this task to the son. Thus comedy ensues from her professional self-doubts and inadequacy, along with her tendency to undercut her authority the very moment she asserts it.

Equally comical is that the son proves less compliant than I have suggested. For one thing, his confusion acts as an undertow impeding the undertaker's work on the corpse. Yet funnier, if only mildly obstructive, is the rebellion he stages against her rule. As mentioned, when she impatiently demands socks for the corpse, the son hastily removes his own and starts putting them on his father's feet. Objecting that he is moving too slowly (though her deeper motive may be to reassert control), the undertaker tears the son away from the corpse and presses him to the floor. Rather than acquiesce, as he generally has, the son wraps an arm around her thighs, wrestles her aside, and defiantly finishes putting the socks on the corpse by himself. This bit of physical comedy is not unprecedented in the scene, since it succeeds the following slapstick sequence: the undertaker shuts the door to the father's room as she momentarily leaves to get the coffin; when the son moves to the door and opens it as the undertaker returns, he collides with the moving door and then the coffin. The results include a bump on his nose and a blow to his foot. Then he hops out of the coffin's way, until the undertaker has him help her stabilise it atop a pair of rickety chairs. In this process, the son finds it opportune to scramble once or twice under the coffin rather than try to get around it. Here as elsewhere in the scene, the son's youthful agility upstages the undertaker even though her greater funeral experience gives her the upper hand.

Hardly diminishing the scene's comic force are the characters' steadfastly deadpan expressions, which probably prompted a reviewer in 2006, the year Kino released the *The Second Circle* DVD, to mention both the film's deadpan aspect and its possible affinity to Jarmusch's *Stranger Than Paradise*: "the unexpected slapstick of the central session, in which the young man scrambles to place the corpse inside a coffin with the complaining help of irritable, businesslike undertaker Nadezhda Rodnova ... suggests a lost *Stranger Than Paradise* blackout skit, or, considering the comically contrasting physiques of ... Aleksandrov and big-boned Rodnova, perhaps even a deadpan Laurel and Hardy takeoff".[57]

It has been said of Buster Keaton that his deadpan look imbued even his most kinetic moments with stillness. The scene in *The Second Circle* discussed above probably contains more movement than any other in the film. Yet even here *The Second Circle* remains a slow movie, as a result of various factors aside from the deadpan. First, most of the movements in the scene are not extensive – each covers only a small space. Moreover, these movements are captured primarily in medium and extreme long shots, which tend to distance and contain the action, rather than magnifying it and heightening impressions of its speed. Further, as mentioned, in the scene a considerable amount of time is taken to move the father's body a short distance – from his bed to his coffin, out of the small apartment, down the nearby stairway, and out of the building. Finally, making up most of the scene are three of the film's longest takes, each exceeding four minutes; thus editing, which tends to confer a sense of motion by rupturing spatial and temporal continuity, is kept to a minimum.

◆

Among the many factors in *The Second Circle* that seem to inhibit the son's movements and even his prospects for survival are the turbidity and darkness of the spaces he enters. When he arrives inside his father's apartment at the start of the film, for instance, a thick mist or vapour, somewhat reminiscent of the falling snow prior to the credits, fills the air of the dishevelled room where the corpse in bed awaits him. Also, the soft sound of static in the room, apparently from the radio, adds to a sense of congestion inimical to both motion and thought. Because deep darkness suffuses the upper half of the composition while the son converses with ambulance medics soon after he finds his father dead, the medics appear headless, and their spoken words seem severed from their bodies. Later in the film, when the son moves to open his father's eyes, a similar darkness consumes the entire space over the father's bed, about three quarters of the frame. The son washing his father in the snow at night, soon after his meeting with the medics, appears well-lit and fully visible in long shot; but when the film cuts to close-ups of the son, shadows obscure his face. The encounter between the son and the female physician authorised to issue a death certificate consists of one long take in which the son and the kindly doctor are crammed into the extreme foreground as both of them face the camera. Despite their proximity to what may be called the surface of the image, both faces – but particularly the son's – are hard to discern in the densely granular, reddish-brown darkness. Such darkness and turbidity, by repeatedly obscuring and inhibiting the son and other characters, contribute to the pervasive sense of uncertainty and anonymity in *The Second Circle*, prompting the viewer to imagine or infer how the son and other characters look, what their feelings are, and even who they are.

Concealing or withholding information, whether as a tactic of visual style, plot or character description, appears natural and inevitable in *The Second Circle*. Indeed, Sokurov's aesthetic seems based on such limits or hindrances, as when he states that "art is only where ... reticence exists. A limitation of what we can actually see and feel. There has to be mystery."[58] He also remarks: "It should be possible for information to be concealed or for the entire image to be gradually withdrawn."[59] Such emphasis on reduction, concealment and withdrawal bears affinity to maxims of Bresson, as when the French director avers, "One does not create by adding, but by taking away."

Sokurov cites what I have termed turbidity as a major means of limiting the information available to viewers. He also suggests that such obscurity encourages the viewer to become more active or involved in the film. "Fog, smoke, vapor, and gliding movement distance the viewer from the overly sharp quality of screen reality [and from key information] ... Ideally", says Sokurov, "the filmmaker would never allow the viewer to comprehend or even perceive the image, at once, in its entirety."[60] Instead, the filmmaker does well to motivate the viewer to investigate the image; and the film's pace should be slow enough to permit such probing: "The most important quality the film image can possess is its capacity to offer the viewer sufficient time to peruse the picture, to participate in the process of attentive looking for something."[61] Furthermore, the viewer not only investigates the picture but also enters into its creation: "Confronted with a true cinematographic work of art, the viewer is never a passive contemplator, but someone who participates in the creation of this artistic world. All works of high art are built on confidence in the delicate consideration and intuition of this person. They always leave something unsaid, or conversely, say too much, thereby concealing some simple truth."[62]

◆

One could argue that William Blake (Johnny Depp), the laconic accountant in Jarmusch's *Dead Man*, exemplifies some of the reticence Sokurov identifies with art. Of his former life in Cleveland, Blake says merely that he recently paid for his parents' funerals and that a woman he was engaged to marry "changed her mind". Though young and handsome, Blake seems not merely reticent but inert. He divulges information in a subdued monotone with a deadpan look. His physical mobility and range of emotional expression are minimal. At the film's outset he sleeps a good deal on the train bearing him west. Although he has not previously been west, neither the extraordinary landscapes shooting by nor the shifting cast of train passengers, who become more rough-hewn and exotic as the train races on, awaken his interest or energy. Then, just hours after he reaches his destination, the industrial town of Machine, and merely 26 minutes into the film, Blake is shot.

The bullet is fired by Charlie Dickinson (Gabriel Byrne), son of a daft mogul (Robert Mitchum) who virtually owns Machine; Charlie is also the spurned lover of Thel Russell (Mili Avital), a woman with whom Blake has happened to land in bed. Blake fires back at Charlie, killing him with Thel's gun, which he has discovered under her pillow. Unfortunately, though, the bullet that has entered the accountant after passing through Thel, instantly killing her, lodges too close to his heart to be safely removed by Nobody (Gary Farmer), the Indian who befriends him. Hence Blake, a rather immobile figure to begin with, finds himself sitting or reclining – whether on a horse, on the cold earth, or in a canoe – for most of the film's remaining 95 minutes as he slowly dies. He rises and walks from time to time, but most of these efforts result in his deploying one firearm or another to kill assailants including law officers, fur trappers and an insidious missionary. On these occasions, and especially when he confronts "Wanted" posters unjustly accusing him of Thel's murder, he appears angry. But for the most part, the dying Blake remains subdued and inexpressive as well as immobile, not unlike the son in *The Second Circle*.

Yet to call Blake reticent may be inexact, for he may conceal or hold back nothing. Possibly he is just empty and without depth. "He's ... like a blank piece of paper that everyone wants to write all over", Jarmusch told Jonathan Rosenbaum,

> which is why I like Johnny [Depp] so much as the actor for that character, because he has that quality. He's branded an outlaw totally against his character, and he's told he's this great poet, and he doesn't even know what this crazy Indian is talking about. Even the scene in the trading post where the missionary ... says, "Can I have your autograph?" and then pulls a gun on him – and Blake stabs him in the hand and says, "There, that's my autograph." It's like all these things are projected onto him.[63]

Jarmusch's view of Blake as a blank sheet on which others write and project is reiterated in Gregg Rickman's essay, "The Western Under Erasure: *Dead Man*". Rickman quotes the director:

> *Dead Man* is only kind of a western because Blake's such a passive character. He starts out as this blank piece of paper, and pretty soon everyone's trying to scrawl graffiti all over him. That's what's going on when Mitchum's saying, "He's an outlaw, he's a killer, he's a scum." And then Nobody does the same thing by telling him not only are you a killer of white men, you're the dead poet William Blake. Everyone's sort of writing and projecting things on to him.[64]

Endorsing Jarmusch's view, Rosenbaum writes: "Depp's luminous Blake, the central white man, is a blank sheet of paper that others – even the original William Blake – cover with their manic scribbles."[65] Moreover, Murray Pomerance's perception of Depp neatly coincides with the view of Blake advanced by Jarmusch and Rosenbaum: "To discover the 'real, real' Johnny Depp", writes Pomerance, "we must be willing to confront emptiness."[66] My aim in citing these opinions regarding *Dead Man* must be obvious: the blankness Jarmusch and Rosenbaum regard as Blake's salient quality, like the emptiness Pomerance sees in Depp, is akin to the "blank affect" Juan A. Suárez finds central to most of Jarmusch's films and that I consider crucial to slow movies generally.

To be sure, *Dead Man* is not a slow movie in every respect. Instead of relying on long takes and long shots, for instance, it includes frequent cutting, close-ups and shot/reverse-shots; and rather than depict only slow movements, it opens with close shots of the massive wheels of the fast-moving train conveying Blake westward. Also, instead of strictly adhering to the natural continuity of time, the film detours to flashbacks of Nobody's experiences as a young Native American abducted by British soldiers and held captive in England, only to be rejected by his own people when he escapes after several years and returns home. Further, in some of the film's most arresting moments, external reality yields to Blake's and Nobody's subjective visions. *Stranger Than Paradise* and *The Second Circle* also accommodate departures from realism, such as the extended blackouts between scenes in *Stranger Than Paradise* and the optical tricks that erase the son in *The Second Circle*. But the departures in *Dead Man* are more emphatic and numerous. Further, *Dead Man* has a grotesque, hallucinatory quality that strains the definition of slow movies proposed in the introduction.

Little in *The Second Circle* or *Stranger Than Paradise* equals in campy grotesqueness *Dead Man*'s trio of fur trappers, including Salvatore 'Sally' Jenko (Iggy Pop), described in one review as a "gaunt old hunter dressed in pioneer-lady drag who regales his comrades with the story of the Three Bears".[67] The scene in *Dead Man* involving Sally and his comrades, Big George Drakoulious (Billy Bob Thornton) and Benmont Tench (Jared Harris), hinges like the rest of the film on killing and dying, but also on reversing the pall of repression that helps mark *Dead Man* as well as *Stranger Than Paradise* as slow movies. Despite its gruesome thematics, the scene begins convivially enough in the glow of a campfire at night with the trappers sharing a jug of whiskey as Sally regales them with the children's tale and cooks their evening meal of beans, possum and spices. But like Blake and Thel's idyllic moment in bed together, the initial harmony of this scene, which arrives midway through the film, devolves into violence enacted in relatively slow, limited movements. In the earlier scene, the gun Blake discovers under Thel's pillow, coupled with her explanation that it is there "because this is America", foreshadows Charlie's attack. As for the trappers, observed from a hilltop by Blake and Nobody in a high-angle long shot, hints of trouble arise in barely audible bits of the fairy tale told by Sally, as when he reports that Goldilocks was scalped for eating the bears' porridge and that her golden hair became "a sweater for baby bear".

Less uncouth yet possibly more ghoulish than his fellow trappers, Sally goes on to recite other tales of horror and violence, explaining first that "The Three Bears" is "a nightmare reminder of evil emperor Nero Augustus ... scourge of all the Christians". Cook, storyteller, sermoniser, logician and scholar, Sally is asked by Big George what "scourge" means. "It's like when somethin' real bad happens, and everyone gets killed, and you can't really do anything about it", replies the hunter from under his bonnet. As to the emperor, Sally continues, "for the entertainment of his guests, Nero would illuminate his whole garden with bodies of live Christians covered in burning oil and strung up on flaming crosses ... At dinner", adds Sally, Nero "would have the Christians rubbed by his guards with aromatic herbs and garlic and sewn up into sacks and thrown to wild dogs". After a momentary dispute as to whether "horrible" or "terrible" is the best word to describe Nero's entertainments, Big George confesses to feeling discomfort in his gut, blaming the whiskey and his age rather than their dinner topics ("I can't drink whiskey like ah used ta' could. My old belly just ain't no account"). Sally assures him that the meal he has just prepared, "food here that even Goldilocks never tasted ... is gonna fix up your old gut", whereupon Big George invites Sally to say "grace out of the Good Book". Perhaps the trio's only member who can read, Sally gladly dons his spectacles and opens a book: "This day when the Lord delivered thee unto mine hand and I will smite thee and take thine head from thee and I will give the carcasses of the host of the Philistines this day unto the fowls of the air and the wild beasts of the earth." In unison the trappers raise their right hands and say "Amen".

Big George now asks what a philistine is, to which Sally replies patiently, "Well, it's just a real dirty person." He barely completes this sentence before the film cuts from the trappers to Blake – short of breath, hand pressed to his chest, face smudged with paint or charcoal – wearily but genially advancing on foot from screen right: "Hello. I smell beans." Benmont aims his rifle at him, but when Blake says he's travelling with Nobody and knows not where, the trappers conclude he's alone and unthreatening, draw him to the pot of beans and the fire, huddle around him, gape at him, touch him where they can (his hand, wrist, arm, shoulder, leg, chest), and ask him about his attire. At once gentle, eager, desirous and brutish, they fasten on his eyeglasses, his suit, his shoes, his hat and Thel's paper rose in his lapel. It is Blake's hair, though, that sends them over the edge. Fresh from his retelling of "Goldilocks and the Three Bears", Sally leads in praising and fondling Blake's locks: "Oh, your hair. Your hair's soft. It's like a girl's." Big George joins in. Having already admired Blake's suit ("pretty") and assured him ("I clean up real good, you know"), he marvels at the hair ("Now how do you get it that way and keep it like that? See this old stuff of mine? It's just, well, it's just like old barn hay"). Then Benmont also fingers Blake's hair, and George quickly objects: "God damn it. You keep your hand off of it ... keep your hands off his hair."

But Benmont will not be deterred, as apparently he was in the past. "You had the last philistine", he snarls at George, utilising the new word Sally has furnished him with. "This one's mine." And possibly recalling the alacrity with which he aimed his rifle at Blake moments earlier, Benmont adds, "I saw him first." Now the two rivals rise and walk some distance to either side of Blake and Sally, and Benmont aims his rifle again, this time at Big George. After multiple dares from George, Benmont shoots him in the foot, which George concedes "burns like hellfire". This shooting triggers more acts: Sally jumps up screaming; George retrieves his rifle, vowing "to kill somebody now"; Nobody suddenly appears and slits George's throat; Benmont readies his rifle again, but Blake shoots him with a gun that has been tucked in Blake's trousers yet overlooked by the trappers as they fondled him. Then Sally prepares to fire, but Nobody accidentally shoots him with George's rifle, causing Sally to crawl away. Rain descends on the camp, and Nobody tosses the rifle to Blake, who takes it with a plate of beans as he slowly walks off and the scene fades out.

Supporting the mayhem is a sense of spatial disorientation that follows an odd break in the scene's visual continuity. The break occurs as George and Benmont rise to face off over who will have Blake. Moments earlier, following some queries about Thel's paper rose, Benmont inexplicably pointed a knife toward Blake's lips. "Look at the edge on that knife. Feel it", he told Blake. This knife remains prominent as Benmont, rising to confront George, moves toward screen right and out of frame at the same instant George exits screen left. The direction each man takes agrees with his prior location in the scene. Throughout their hovering over Blake's body and attire, with Blake directly facing the camera, Benmont has been located on screen right, to Blake's left, while George has been located on screen left, to Blake's right. These respective locations accord with the positions relative to screen right and left that Benmont and George occupied before Blake's arrival, as they listened contentedly to Sally's stories of violence. Sally alone occupied the centre of the screen for these gruesome tales, while Benmont and George sat several feet away on either side of him. The arrangement allowed each man to face Sally as he talked and cooked, while they also faced each other. But in the shot immediately succeeding the one in which the two rivals rise for the duel, Benmont appears alone on the left, facing screen right, the knife no longer in his hand; and in the next shot, George stands alone in what appears to be Benmont's former position on the right, facing screen left. Thus, as the violence commences, neither man stands where he was before and where the viewer expects to find him; nor does either man face in the expected direction.

The ensuing violence feels all the more implausible, both in itself and as an antidote to repression, because unexplained spatial shifts multiply: Blake looks up in alarm toward screen left as he says "Nobody", but Nobody slits George's throat on screen right. Blake aims screen right when he shoots Benmont, though the latter is on screen left. In accidentally shooting Sally, Nobody points the rifle to the right, whereas Sally would seem to be on the left. Moreover, unlike earlier in the scene when Sally regaled George and Benmont, no establishing shot encompasses the five violent characters and clarifies their spatial relationship.

That these odd trappers who feast on tales of carnage and injustice fall into mayhem seems inevitable. Possibly more surprising is the shift in George's focus as he aims his rifle after promising "to kill somebody now". While at first he appears to aim at Benmont, who is the logical target since Benmont has just shot him, George then moves his rifle to the left, apparently towards Blake, and says, "Well, God damn it, I guess nobody gets you." Why George would choose to murder the innocent Blake rather than retaliate against Benmont is unclear. Perhaps the former accountant must be punished for having aroused, though innocently, unbearable lust and jealousy in the trappers.

In any case this lengthy scene seems more significant than most commentary on the film has suggested. Here *Dead Man*'s ever-simmering blend of horror and farce explodes on a larger scale than elsewhere in the film, though *Dead Man* does not lack other comic, horrific characters. Consider, for instance, the train's grimy fireman (Crispin Glover), who stops tending the furnace in order to take a seat facing Blake in the passenger car, where he informs him that he has arrived in Hell. The fireman predicts, moreover, that Blake is as likely to find his own grave as a job in Machine, which the unbidden pessimist calls "the end of the line". Another standout is John Dickinson, the gruff old magnate with cigar in one hand and rifle in the other, who wants Blake gunned down for killing his son Charlie and riding away on Dickinson's beloved horse. As if in a trance, Dickinson initially ignores the three killers in his office he has hired to kill Blake and instead directs his grievances to a stuffed, open-mouthed bear that towers over him. Then there is Cole Wilson (Lance Henriksen), probably the fiercest and most conscienceless of the hired guns, who ends up shooting the others and eating one of them, savouring in particular a crinkly hand. It was this victim who in better days described Cole as a "living legend ... fucked his parents, killed them, cut them up, ate them". Cole's (and this film's) ill ways also surface when Cole comes upon two bald-headed marshals stretched dead on the ground, having been slain in self-defence by Blake. Cole tramples the head of one of the marshals, which bursts open like a hollow shell, spurting blood.[68]

Unnerving as well is the town of Machine, the westbound train's last stop, with its miserable main street of hostile faces and gritty sights, including fellatio at gunpoint, a horse urinating, coffin-making, and heaps of animal skulls. Inside Dickinson's blighted Metalworks factory, which dominates the town, things are no better. A worker next to a factory wheel brings to mind images of industrial bondage in *Metropolis* (Fritz Lang, 1927). Blake himself evokes at one point the estranged Cesare, somnambulist and mesmerised killer in *The Cabinet of Dr. Caligari* (Robert Weine, 1920). The moment comes after Dickinson confirms with his pointed rifle that the accountant's position Blake was promised has been filled. On his way out of the factory, the homeless Blake suddenly presses his back against a curved, black-splotched wall in a pinched, winding corridor to make room for a passer-by. Here in particular his straitened state evokes Cesare.

Commenting on Cole's brutal treatment of the marshal's head, Jarmusch told Jonathan Rosenbaum, "It's stylistically over the top, but it seems to fit with that guy's character ... The cannibalism, too, is over the top."[69] Admiring critics have deployed terms like surreal, nightmare and grotesque to suggest *Dead Man*'s tendency to go over the top. Rosenbaum, for example, calls the film a "classic western reconfigured as some sort of nightmare".[70] He describes Machine as a "nightmarishly squalid settlement"[71] and the train fireman's harangue to Blake as "a surrealist monologue".[72] Stephen Holden in the *New York Times* considers *Dead Man* a "sardonic nightmare vision of the Old West", adding that the film's "grotesquerie ... is so sensational it sets up expectations that the movie might be the surreal last word on the Hollywood western and its mythic legacy".[73] Obviously *Dead Man* stretches the boundaries of minimalist realism. Though Rosenbaum focuses on *Dead Man*'s historical rather than stylistic range, he notes the stylistic shift: "without quite contradicting the minimalism that had informed his style in ... previous films, [Jarmusch] broadened his canvas [in *Dead Man*] to take in a lot more".[74] Indeed, *Dead Man* both evokes rather minimalist films, including works by Ozu, Bresson and Akerman, and brings to mind films of more flamboyant emotion and imagination, such as *The Cabinet of Dr. Caligari*, *Metropolis*, *Strike!* (Sergei Eisenstein, 1924) and *Un Chien Andalou* (Luis Buñuel and Salvador Dali, 1928).

In *Stranger Than Paradise* such flamboyance was represented by the voice of Screamin' Jay Hawkins, which of course Willie sought to banish. And though Hawkins' body was absent from that "repressed" film, it can be seen in a YouTube music video as Hawkins performs "I Put a Spell on You", the song that repelled Willie. Striking the keys of a piano and stomping around in a polka-dot cape and bulky necklace, Hawkins seems to be in a wild trance. Animal tusks project from his flaring nostrils, and he brandishes a wand on which sits a skull with a lit cigarette in its mouth. Swirling smoke and shooting flames add to the performance's violent, ritualistic air. Though Hawkins sings of unconditional love – "I love you / I don't care if you don't want me" – he bears some likeness in this video to *Dead Man*'s bestial, grotesque villains, including Cole and the trappers. These characters are Hawkins' evil kin, who realise his savage potential but not his capacity for affection and devotion. The wild passion repressed in *Stranger Than Paradise* surfaces in perverted form in *Dead Man* – in the cold brutality of these villains stripped of love.

Despite its broadened canvas as compared to Jarmusch's earlier films, *Dead Man* remains a reductive movie, almost obsessively charting the absence or diminution of moral, spiritual and physical life. As noted, Blake already appears blank, rigid, deadpan, emotionally numb or dead to himself and the world even before Charlie Dickinson shoots him, causing him to spend the rest of the film physically dying. Moreover, though Blake occasionally regains his physical strength after he is shot, he rarely appears emotionally or spiritually enlivened. In the film's closing moments, for instance, as Nobody sends him off in a canoe finally to die, Blake seems no less literal, nor more sensitive to his friend's social and spiritual beliefs, than when they first met. "It's time for you to ... go back where you came from", says Nobody. "You mean Cleveland?" Blake asks blankly. "The place spirits come from and to which they return", replies Nobody.

Blake is also unyielding on the subject of tobacco. Several characters including Thel, the hired killers, Nobody and the trappers ask for it in the course of the film without success. The request is directed to Blake in most cases, and he responds that he doesn't smoke. By the film's end Nobody, who outlives just about everyone, including Blake (though Blake may still be breathing in the vanishing canoe as Nobody and Cole shoot each other on the shore), has reiterated his desire several times. His devotion to tobacco, as explained by Jarmusch in interviews, reflects Native American belief that its use supports friendship as well as physical and spiritual health. Still, when Nobody tells Blake he has placed tobacco in the canoe for Blake's final journey, the dying man only replies yet again that he doesn't smoke. This time he conveys a bit more warmth and intimacy than previously; but the overriding sense remains that of "psychic stasis rather than growth"[75] – a phrase Rickman applies to life in the West generally as portrayed in *Dead Man*.

Perhaps the keenest sign of growing sensitivity and self-awareness in Blake prior to his closing dialogue with Nobody appears after he encounters a slain fawn in the forest. As he bends over the creature, his finger takes its blood from a moist bullet hole in its neck. Blake's finger then moves to his own chest, and seems to blend the animal's blood with his own, the dead with the dying. Next Blake paints a vertical bar in blood over his forehead, nose, lips and chin, and lies down and curls up beside the fawn. He briefly embraces it with one arm, turns on his back, then falls deeply asleep under a canopy of leafless branches that spin over him, partially in double exposure.

Although this lyrical scene suggests a heightening of Blake's capacity for empathy, rest and renewal, the overwhelming tide of the film discourages hope. *Dead Man* for the most part adheres to death and to the quiet certainty that human existence comes to naught. Stephen Holden asserts that the film depicts an "infernal landscape ... a frontier crawling with violence, death and decay".[76] The "westward journey", says Rosenbaum, yields "death rather than rebirth ... pessimism rather than hope".[77] In the West, says Rickman, people lose rather than find themselves.[78] Scant renewal, regeneration or enlightenment occurs here. Even "psychic stasis" seems too much to claim amid the devastation and decay. Blake's blankness and emptiness parallel the nullity around him, the absence of life, civility and civilization. His vacuity befits the abandoned tepees and empty wagons espied from the westbound train and, along with fires, charred ruins and a human skeleton, from the boat bearing Nobody and Blake to the Makah village. Blake's blankness relates also to the ubiquitous skulls that appear on Machine's main street, on Dickinson's desk and along the route travelled by Nobody, Blake and the hired killers. The blankness also relates to the dead marshal's hollow head and to the empty waters and sky framing Blake's final voyage in the canoe. The death or failure of human community marks both Blake's void and the experience of the people around him. Thus Blake's rescuer Nobody tells of having been rejected by his own people and "left to wander the earth alone"; and Dickinson's three hired killers are sceptical of uniting to kill Blake because each has always worked alone.

Death, void, nullity and aloneness define this environment. Rickman writes of "the void of [Blake's] empty and meaningless fate"[79] and predicts that "Blake's ultimate fate is to be erased from memory".[80] He adds that "the fates of all the characters and the West itself are all equally null".[81] Jarmusch turns to such themes in other films as well, of course. A thug remarks in *The Limits of Control* (2009), for instance, "He who thinks he's bigger than the rest must go to the cemetery. There he will see what life really is. It's a handful of dirt."

Suárez describes *Dead Man* as a "meditation on death and dying".[82] The claim that death and dying are central to this film, as well as to other slow movies, including Sokurov's *The Second Circle* and *Mother and Son*, Cristi Puiu's *The Death of Mr. Lazarescu* and Béla Tarr's *The Turin Horse*, seems indisputable. Somewhat surprising, though, may be Suárez's description of *Dead Man* as a meditation, since the film's violence and flamboyance might be considered to disrupt meditative activity. Further, neither Blake nor any of the other characters seems strikingly thoughtful. Even Nobody, probably the film's most soulful individual, proceeds on autopilot much of the time, issuing stock phrases like "stupid white man". Yet *Dead Man*'s deadpan refutation, or erasure, of rosy visions of the West both reflects and prompts thoughtfulness. Further, the film clearly provides time in which to think. Blake's dying, his journey with Nobody and their pursuit by the hired killers all proceed slowly, with frequent pauses, dead moments and blackouts. Suárez notes that *Dead Man* is "frequently taken up with pauses and intervals – leisurely riding and talking – and with contemplation of nature rather than with action".[83] He adds that "what action there is is slowed down and bled of dramatism ... the various shootouts have a spaced-out, listless quality".[84] During most of the film, moreover, the journey points nowhere, to no particular destination. In concert, then, *Dead Man*'s retarded, rather aimless trajectory, its focus on death and dying, and its deadpan rejection of myth are likely to foster thoughtfulness in the spectator, as slow movies generally do.

That *Dead Man* allows the spectator time and cause for thought appeals to many critics, including Suárez, Rosenbaum, Rickman and Holden, but not to all. Roger Ebert describes *Dead Man* as "a strange, slow, unrewarding movie that provides us with more time to think about its meaning than with meaning".[85] Indeed, the approaches to space, time and action in many slow movies often distance rather than absorb the viewer, who may feel stranded and disengaged, saddled with too much time and self-reflection. Yet this dilemma, as in the reception of plays by Beckett and Bertolt Brecht and films by Bresson, may ultimately enliven rather than disappoint and frustrate the viewer. In any case, Ebert's dissatisfaction underscores the point that slow movies, more than most mainstream films, may focus attention on the spectator as much as on the artist and the work of art. This adjustment relates to a shift prompted by modern and avant-garde art generally, as described by Jean-François Lyotard in 1988: "Henceforth it seems right to analyze the ways in which the subject [i.e. the viewer] is affected, its ways of receiving and experiencing feelings, its ways of judging works ... No longer 'How does one make a work of art?', but 'What is it to experience an affect proper to art?'"[86] It is to this last question that our study returns in the next chapter, "Stillness".

Stillness

Elephant and *Mother and Son*

"Given his plaintive desire [in Elephant*] to keep things moving forever, even while arresting that flow, Van Sant could have appropriated the title of another high school movie: Time Stands Still"*

– J. Hoberman, *Village Voice*[1]

Like Jarmusch and Sokurov, Van Sant has taken rarefied pleasure in achieving various sorts of distance and detachment in his cinema – particularly in *Gerry, Elephant, Last Days* (2005) and *Paranoid Park*, four works he directed between *Finding Forrester* (2000) and *Milk* (2008), two of his more mainstream films. Regarding *Gerry*, a slow movie about two hikers who lose their way, Van Sant told Gerald Peary, "A lot of movies don't want you to have space to drift off and reflect on what you are thinking. Or for you to get lost, which is what this film is about … I know we won't be welcomed with open arms, but D. W. Griffith wasn't either, when he brought in the close-up." Discussing his subsequent film, *Elephant,* Van Sant cited more of his aesthetic preferences that account for stratagems of distance and detachment in his work: "Hollywood busies itself with ultra-scene changing, getting quickly in and out of places", said Van Sant. "But a lot of stories happen in our lives when we park six blocks away and walk. If we can show walking slowly to a mailbox and back, it can be a brilliant, brilliant film."[2] His mention of "walking slowly to a mailbox" brings to mind both Jarmusch's "a guy walking his dog" and Bresson's "the flattest and dullest … have

in the end the most life". In each case the filmmaker risks distancing and even losing the audience by forgoing actions and locales typically regarded in mainstream
cinema as dramatic and exciting.

Further, Van Sant's desire that spectators "have space to drift off and reflect",
or "to get lost", resembles Sokurov's taste for "fog, smoke, vapor, and gliding
movement [that] distance the viewer from the overly sharp quality of screen reality". Both Van Sant and Sokurov create films that encourage the spectator to drift
off, yet also to think about and fill in aspects of plot, space, time and character
deliberately left unclear by the filmmaker. Possibly such withholding of clarity
and definition bears on Lyotard's notion that a central interest of avant-garde art
is "to bear witness to the indeterminate".[3] In any case, Sokurov's desire that art's
reticence quicken the spectator's involvement ("the viewer is never a passive contemplator, but someone who participates in the creation of this artistic world")
parallels Van Sant's commitment to the "open film", by which he means cinema
that prompts multiple interpretations along with drifting. Van Sant referred to
Paranoid Park shortly after its release in 2007 as an "open film", contrasting it
to his films of "very specific intentions" like *Good Will Hunting*, winner of the
Academy Award in 1998 for best original screenplay.[4] Probably Van Sant was
already describing the open film in 2004, in remarks about *Elephant* after it won
the prizes for best picture and best director at the Cannes Film Festival: "Modern-
day cinema takes the form of a sermon", he said. "You don't get to think, you
only get to receive information. This film is not a sermon. The point of the film is
not being delivered to you from the voice of the filmmaker. Hopefully, there are
as many interpretations as there are viewers."[5]

Thus both Sokurov and Van Sant may be said to represent "post-structuralist
thinking" as described by Thomas Elsaesser and Malte Hagener:

> By shifting the focus from the idea of structures as objectively given and "out-
> there", and envisaging narratives as processes of open and indeterminate exchange
> between reader or viewer and text or sound-and-image track, post-structuralist
> thinking is not only on its guard against totalizing or centralizing theories of
> meaning, but also concerned to give the recipient or narratee a more active, inter-
> ventionist or inter-active role.[6]

Perhaps even more than Sokurov, Van Sant invites viewers to inject or read into his
open cinema their own thoughts and emotions. Though the distance each director
establishes in his films may prompt the viewer to "drift off and reflect", the ultimate goal is to lure the viewer into an uncommon involvement or "exchange".

Born in 1952, less than a year after Sokurov and one year before Jarmusch,
Van Sant has cited the Russian director as a major influence on his work. He
has cited other directors as well, including Béla Tarr, whose *Satantango* (1994)
Van Sant viewed at New York's Museum of Modern Art in the 1990s. Van Sant

acknowledges the Hungarian in the closing credits of *Gerry*, a film in which long takes of characters walking are perhaps even more pervasive than in *Satantango*. While attending the festival at Cannes for the screening of *Elephant* in 2003, Van Sant was asked about Tarr's example: "He continues to be an influence", replied the American. "The overlapping of moments, the repeats, repeats, in Tarr's *Satantango*, inform part of this film. His long pieces of film [i.e., long takes] are still inspirations, but also the works of Tarkovsky, Jancsó, and Sokurov."[7]

Another filmmaker whose work obviously informed Van Sant's *Elephant* was Alan Clarke, the Englishman who in 1989 made the remarkable forty-minute *Elephant*, depicting sectarian murders in Ireland. A visual catalogue of perhaps twenty killings, Clarke's *Elephant*, which Dennis Lim described as "near-Bressonian",[8] is minimal and detached in the extreme, composed largely of long shots and long takes of impassive assassins striding – almost as if in *Gerry* or a film by Tarr – up to their victims and abruptly firing their guns, often multiple times. Only fleeting and remote contact occurs between the anonymous murderers and their prey, who are sometimes shot in the back. The deadly events advance inexorably, mechanistically, without dialogue, explanation or public notice, frequently in Deleuzian empty spaces – big, bleak parking lots, garages, warehouses and corridors devoid of people. Indeed, the main theme of Clarke's film would seem to be humanity's absence from the world as well as the absence of non-lethal bonds between people.

Regarding his own *Elephant*, based loosely on the Columbine High School killings, Van Sant has mentioned the influence of yet another cold-eyed filmmaker, documentarian Frederick Wiseman, and has cited reasons like those underlying his admiration for certain European directors. According to the dispatch from Cannes in which Van Sant spoke of Tarr, Tarkovsky, Jancsó and Sokurov, he invoked Wiseman when asked if he wanted "the audience to feel emotionally for [*Elephant*'s] high-schoolers". "It's not that I don't want you involved in the characters", replied Van Sant, "but I want you involved by watching them, an observation, the way documentarian Frederick Wiseman sits back and lets things occur. We could have invented a more traditional psychological narrative. I have my ideas why Columbine happened, but that's not this film. I wanted a poetic impression rather than dictating an answer. I wanted to include the audience's thoughts."[9] Van Sant thus reiterated his desire to include or involve the audience in a distinctive way, and went on to affirm certain typical slow-movie traits: the establishment of distance, or at least of a neutral, observational air; avoidance of subjectivity, psychological explanation and emotional expressiveness; and stress on poetic richness and ambiguity, usually at the expense of clear, strong narrative action, logic and resolution.

Van Sant's *Elephant* reflects these artistic dispositions while following several students for a day as they walk through their high school's long, broad corridors, attend classes, traverse the adjacent grounds and engage in quotidian conversations – until two classmates armed to the hilt with guns and explosives open fire with barely twenty minutes remaining in the film. Though the film depicts aspects of the killers' lives leading up to the massacre, most of the students who are slain are anonymous and appear just briefly – when struck by bullets in the blurred background of long shots. Accorded greater visual attention during the shooting are students who have received names and attention prior to the assault. Yet like the anonymous victims, these featured students do very little prior to the violence, and they remain passive and helpless during the attack as well. Hardly strong narrative agents, these more prominent characters function much like the minor ones: as fodder for the killers.

One such student who receives more cinematic attention than his modest actions seem to warrant is Nathan (Nathan Tyson). Initially he appears in a static long shot among several young males playing a low-key football game on the high school's large playing field. Two groups of female students exercise in the remote background. A few other male and female youths jog across the shot, which begins eight minutes into the film. A minute and a half into the shot, after Nathan and other players have momentarily left the stationary frame, Nathan returns and occupies the central foreground, where he dons a red, hooded sweatshirt he has apparently left on the grass, and then walks towards the high school building. He enters the building, walks a short distance, climbs a flight of stairs, goes down a long corridor, emerges from the building, enters another wing, goes down another corridor, and eventually meets his girlfriend Carrie (Carrie Finklea) near the school's central office, where they intend to sign out from school until one-thirty that afternoon. While heading towards Carrie, Nathan passes a trio of female students (Brittany Mountain, Jordan Taylor and Nicole George), one of whom casts him a lustful look he clearly savours. Otherwise, his journey is without incident. Yet almost four minutes have elapsed between his return to the frame to don his red sweatshirt and his meeting with Carrie, and a half minute more passes before they reach the sign-out counter. Thus Nathan appears on screen almost continuously for six minutes – more than forty per cent of the film to this point – for no obvious dramatic reason.

Moreover, his time on screen interrupts potentially stronger narratives, initiated during the film's opening minutes, John (John Robinson) and Elias (Elias McConnell). John appears first, or rather the car piloted by his drunken father (Timothy Bottoms) does. As, in high-angle long shot, the car skids to a halt on a sunlit residential street shortly after it caroms off a parked vehicle, John's name appears on a black screen. Only then does John appear – emerging from the car, checking the damage to its front, and warning his father, "Mom's gonna kill you". Next he commands his father to let him take the wheel, whereupon John drives them to the high school, where he is late for class. He instructs his father to remain in the car until John's brother Paul arrives to drive him home. Then, as John phones Paul from inside the school, he is directed by Mr Lewis (Matt Malloy), the school principal, to meet him in his office.

This introduction of John occurs in just three long takes. At the end of the second, in which John checks the damage caused by the minor crash, takes the wheel and drives towards school, Elias is introduced in a separate long take, which will be followed by John's arrival at the school. As Elias's long take begins, he strolls with his still camera over fallen leaves in a tree-shaded section of the park apparently adjacent to the playing field where Nathan will soon appear. Encountering a young man and woman, teenage sweethearts, Elias explains he is doing random photographic portraits for his portfolio, and after he tells them what a portfolio is, they agree to pose for him. As he takes the pictures, Elias in an easy-going but firm tone directs the couple: "Be a little happier ... come on ... yeah ... there you go ... kinda look away ... make a funny face, you know ... one more ... keep walkin' ... keep walkin' ... maybe one kiss ... perfect."

When his teenage subjects offer "to get naked" for him early in the shoot, Elias declines: "I'm not for the outdoor naked thing." But he is not so reserved as to deny them "maybe one kiss" as he concludes the session and announces he must be off to school. His responses regarding nudity and the kiss seem to reflect his good sense and moderation, though also, perhaps, some sexual ambivalence. Elias rules out prurience such as the photographer Thomas (David Hemmings) embraces in *Blow-up* (Michelangelo Antonioni, 1966), but he does not go to the extreme of banning all sexual expression in public. His temperance supports his serenity. Although Elias later alludes to having problems with his parents, his encounters on screen prior to the massacre at the end of the film are free of social tensions and disagreements; and of course, just as he does not emulate Thomas, he displays almost none of the anguish and perversity of other movie photographers such as L. B. Jeffries (Jimmy Stewart in Hitchcock's *Rear Window*, 1954) and Mark Lewis (Carl Boehm in Michael Powell's *Peeping Tom*, 1960). A further reason for his contentment may well be that, unlike such predecessors, Elias relates photography, his core passion, not to commerce, fashion and sport, nor to voyeurism, death and dread, but to something vaguely purer and higher, to art such as he finds in "galleries", as he tells the teenage couple.

As with John, Elias's name on the black screen precedes his actual appearance in *Elephant*. By contrast, Nathan's name appears only at the end of his first six minutes on screen, when he and Carrie enter the office where they will sign out. Further, his name on the black screen is joined by Carrie's. That he is identified belatedly and with his girlfriend seems consistent with his insignificance as a narrative agent compared to John and Elias. Unlike them, for most of his initial time on screen Nathan undertakes no action other than walking, and he utters not a word. Nor does he enter into a problem or conflict, such as John does in attempting to deal with his father and the ludicrously stern Mr Lewis.

Elias, like John, speaks and acts. Moreover, one can easily imagine that his acts and motives resemble those of Van Sant in directing *Elephant*. Van Sant, too, seems to be creating portraits of ordinary youngsters who might be encountered randomly in everyday life. Further, in shaping these portraits, which contain minimal action, drama and emotion, after having directed in a more conventional style mainstream hits like *Good Will Hunting*, Van Sant seems inspired, as Elias is, by personal and artistic rather than commercial goals. Will Elias achieve artistic recognition comparable to that accorded Van Sant for *Elephant*, virtually an experimental film that won the Palme d'Or at Cannes? Van Sant as a student at the Rhode Island School of Design aspired to be a painter, but shifted to filmmaking after studying films by Andy Warhol, Stan Brakhage and others. What course will Elias take? The viewer grows invested in him owing to the good sense and artistic dedication that set him apart from his schoolmates. Although he appears in little of the film and his completed photographs are not shown, what he says and does, as Van Sant's surrogate or not, matters.

While the same cannot be said of Nathan, who confronts little if any challenge or responsibility during his first six minutes in *Elephant*, as the film tinkers with time and motion both in the course of introducing Nathan and thereafter, it poses challenges for the spectator if not for Nathan. In fact, hovering throughout the film is the question: will *Elephant*'s unconventional tactics alienate the audience, or will viewers adjust and get involved in unusual ways, as Van Sant would prefer? An example of the film's departures from convention while introducing Nathan arises during the football game. As the players compete in the middle distance, a bespectacled young woman, eventually identified as Michelle (Kristen Hicks), jogs into frame and stands in the central foreground, where Nathan will retrieve his sweatshirt later in the shot. Ungainly and daft-looking, she undertakes a series of movements, which, though small and inconsequential, project the film momentarily into an ethereal, dream-like realm. One reason is that her gestures, the football game, the exercises in the background and all other activities in the frame enter into slow motion for the duration of her stay on screen. This slowdown is relatively modest – less extreme than occurs in, say, renderings of violence in many a western or gangster film. But in such genre films the altered pace seems driven by the rising drama and horror of the events being depicted. By contrast, the action in *Elephant* here seems relatively placid and quotidian. The suddenly slow, soft, gliding motion seems to occur without cause or explanation.

Further, the woman's manner is enigmatic, even a bit vertiginous, quite apart from the slow motion. Having entered from the left, she first faces right, then slowly turns left, with her head angled back, and her eyes straining upwards. Next she looks left without simultaneously peering up. Then, as her body faces the audience, she tilts her head back and resumes her upward search while turning right. Her head next cranes left, but only to a point where she would be looking into the camera were her head not angled back, perusing the sky. Last, she draws a deep breath and trots off, exiting screen right. What is this woman up to as – oblivious to the human activity around her – she silently probes the vacant atmosphere, while glimmers of curiosity, wonder, anxiety and dismay cross her face? Is she expecting rain? Taking in nature's splendour? Stretching bits of her anatomy in advance of joining the women exercising in the background? Whatever her intent and level of awareness, and even though she seems narratively extraneous, she occupies the central foreground of the image. Here, though she does not look directly into the camera, she seems to be aware of it, even to pose for it, to acknowledge its presence more than any other character has. She thus encourages the viewer to consider the camera's role in the film's inchoate plot.

Erwin Panofsky regarded motion as fundamental to the pleasure afforded by motion pictures: "the primordial basis of the enjoyment of moving pictures", he said, "was not an objective interest in a specific subject matter ... but the sheer delight in the fact that things seemed to move, no matter what things they were".[10] If so, what better way to indicate that *Elephant* is a *different* kind of moving picture than to alter, suspend, impair or slow its movement for no clear narrative reason? Panofsky also wrote that "an aesthetic interest in the formal presentation of subject matter" had no part in the primordial basis of the enjoyment of moving pictures.[11] The manner in which Michelle appears on the playing field, however, suggests that "formal presentation" is of utmost concern to Van Sant. Another indication of such a concern is the choice of Beethoven's slow, meditative *Moonlight Sonata* on the audio track. The piano begins even before Michelle enters the frame, and it continues after she departs, as the camera tracks Nathan crossing the field and walking through school corridors. Counterpointing his brisk pace and that of other athletes on the playing field, the slowness of both the sonata and Michelle's unnatural gestures contributes to a key formal tension in the film identified by J. Hoberman: "to keep things moving ... even while arresting that flow".

The contrast provided by Michelle and the music anticipates the violent conflict of movement and arrest yet to come in the climactic massacre. Following her debut in the film, Michelle reappears and grows more relevant; before long a blackout bearing her name fills the screen. But not until her final appearance in *Elephant* does she almost face the camera again while occupying the central foreground of the image. And it is here, in a brief medium close-up in the school library, that she becomes the first student shot dead in the massacre. Having first seemed peripheral to the action, she becomes painfully central to the narrative climax, albeit as passive victim rather than narrative agent. The sonata, too, foreshadows the climax, since the only character seen performing this composition is Alex (Alex Frost), who masterminds the massacre and goes on to kill Michelle in the library. The broad outline of what must happen in *Elephant* is known from the outset: a massacre must occur, since the Columbine killings form the basis of the film. The question is *how* they will occur – how, for example, the incongruous sonata, arrests of motion and Michelle's trance-like moves on the playing field will play out. In *Elephant*, "formal presentation" is key.

Slowing such as occurs in the sonata and in Michelle's initial appearance proves integral to the film. Motion is not only retarded at times, but also suspended, as when the black screen bearing the names of characters interrupts the action. Further, physical acts and dialogue recur, so that time, while seeming to advance, is shown to be frozen; or events that seem to be occurring in the present turn out to belong to the past. Such temporal ambiguity and intricacy mark the film's tension between motion and arrest as well as its dream-like quality, both of which bring to mind not only Tarr's *Satantango* but also *Last Year at Marienbad* (Alain Resnais and Alain Robbe-Grillet, 1961), a film rarely mentioned in relation to *Elephant*.

As Nathan passes the ogling trio of female students in the high school corridor, a slowing more pronounced than that of Michelle on the playing field occurs in two phases. First the camera registers the trio's slowing movements as they look and talk, and then, without a cut, it pans to the slowing of Nathan's gait and of his head turning towards them in acknowledgment of their lust and longing. Also curious in this encounter is that while the lips of the female student who adoringly says "He's so cute" move in slow motion, her words issue at normal sound speed.[12] Then the lips move slowly again, apparently repeating "He's so cute", but no sound emerges. Next, following a pause, the lips resume their slow motion, this time shaping "Wow", but again nothing is heard. In short, the usual link or synchronisation between sound and image is suspended as the motion slows, and the depiction of ordinary people doing ordinary things diverges from what might be called "the cinematic ordinary". Such disturbances in the film's form and technique undermine the juvenile ordinariness of the characters and their story, adumbrating the cataclysm to come.

After Nathan acknowledges the female trio, his normal pace resumes as he continues down the corridor. Then he reaches Carrie, and they enter the office where they are to sign out. Approaching the sign-out counter, Nathan says, "Excuse me, Miss", just as the black screen bearing his name and Carrie's interrupts the image. Following this "blackout", Nathan, onscreen again, tells the offscreen clerk, "We need to sign out", whereupon a woman, in voice-over, explains that a photograph, presumably on a wall offscreen, was taken in Hawaii on the island of Maui. Curiously, though, no voice has been heard to inquire about the photograph. Here, then, begin fresh manipulations of sound and time that retard the narrative and disorient the viewer.

Elephant cuts from the statement about the photograph and Maui to Mr Lewis, the high school principal, still glaring at John in his office as he was six minutes earlier in the film. Has Lewis been fixed in this grim pose all this time? Did his interaction with John simply freeze when the film cut to the playing field? Indistinct sounds, apparently from the adjoining room containing the sign-out counter and photograph, continue over Lewis's glare and his abrupt termination of the meeting. Rising, he dismisses John and warns him not to be late for detention. John passes in front of Lewis and emerges from Lewis's office into the sign-out room. At this point Nathan, in voice-over (for he is absent from the shot that shows John entering), is heard again saying, "Excuse me, Miss. We need to sign out." Then we see and hear John inquire about the offscreen photo, and we hear the voice from offscreen identify the photo exactly as before.

In terms of narrative progression, the scene just concluded between John and Lewis seems to occur immediately *after* the one in which Nathan first approaches the counter and announces his desire to sign out. But how could John ask about the photograph in the sign-out room if he has not yet left Lewis's office? Might his existence be multiple, like that of a character in Jorge Luis Borges's "The Garden of Forking Paths"?[13] Perhaps, then, the meeting between Lewis and John concludes just *before* rather than after Nathan and Carrie approach the counter, allowing John, though out of frame, to approach the counter at the same moment they do. But in this case, the scene between John and Lewis represents a move back in time rather than forward. And in either case the film repeats, though from a different visual angle or perspective, the scene (and period of time) in which Nathan makes his request and a woman's voice explains the Maui photo. Such repetition from an altered perspective may be found elsewhere in film history, of course – in *Life of an American Fireman* (Edwin S. Porter, 1902), for instance, as well as in *Satantango* and *Last Year at Marienbad*.

Perhaps somewhat more unusual and unnatural is a subsequent manipulation of time, sound and action as Nathan and Carrie sign out. At the end of the second version of the sign-out scene, in which John, onscreen, asks about the photo, Nathan and Carrie, to whom the camera has panned, step backwards into the doorway as they prepare to leave, and Nathan, in response to an offscreen voice inquiring when they will be back, says, "Right around one-thirty". At this point we are fifteen minutes into the film. After an adult male employee in the sign-out office mentions a gathering, possibly to occur at his home in celebration of his birthday, the film cuts to John walking down a school corridor and then into a large, empty room, where he starts to weep. A female student (Alicia Miles) enters and tries to comfort him, but he claims not to know what is troubling him. She departs, promising to return, and the screen goes black, except for her name in white: "Acadia". As she enters a classroom where an African American teacher and his students discuss perceptions of homosexuality, the camera pans across their faces. Then the pan advances slowly over just the blackboard, while a woman, in voice-over, asks, "What time will you be back?" Nathan, in voice-over, starts to reply: "Ah…"

The film cuts back to the doorway of the sign-out office, revealing Nathan and Carrie again, as Nathan completes his reply: "Right around one-thirty." Minor differences of sound and image exist between this version of their departure from the office and the previous one. Here the question "What time will you be back?" is louder and clearer than previously. Moreover, as Nathan now says "Right around one-thirty", he and Carrie, while backing away as before, are already out-side the office, rather than just inside the open doorway as they were previously. Most important and unusual, however, is that three minutes and forty-five sec-onds have passed since this exchange about the hour of their return last occurred. Have Nathan and Carrie, perhaps like the glaring Mr Lewis before them, been frozen in time? Has their story stopped, even while the stories of other characters such as John and Acadia have moved ahead? Further, does this third exchange about the anticipated time of their return, which jarringly interrupts the scene in the classroom, suggest if not foretell that Nathan and Carrie, perhaps along with other students, are trapped inside the school forever, doomed to an eternity of what Mr Lewis has called "detention"?

In any case, by returning to Nathan and Carrie as they leave the sign-out of-fice, *Elephant* seems to return to an earlier point in its narrative, which is to say that it goes back in time, as it has before and will again. The story of Nathan and Carrie then proceeds, as they converse in the corridor about their friends and social calendar. The most dramatic fact to emerge in this conversation is that Carrie may be pregnant. But even this momentous prospect, given the couple's blandness, packs less of a punch than the bold intrusion a moment earlier of the line, "What time will you be back?" There as elsewhere, the film's impact derives from its unusual "formal presentation", to cite Panofsky's phrase, rather than from the information it divulges.

The film cuts from Nathan and Carrie conversing to Elias walking in another of the school's corridors. Michelle, still without a name, walks in the same di-rection as Elias but far behind him. Elias sees John walking towards him in the corridor; the two young men greet each other; Elias asks to take John's picture; and John poses with one hand on a railing by the window and the other on his hip. Michelle started to jog as Elias asked to take John's picture, and she passes him and John at almost the very moment the picture is snapped. Then John asks Elias whether he will be going to the concert that evening, to which Elias replies that his parents are being "bitches" and will not allow it. The young men part, and Van Sant's camera follows John as he resumes walking down the corridor.

This scene of John, Michelle and Elias is repeated twice in the course of the film, with colour, focus, ambient sound and viewpoint altered each time. The camera remains with John at the end of the first version, with Elias at the end of the second, and with Michelle at the end of the third. The third begins with a close shot of Michelle's upper back, rather than the medium long shot of Elias facing the camera as in the first version. Moreover, Elias at the start of the third is a small, spectral figure in extreme soft focus floating in the remote background, instead of a body in sharp focus and closer than Michelle to the foreground of the image, as in the first version. Despite such formal shifts, though, the ac-tion and dialogue remain the same for each version of these students crossing paths in the high school corridors. Similarly, Nathan is shown passing the trio of female admirers twice, though at normal speed the second time, and with the camera ending up on *them*, not Nathan, as they walk toward the cafeteria. "The high-schoolers walk and walk and walk prior to the climactic shootings, when many of these walkers become human targets", remarks Gerald Peary.[14] Such endless walking in what increasingly seems a cinematic maze calls to mind the words introducing *Last Year at Marienbad*, intoned by a male voice described in the screenplay as "rhythmical but without any particular emotion": "Once again [pause] I walk on, once again, down these corridors, through these halls."[15] In *Last Year at Marienbad*, too, a film more literary and theatrical than *Elephant*, the action and motion, instead of advancing, seem fixed in a spatiotemporal vice. While *Elephant* is based on real events, it nonetheless suggests a phantasmic realm reminiscent of *Last Year at Marienbad*'s.

When the camera follows John at the end of the first version of his encounter with Elias, he continues down the corridor, soon exits the school, and calls to a dog a few yards away (all in one long take that began when Elias first appeared in the corridor). After the dog goes to John, the entire action shifts without a cut into slow motion as the dog leaps up. Simultaneously Alex and Eric (Eric Deulen), the killers bound for the massacre, make their first appearance – in the distance, far beyond the slow-motion leap, toting bags packed with guns and explosives. The pace of the moving image returns to normal as Alex and Eric approach John. Wearing black gloves and other dark clothes, Alex sullenly warns him to leave the area. John asks, "What are you doing?", precisely his question as his father drove recklessly, and turns to watch them continue towards the school. As they open the school door through which he exited a moment earlier, a blackout bearing their names appears, and over the blackout a student's voice is heard: "When the electrons jump from…" The film cuts to a science class discussing the relationship between the energy of electrons and their orbital distance from a nucleus. A student seated at the front of the class completes his electron question, and a pan to the rear of the room reveals Alex in casual attire rather than the dark militant dress in which he started to enter the school. It soon becomes evident that "When the electrons jump from…" marks – much like "What time will you be back?" – an abrupt shift to the past. But here the past does not comprise events already observed within the film, but unseen events, prior to the beginning, before the swerving car. This alien past seems integral to the present, though, since no indication of a flashback precedes it (and since it repeats no earlier events in the film). Further, the past events that now unfold are seamlessly intercut with both the present as it becomes future and repetitions of occurrences we have previously beheld, particularly the picture-taking convergence of John, Elias and Michelle. In sum, the voice-over inquiry about jumpy electrons in tandem with the blackout bearing the names of Alex and Eric marks several phenomena at once: a substantial jump back in time; a confluence of past, present and the indefinite tense of the black screen; and a halt to action in the present – in this sense, a halting of time.

Alex, the principal character from the alien past that invades *Elephant* and mingles with the present, appears in the science classroom twenty-two minutes into the film – with one hour remaining. In the next scene he appears in a school lavatory, where he wipes off the white muck a student in the science class has hurled at him; then he appears in the school cafeteria scribbling plans for the massacre in a small notebook. After these two scenes, he appears solely in the spacious home of his parents until he leaves to attack the school. We observe him over several days, which are not necessarily consecutive, in the kitchen, den, living room and garage, but principally in a basement living area equipped with a bed, piano, couches, laptop computer, bathroom and shower. Eric joins him for most of these domestic scenes, which are intercut with characters and actions at the school on the day of the attack. One night Alex plays the piano as Eric arrives. They sleep on adjacent couches as the weather turns stormy and thunderous. Then they have breakfast in the kitchen, served by Alex's mother as his father prepares to leave. Amid such ordinary activities, Alex and Eric prepare for the massacre.

While Alex plays the piano, Eric focuses on digital animation on the laptop screen that allows him the illusion of shooting moving human targets. Alex shifts from the piano to the laptop to access "GunsUSA". Later, as he and Eric await UPS delivery of their weapons, they watch a television documentary describing the Nazis' propaganda machine and debunking Hitler. Alex and Eric practice-fire their new weapons into a heap of firewood in the garage. They take a shower and kiss for the first time. Alex dresses, lays out a map of the school in his basement preserve, and reviews with Eric his detailed plans for the attack. More than one-third of the film (or close to thirty minutes) passes between Alex's first appearance in his home and his departure with Eric to attack the school. At no point, though, do these characters say why they are planning to murder their classmates; their violent trajectory seems as arbitrary and motiveless as the film's aberrations of time, space and motion.

The absence of explanation in *Elephant* is matched by the lack of emotional expression. As Alex's mother perfunctorily serves the youths breakfast while the father prepares to leave, only the lower part of the mother's face appears briefly in the background, and the father's is cropped out entirely. The parents exist mainly as featureless, anonymous bodies with uncaring voices. And for the most part, Alex and Eric show little more emotion than the parents do. When Eric remarks at breakfast that Alex's mother smells bad, his tone is snide and cold. Alex scarcely reacts to this unprovoked insult, and his mother, offscreen, replies only that the two youths are free to go elsewhere for breakfast. When Alex enjoins Eric to "have fun" at the massacre as the two set out from home for the school, his injunction sounds pallid as well as incongruous. Later, as Alex trots through a school corridor firing his rifle, his mouth opens briefly and tentatively in a smile, but his overall expression remains blank and joyless. Toward the end of the massacre, he and Eric come upon each other after they have forged separate paths of havoc through the school. Alex, seated in the cafeteria among fallen bodies, asks his friend, standing in the nearby corridor, about his progress. Eric announces with some satisfaction that he has killed Mr Lewis, but Alex interrupts his cohort, shooting him dead for no reason, and without remorse or other evident emotion.

Perhaps not every character in *Elephant* exhibits a flat, affect-less condition such as Fredric Jameson finds endemic in postmodern culture, and which brings to mind *Dead Man*'s William Blake, among others. As noted earlier, John evinces sadness, Acadia is caring, and Elias shows good will. Yet their emotions often seem shallow, restricted, hemmed in, and they are unable, or disinclined, to talk about the nature and origins of their feelings. Better off materially than, say, the youths in Van Sant's *To Die For* (1996), *Elephant*'s characters are more inhibited emotionally than their counterparts in that film as well as in most mainstream cinema. The interviewer who asked Van Sant at Cannes whether he wanted "the audience to feel emotionally for [*Elephant*'s] high-schoolers" possibly assumed that movies always seek audience involvement, and even identification, with their characters. Certainly Hollywood films do, argues Carl Plantinga. They comprise, he writes, "a particularly emotional cinema ... mainstream films avoid audience boredom at all costs and attempt to elicit strong, clear (if also sometimes mixed) emotions throughout the viewing process".[16] But *Elephant* counters such emotional cinema that seems bent on avoiding audience boredom at all costs. Van Sant's film tends to be unemotional, as well as unpredictable and inexplicable. Rather than wooing the audience, it keeps the spectator at bay.

Of course, Van Sant in *Elephant*, which might be considered a docudrama, does not just sit back and let things occur. Indeed, his conspicuous manipulations of time, space and motion veer towards the wizardry of Georges Méliès and Dziga Vertov's *Man with a Movie Camera* rather than adhering to objective documentary practice. Yet *Elephant* also deploys techniques commonly associated with both realist cinema and slow movies. Not the least of these are long takes, which Bazin argued preserve the natural continuity of the time and space of everyday life. In *Elephant*, though, long takes not only bolster the realism but also serve to keep the audience distant and the film's emotional temperature low. For as in *Stranger Than Paradise*, long takes in effect suspend shot/reverse-shot editing and point-of-view shots, which in mainstream cinema tend to heighten the impression that a film's characters possess narrative agency and subjectivity and make emotional as well as physical contact with one another. Moreover, as mainstream movies cut in shot/reverse-shot fashion from one character to another, the audience may grow more intimate with each character, leading to greater identification. In all of *Elephant*, though, such editing occurs in a sustained manner just once, at the climax in the school library as the long-awaited massacre begins.

The unusual shot/reverse-shot sequence in the library centres on Alex and Elias. Although the two have not met previously in the film, their lives have been juxtaposed. For instance, as Alex scribbled notes in the cafeteria, he experienced a crescendo of ambient noise and drew his hands to his head; the film then cut to Elias, who by contrast appeared untroubled as he entered the school on his way to the photo lab to develop his pictures. In the lab, chatting softly and amiably with fellow artists about focus, composition, colour, light and contrast, Elias seemed more serene than ever. Alex looked similarly at peace just once: while performing the *Moonlight Sonata* in his basement quarters. But his calm exploded when he started to strike the wrong keys.

Now, upon entering the library, Alex looks as he has most of the time: somewhat sad and puzzled, and nearly as isolated and inexpressive as *Dead Man*'s Blake. As he strides with Eric toward Michelle, who is employed in the library shelving books, Alex turns to his left, towards Elias (who entered the library after taking John's picture); and in this gesture Alex virtually announces or declares himself to Elias, whose back is to him. Then we hear the cocking of Alex's firearm, offscreen. Cut to Elias turning around. Cut to Alex and Eric, observed from behind, repeating the end of their prior motion when they advanced towards Michelle. Cut to Alex as Van Sant's camera pans from his back to his face. Cut to Elias, who raises his own camera and apparently aims at Alex. Cut to Alex. He seems to pose for Elias's camera as we hear it click. Then Alex turns to Michelle. Cut to a medium close-up of her being struck by gunfire at close range, her blood splattering the books behind her. Cut to Alex turning to his left again, but past Elias, before felling additional victims in the blurred background.

Elias himself is not shown being shot. His death would be unwelcome and surprising, not just because he is an almost angelic figure and the director's surrogate, but also because he has been engaged in achieving through peaceful means – that is, by taking still photographs – the arrest or suspension of motion and time that has comprised perhaps the film's salient formal interest. Alex, too, has seemed impelled to halt motion and time, but only through mass murder. Thus, two contrary approaches to stillness, as distinct from each other as the clicking of a camera and the firing of a gun, collide in the climactic encounter in the library.

The use of shot/reverse-shot editing to delineate this encounter demonstrates anew the dramatic significance in *Elephant* of what Panofsky termed "formal presentation". Suddenly the exceptional long takes that have been the rule in this film are suspended, and the editing that supplants them, though commonplace in mainstream cinema, seems almost shocking because it has not occurred previously in the film, now all but over. The narrative leading up to the massacre in *Elephant* is uneventful, and the fact of the massacre is predictable. Hence the film's plot accounts just partially for *Elephant*'s drama and excitement. More consequential is its formal presentation, including its uses of the camera and editing, which upend typical assumptions about what is ordinary and extraordinary in motion pictures. *Elephant* first bans the ordinary (shot/reverse-shot editing) and installs the exceptional (extensive long takes), which becomes the new ordinary; then, towards the end, the film deploys the rejected ordinary, which now feels novel, even extraordinary.

◆

Formal presentation plays an equally prominent role in Sokurov's *Mother and Son*, with the result that the Russian film, like *Elephant* and other slow movies, seems as likely to distance and disorient the audience as to engage it. Susan Sontag, probably the most persuasive and celebrated US advocate of Sokurov's cinema, considered him "perhaps the most ambitious and original serious filmmaker of his generation". His movies convey exceptional "moral depth", she said, yielding "an unforgettable emotional experience".[17] Yet *Mother and Son*, Sokurov's first major international success, widely praised for its moral and emotional force, left Andrew Sarris cold, though he considered it an exceptional work. "See *Mother and Son* if you are looking for something completely anti-formulaic", wrote Sarris in the *New York Observer*. At the same time he found aspects of the film's formal presentation overdone and off-putting: "There is a prodigious effort involved in the degree of control the director exerts on the human face, voice and body, and all the God-given manifestations of the natural world." Sokurov's forms of control, argued Sarris, reduced the naturalness and credibility of the physical setting and the human characters. Such distortions and constraints alienated Sarris, who might otherwise have sympathised and identified with the characters: "I recently lost my own beloved mother, and I should be the ideal spectator for *Mother and Son*, guilt, grief and all. But I was never moved, possibly because the son's sorrows were rendered with such rhetorical excessiveness that I felt he was suffering enough for both of us."[18]

Among reviewers more favourable to *Mother and Son* was the *San Francisco Chronicle*'s Edward Guthmann, who called the film "a surpassingly emotional experience that stands completely alone among recent films … Instead of … extra sentiment and syrup, *Mother and Son* delivers pure emotion – heartbreaking and rhapsodic … refiguring cinema as an act of reverence – a form of visual poetry … that celebrates family love and the strength of the spirit."[19] Although Sarris and Guthmann responded differently to *Mother and Son*, they probably would have agreed that the film, despite its checks and constraints, projects emotion more emphatically than *The Second Circle* does. By word, look, touch and deed, the son and his dying mother repeatedly testify to their mutual caring, whereas such avowals are largely absent in *The Second Circle*, in part because the father has died by the time the son arrives (and, in any case, the two were never close). Moreover, the natural environment in *The Second Circle* hardly compensates for the absence of human warmth and community in this film. The flat, cold setting evokes less wonder, less emotion of any sort, than do *Mother and Son*'s majestic landscapes, reminiscent, as critics have noted, of Northern Romantic paintings by Caspar David Friedrich. Yet despite the greater emotion and natural beauty in *Mother and Son*, Sarris's point is not easily dismissed: the film's stilted effects do produce sensations of excess and unreality, as a result of which the audience's emotional engagement may be retarded, if not arrested.

The extraordinary opening image provides evidence of both Guthmann's "pure emotion" and Sarris's "excessiveness", a combination that may simultaneously attract and repel the spectator. The son lies in bed at an angle to his mother, with his head above hers, his eyes peering past her in unexplained rapture, while her eyes stay closed. In sharper focus than the rest of the image, both faces appear in the upper half of the frame, as if in the distance, in long shot. The wavy grain of the mother's blanket spreads beneath them in the foreground across more than a third of the frame, conferring on the scene an undulant air, as if mother and son were at sea. With his wide-eyed gaze betokening unusual purity and intensity, the son remains incredibly still. Possibly asleep, his mother also remains still but for the slight rise and fall of her blanket as she breathes. Indeed, for the first twenty-five seconds of this shot, which will last five minutes, mother and son are so immobile that the image suggests a still photograph or a painting. Particularly "posed" – as Sarris would say – is the son's body stretching horizontally across the screen, perpendicular to the frame's vertical borders, and nearly perpendicular to his mother's body. Thus positioned, the son in his stillness appears almost suspended in mid-flight like some character in *The Matrix* (Wachowski Brothers, 1999). His black-clad body seems endowed with wings as it merges into the black, cape-like shadow on the blurred, darkly mottled wall in the background. Further, the image as a whole has a dense, painterly and anamorphic look, lending weight to Lauren Sedofsky's view that Sokurov's "paradigm is indeed painting" rather than film,[20] and adding to the scene's controlled, immobile and "excessive" feeling, which persists throughout *Mother and Son*.

"I don't remember a film that has captured this sense of deep intimacy and communion between a parent and an adult child", wrote Guthmann.[21] Yet often the rendering of this intimacy as it verges on rapture seems unconvincing and overdone. "Creation – you are wonderful", exclaims the son almost too poetically and self-consciously (though subtitles may be the problem) as he converses with his mother. Then he tells her, "You and I – we love each other", a redundant declaration given their extremely intimate positioning and fondling. What explains such "rhetorical excessiveness", which bears on the son's wonder as well as his suffering, and on the film's action and mise-en-scène more generally?

Perhaps the son's declaration, "You and I – we love each other", indicates a need for reassurance about their love, or a desire to overcome some nagging disparity between the love they have attained and one yet more ideal that he imagines. The mother alludes to such divides between real and ideal when she and the son discuss their recent dreams just before he tenderly combs her hair. Mentioning first a "suffocating nightmare" from which she awoke "terror-stricken", the mother goes on to lament that "God, dwelling in my soul, affects only my consciousness ... He never extends to the outer world, to the course of things ... My heart is heavy from such imperfection." The son reports having had a nightmare similar to hers, and concludes adoringly that they "have the same dreams". But while his notion of having the same dreams supports the ideal of intimacy they share, it is unlikely to be literally accurate. Rather, the son's statement suggests a deeply held wish striving to become fact, striving to extend "to the outer world" as the mother would have God do. In a similar vein, *Mother and Son*'s "rhetorical excessiveness" may reflect Sokurov's intention to create a cinema in which the immaterial world becomes increasingly tangible, a cinema in which ideals and aspirations transform the surface of the image, or "the skin of the film".[22]

The strong tactile sensations evoked in *Mother and Son* result partly from the frequent and intimate physical contact between the parent and her child. Their bodies press together as they lie in bed and as the son cradles her in his arms or hoists her over his back in order to carry her across the hills and forest near her home. Tactile and bodily sensations are also central in *The Second Circle*, as when the son painstakingly scrubs his father's naked corpse in the snow on a cold night, or when the father's face assumes features of the son's later on. But the physical contact between parent and child in the earlier film is less constant and, obviously, less alive. Yet another factor contributes to the greater tactility of *Mother and Son*: Sarris refers to this factor when he remarks that "Mr. Sokurov goes so far as to distort his images with the equivalents of brushstrokes and mirrored reflections"; similarly, Guthmann comments that "Sokurov shoots through mirrors and panes of hand-painted glass positioned at various angles."[23] Such manipulations, along with Sokurov's anamorphic lenses, inevitably yield unusual effects. Bulging, compressed, distended and glassy, the images often appear liable to crack or burst open, though at times they look soft, hazy, even vaporous and ethereal. Conventional realism and linear perspective, or what Sokurov has called "traditional illusionistic volume",[24] give way to a palpably different vision, which to Guthmann suggests "the heightened dreamlike reality of the dying mother and son".[25] The vision also may portray the realisation, or extension into the outer world, of the son's ideal of love and the mother's notion of God and spirit. *Mother and Son*'s tactile world suggests, in any case, the convergence of ordinarily separate and elusive realms of being.

In this cinematic universe like no other, Sokurov's abrogation of "traditional illusionistic volume" is crucial. He has made clear, often in relation to the value he places on reticence and mystery in art, his preoccupation with the image's essential flatness: "art is only where ... reticence exists. A limiting of what we can actually see and feel. There has to be mystery and the flat image provides the mystery."[26] Repeated occurrences of flat and compressed compositions in *Mother and Son* forcefully remind the viewer of Sokurov's commitment to the flat image – to what Lauren Sedofsky has termed "limited visibility … the unprecedented eradication of linear perspective … plane-bound deviations from the Albertian model".[27] Interviewed by Sedofsky in 2001, Sokurov cited the development in Russia of lenses resistant to mainstream cinema's three-dimensional bias, and implied that such lenses were used to shoot *Mother and Son*:

> The question is whether we need a three-dimensional space at all. The development of pictorial art reposes in the artist's understanding of the flat surface [i.e., the flat screen or canvas] as a canon, an objective reality that should not be fought … Since camera lenses are generally designed specifically to create the impression of volume, we have had two developed in Russia specially for our films. They reverse traditional illusionistic volume and emphasize the illusion of a plane. These are the first steps, but we still have a long way to go before we have significant artistic resources for the flat film image.[28]

Yet possibly even more important to him than attaining the flat image is that he exert more formative control of his films than conventional lenses allow. Hence he decries the "good-looking picture … created essentially by neither the director nor the cameraman but rather by the frozen liquid of optical glass".[29]

In underscoring his own vision rather than one dictated by conventional cameras and lenses, Sokurov brings to mind Stan Brakhage, whose book of the early 1960s, *Metaphors on Vision*, begins, "Imagine an eye unruled by man-made laws of perspective",[30] and goes on to recommend subversive steps like "deliberately spitting on the lens or wrecking its focal intention".[31] Brakhage adds: "One may over or underexpose the film. One may use the filters of the world, fog, downpours, unbalanced lights, neons with neurotic color temperatures, glass which was never designed for a camera."[32] While Sokurov was to deploy "panes of hand-painted glass" in filming *Mother and Son*, Brakhage painted directly on celluloid for *Dog Star Man* and other films. Brakhage concluded one of his lists of subversive measures in *Metaphors on Vision* by exulting that the avant-garde filmmaker "may become the supreme trickster, with hatfuls of all the rabbits listed above breeding madly".[33]

Between Brakhage and Sokurov, two tricksters, exist differences as well as resemblances of outlook. The human eye Brakhage exalted over the camera eye, for instance, he identified with a newborn's innocent, untutored way of seeing ("How many colors are there in a field of grass to the crawling baby unaware of 'Green'?" he asked in *Metaphors on Vision*), whereas Sokurov makes paramount his own highly educated eye and soul, steeped in literary, musical and visual works of "old masters", such as – in the case of painting – El Greco and J. M. Turner as well as Caspar David Friedrich.[34] Embracing his connection in particular to artistic giants of the seventeenth through nineteenth centuries rather than to his contemporaries, Sokurov casts himself as "resolutely traditional",[35] as indebted to the past and mindful of the continuity of time, experience and art. "The purpose of art", he tells Sedofsky, "is to repeat the most fundamental ideas, year after year, decade after decade, century after century. Because people forget."[36] And to Joan Dupont he declares, "The mechanism of art is always memory."[37]

Perhaps Sokurov's abiding respect for the continuity of time and experience helps explain his preference for long takes over Brakhage's rapid montages. Indeed, he describes himself as "sick of editing" when he limits his feature-length *Russian Ark* to a single take. "I do not want to experiment with time … to squeeze or segment time, but to go with the flow."[38] His belief, moreover, in the essential stability of art and experience, both of which he views as based on eternal, fundamental ideas, may explain the slow deliberateness of his films in contrast to the excited motion of Brakhage's cinema. Probably *Mother and Son* proceeds all the more slowly because it addresses death. A mother's life ends in *Mother and Son*; "flow", such as Hoberman cited in his review of *Elephant*, is arrested.

As indicated in chapter one, Sokurov maintained that a major purpose of art was to help humanity prepare for death, for an end, in a sense, to motion and time. The immobility of the mother and her son during the first twenty-five seconds of Sokurov's film sets the stage for additional pauses, centred on the son more than the mother. Not long before her death, for example, a low-angle shot of the son shows him standing frozen for fourteen seconds observing her. This "caesura" occurs sometime between his handing her a bottle of fluid and entreating her to eat. In other instances his body pauses or freezes in mid-stride: for example, when he sets out to find letters and books to read to his mother as she lies on the bench near her house, and at least once as he prepares to lift and carry her down a forest trail. When motion resumes, it is just as slow and gradual as before, whether over the forest trail or on the path between the mother's house and the nearby bench. "Everything", including each motion of the camera and characters, "happens slowly".[39]

The concluding scenes of the son grieving for his mother, both just before she dies and after, are no different – they proceed slowly, quietly, softly, suggesting a cautious minimalism contrary to the "rhetorical excessiveness" claimed by Sarris. The son steps gently from his mother's home, for instance, having vainly encouraged her to accept food, and enters the luxuriant countryside and mountainous forest where previously he transported her. Viewed primarily through panes of glass and anamorphic-like lenses[40] in extreme, high-angle long shots, he looks exceptionally small and vulnerable in the wondrous, curving vastness devoid of other human presence. Finally he appears in a closer, eye-level long shot: his body pressed against a burly tree in the forest, he sobs softly in the wind as the distant chant or lullaby of an unidentified woman drifts in and out of hearing. Then he sits at the base of the tree (and at the bottom of the frame), where his lamentation turns into a moan, and then into a hesitant, broken humming or echoing of the distant tune. He points his face skyward, as if to espy the chanteuse in the misty sunlight and tremulous shadows of the woods.

When he returns home to find his mother dead, the film shifts from anamorphic extreme long shots to an anamorphic close-up lasting three minutes without a cut, almost to the very end of the film. Filling the lower half of the frame is the sallow flesh of the mother's elongated lower arm, wrist and hand at rest on her blanket. Soon the son's right hand, elongated like hers as it enters the anamorphic frame, moves slowly down the mother's arm onto her fingers, all the while pressing into her parched flesh. Then the son's face, as his hand withdraws, slides up the arm and out of frame, leaving his thick, elongated neck tautly stretched over the mother's lower arm and the back of her hand. His left hand creeps into the frame and presses into the backs of her fingers while his neck remains in place; then his hand hops a bit further up her arm, presses again, and retreats, leaving his neck alone braced along her arm across the full width of the screen. Finally a strong spasm grips the skin, tissues and muscles of his neck, and a desperate, strangled scream emerges, as if he has been fatally stabbed. The long take ends with a dissolve to a close shot of the son and his mother in bed. He faces down, his mouth below the bottom of the frame. "Wait for me", his voice entreats the mother. "We will meet where we agreed." So ends the film.

By the time this final shot with its promise of reunion ends, almost twenty minutes (nearly a third of the film) have elapsed since the son slowly descended the steps of his mother's house and made his way alone into the countryside and forest. No other words have been heard, except perhaps indistinctly in the distant chant of the unknown woman. Further, few sounds of any kind have issued from the son during this time. Only his footsteps have been audible, and then his low sobs and moans by the tree in the rushing wind. Equally restrained during his journey has been the spare, delicate interplay of natural and mechanical sounds, including the flapping of a large bird's wings, fragments of dissonant piano music, a train whistle, a bell, waves of water and a dog's bark. Consequently Sarris's charge of "rhetorical excessiveness" fits neither the son's suffering nor the soundtrack, especially in the final portion of the film.

As suggested, though, Sarris's phrase seems more apt if applied to the film's visual composition. The appearance I have called anamorphic, which in fact ensues from post-production adjustments as well as from "distorting" lenses, angled mirrors and painted glass, often does feel strained and excessive. Rather than simply indicating benign uplift, for example, the distorted if majestic landscapes dwarfing the son betoken stress and estrangement. And the son's posed, hesitant stance and gait in these environments add to the unease. Sokurov has referred to landscape as an unsympathetic "witness of death … Not every human face contains some artistic essence, but every landscape does. Each one is the indifferent countenance of nature looking at human beings, some lofty art that doesn't care whether humanity exists or not. There is a special pain and tragedy in it."[41] Possibly there is also special heaviness in the natural world in *Mother and Son*, laden as it is with optical manipulations. Michael Sicinski has written that Sokurov in *The Second Circle* "manages to invest the swirling grain of the film stock with the anguished, punishing weight of iron slag; it is a film that exhausts the eyeballs down to the bottom of the orb".[42] Sicinski also avers that such weight and anguish dissipate in *Mother and Son*'s "expansive pictorial beauty and ... unbridled simplicity".[43] But I suggest that the weight and anguish persist, though in an altered form, in the later film, and that its pictorial beauty is anything but simple.

Perhaps buttressing his claim for *Mother and Son*'s lightness of being, Sicinski remarks that "under Sokurov's flattened gaze and attenuated pacing, the union of mother and son (the former frequently carried like an infant in the latter's arms) is a structure that cancels time altogether. Here Sokurov achieves the sublime, nearly lifting cinema out of the realm of the temporal arts."[44] But Sokurov also lifts the characters in *Mother and Son* out of the realm of human connection and community. Indeed, the film's universe may be yet more insular than *Elephant*'s, wherein no hint appears of the firemen, police, neighbours, journalists and medical personnel who hastened to the actual massacre of 1999. The son asks his mother in *Mother and Son*, "Is it nice living here?" The query both casts him as something of a stranger despite his physical and emotional intimacy with his mother and underscores the strangeness of an elderly person like her living alone far from other people. Given the unnatural slowness and visual oddness of *Mother and Son*, the film seems no less detached from the world than its two characters. Perhaps for this reason *Mother and Son* brings to mind Lyotard's notion that "avant-garde art abandons the role of identification that the work [of art] previously played in relation to the community of addressees".[45] But if, like *The Second Circle* and other slow movies, *Mother and Son* resists "the role of identification", it nonetheless stirs wonder in the "addressee".

Long Shot

Distant and *Climates*

"How is it that the same movie [in this case, Nuri Bilge Ceylan's Distant] can seem tedious on first viewing and absorbing on the second? ... Perhaps in the hurry of Cannes, with four or five films a day, I could not slow down to occupy those silences."

– Roger Ebert[1]

"The central thematic [in Antonioni's tetralogy] ... is the perilous state of our emotional life ... a life lacking in purpose, in passion, in zest, in a sense of community, in ordinary human responsiveness, in the ability to communicate, in short, a life of spiritual vacuity."

– Seymour Chatman, *Antonioni, or, The Surface of the World*[2]

Although Roger Ebert apparently adhered to his low opinion of *Dead Man* cited at the end of the first chapter, his change of heart about *Distant* confirms that our reactions to movies, along with other aspects of our experience, are susceptible to change. Reacting in 1985 to the critical outcry of the early 1960s against Antonioni's seeming breaches of narrative logic, causality and resolution in his "great tetralogy" (*L'Avventura* [1959], *La notte* [1960], *Eclipse* [1962] and *Red Desert* [1964]), Seymour Chatman wrote, "at this distance in time it is difficult to understand all the critical fuss that greeted the films".[3] History often acts to mute, elevate or otherwise amend prior critical opinion. Hence, provided "the recipient or narratee" remains "active", as Elsaesser and Hagener have noted, the "exchange between reader or viewer and text or sound-and-image track" remains "open". Our experience of a film – of tone, rhythm and action, for example – may change. Moreover, a recent slow movie such as *Distant* may alter our perception of older slow films such as those of Antonioni.

Hardly unusual in slow movies, in addition to their sparse, inexpressive dialogue, are periods of silence, devoid of all spoken words if not of all natural sounds, like those Ebert eventually "occupied" in *Distant*. The absence of words can be calming, as in Abbas Kiarostami's *Five Dedicated to Ozu*, a slow movie entirely free of dialogue. But frequently, as in *Distant* and to a lesser extent *Climates*, absences of spoken words and scarcities of other sounds, along with visually bare or empty spaces, betoken vacuities of purpose, passion, community and spirituality such as Chatman identified in Antonioni's tetralogy. Resemblances between Antonioni's work and Ceylan's have been suggested by film critics including J. Hoberman of the *Village Voice*, Philip French of *The Observer* and Manohla Dargis and A. O. Scott of the *New York Times*.[4] "Mr. Ceylan has clearly been influenced by any number of modernist auteurs, including Michelangelo Antonioni",[5] writes Dargis; French states that Isa (played by Ceylan), the central male character in *Climates*, "has something of the ... spiritual emptiness of the heroes of Antonioni's *L'Avventura* and *La notte*".[6] Hoberman, too, focuses on "emptiness" in Ceylan's films. "The remote Mahmut is a modern man", he says of the older of *Distant*'s two main characters. "He's distanced from his own feelings ... The emphasis falls on the space between people – and their failure to bridge that void ... Is it possible to make a rich and satisfying movie about loss and emptiness?"[7] Similarly, French comments that *Distant* is "a contemplative picture about loneliness, alienation and the death of community life", a film "about desolation and loss".[8]

Like these critics, Asuman Suner considers Ceylan a filmmaker intensely concerned with absence, loss, silence and emptiness. But in order to illuminate Ceylan's concern she turns, in *New Turkish Cinema: Belonging, Identity and Memory*, primarily to Deleuze's *Cinema 2: The Time Image* rather than, say, to the cinema of Antonioni or another filmmaker. Yet Deleuze's account of time-image cinema often resembles Chatman's description of Antonioni's work quoted at the start of this chapter. In positing time's displacement of action, motion and causality as cinema's predominant subject after World War II, for example, Deleuze underscores not just time's heightened presence in films in which nothing much happens, but also various instances of absence and emptiness. As noted in the introduction, he speaks of "empty time", the "halting of time", "empty" or "deserted" space, and ultimately, as Suner stresses, of empty humanity. "Speaking of the representation of empty or deserted spaces in time-image cinema", Suner writes, "Deleuze contends that characters wandering around these spaces are themselves emptied."[9] She then quotes his description of such characters: "They are suffering less from the absence of another than from their absence from themselves."[10] Deleuze also stated that the notion of empty or deserted space "refers back again to the lost gaze of the being who is absent from the world as much as from himself".[11]

Deleuze's book about time-image cinema and contemporary human experience originally appeared in 1985, the same year as Chatman's study of Antonioni; further, in the same paragraph from which Suner quotes, Deleuze cited Antonioni's *Eclipse* and *The Passenger* (1976) as representative of the absence and emptiness he was describing. Yet Suner refrains from linking Ceylan to Antonioni. Instead she simply reports that "Ceylan cites Ingmar Bergman, Andrei Tarkovski, Robert Bresson, Yasujiro Ozu, and Abbas Kiarostami among his major sources of inspiration".[12] While Antonioni appears neither on this list nor in the index of Suner's book, strong resemblances of form and content between his films and Ceylan's such as critics often cite are difficult to deny. There are also immense differences, though, which perhaps prompt Suner's silence about Antonioni; and these differences may illuminate not only Ceylan's distinctiveness, but also that of recent slow movies as compared to their precursors.

We might sum up major differences between Ceylan's films and Antonioni's by stressing that Ceylan's are in various ways leaner or more minimal. Especially in *Distant*, the main characters, psychologically flat and stiff, are less verbal as well as less emotive than those in Antonioni's tetralogy. Silences in *Distant* are more complete, often devoid of music as well as dialogue, and with fewer and softer natural sounds. Motion, whether of the camera or characters, is more limited. Long takes are more numerous and sustained. The rendering of material and spiritual loss and emptiness, while no less constant than in Antonioni's tetralogy, is quieter and more restrained, or less emphatic and melodramatic. Also, Ceylan's major characters represent a less privileged social and economic class than do those in Antonioni's tetralogy.

◆

Much as Ebert in 2004 addressed what he called "those silences" in *Distant*, Jonas Mekas probed the silences in Antonioni's *Eclipse* in 1962. "You have heard much about the silence in Antonioni's films, particularly in *La notte*", he observed. "*Eclipse* is still more silent. There is a gradual disappearance of dialogue from *L'Avventura* to *Eclipse*." Presaging the views of Chatman and Deleuze published in 1985, Mekas argued that silence in Antonioni's cinema signalled a yet deeper absence, loss or vacuity: "they say Antonioni rediscovered silent cinema, he is going back to the true principles of cinema. They look at it formalistically. But ... Antonioni's silence comes from his content." This content, insisted Mekas, went beyond the dilemma of communication often considered Antonioni's salient theme. "Antonioni's films aren't about communication, as all critics have conspired to insist. His films are about people, about *us*, who don't have anything to communicate, who don't feel a need to communicate, whose human essence is dying. Antonioni's films are about the death of the human soul."[13]

Silence betokening absence, loss and emptiness – and possibly even "the death of the human soul" – pervades both the final scene of *Distant* and the celebrated seven-minute "coda", as Chatman called it, of *Eclipse*. Yet while both endings are devoid of dialogue, they differ significantly in style and tone, as do the films they conclude. Let us start with *Distant*. For the entire last scene of the film, Mahmut (Muzaffer Özdemir) sits alone on a bench in a largely empty outdoor space in Istanbul facing the river as boats go by. His expression is blank, mirthless, nearly lifeless, as it has been throughout *Distant*. For an instant he almost smiles. He lights a cigarette, adjusts his posture, looks faintly pensive. Mostly, he just maintains his blank, affect-less look until the camera finally inches towards him, from medium shot into close-up, and the final image fades out. Except for one broader slow movement, the camera, like Mahmut, remains rather still in this scene. Frugal editing supports this stillness: since the scene lasts three minutes and seventeen seconds and contains only six shots (including one of a boat and another of a building far to Mahmut's right), the average shot length is 32.8 seconds. Further, not just the scene's silence but also its stillness is served by the absence of music as well as the absence of dialogue; also, just a few nonhuman sounds occur – emitted by boats, birds, wind and water slapping against the shore.

Although Mahmut has been mirthless, taut and silent throughout the film, he has special cause to be restrained or subdued in this final scene. For he has confronted in the two previous scenes fresh reminders of the emptiness of his life and of his absence from himself and the world. In the first of the previous scenes, he returned to his apartment to find his young cousin Yusuf (Emin Toprak) gone. A country bumpkin who just weeks earlier hitch-hiked to the great metropolis of Istanbul to find work on ships that would take him around the world, Yusuf was never a welcome guest in Mahmut's apartment, perhaps because he reminded Mahmut, somewhat as Eva does Willie in *Stranger Than Paradise*, of a former self he would rather forget (Gönül Dönmez-Colin says Yusuf reminds Mahmut "of the roots he thought he had severed while trying to build a new identity in the urban environment").[14] Mahmut too had abandoned rural life and travelled to Istanbul to make a new life. He took up photography, got married and divorced, relinquished hope of a career in art, and fell into solitary assignments as a commercial photographer. Recently he has been photographing ceramic tiles that hold no real interest for him. Yusuf disrupted Mahmut's routine, but provided most of what little company and dialogue he had. Now the photographer must return to his former silence and isolation and ruminate on why he could not open himself to his kin. This question's urgency has increased as a result of the second scene in question (following Mahmut's discovery of Yusuf's departure and preceding the closing scene at the river), in which Mahmut has driven to the airport and, from behind pillars and walls, furtively observed his former wife – who underwent an abortion when confronted by his refusal to have a child – depart for Canada with her new husband.

Like *Distant*'s final scene of Mahmut alone on the bench by the river, *Eclipse*'s famed ending bears witness to absence and solitude. Obviously contributing to this sense of desolation is the absence of the two main characters, who unexpectedly vanish from the film. In the scene prior to the ending, young, beautiful Vittoria (Monica Vitti), who works as a translator, and Piero (Alain Delon), her mother's dashing stockbroker, conclude their amorous frolic on a couch in Piero's boss's office by agreeing to meet at 8pm at their usual place: a white-striped pedestrian crossing where they almost kissed for the first time and subsequently rendezvoused. Moments later begins the film's closing montage of images anchored to the crossing and its surroundings. Fifty-eight such images appear, lasting seven minutes in all, without a word of dialogue as day yields to night. This lengthy montage provides no explanation of the lovers' absence. Nor is it clear, as Ian Cameron has noted, that the events pictured in the montage occur on the same day the lovers promised to meet.[15]

The ending seems vague, ominous and desolate for reasons other than the unexplained absence of the lovers. Although posh neighbourhoods exist within the outlying business and residential district of Rome in which the lovers' white-striped crossing is located, the crossing's immediate environment as presented in the closing montage is decidedly "shabby and forlorn".[16] On the street corner devoid of people where Vittoria once awaited Piero are only a water barrel, still containing the small stick and empty matchbook discarded by the lovers during their first encounter, a heap of chipped air bricks, and a wall of straw matting over a building site. The dreariness is all the more emphatic because each component – the barrel, the heap of bricks, the matting – has at least one separate shot of its own. No more inviting and romantic than these images are close-ups of empty asphalt pavement, ants crawling over tree bark, scaffolding rods protruding through the matting, and water, at times containing bits of refuse, alternately running and trickling between a hole in the barrel and a curbside sewer. This locale's "message", observes Chatman, is that "nothing warm and intimate, perhaps nothing human can happen here".[17] "It is a void", he writes, "not an intended place."[18]

As with the locale, a cold void marks the vaguely apprehensive faces of isolate individuals who turn up during the closing montage in lieu of the lovers. The face of one individual appears particularly barren and severe in three extreme close-ups; then a full shot reveals a tall, gaunt man with white hair who promptly exits the frame. Other individuals are pictured less abstractly, but to equally piercing effect: a woman peering from behind an iron grating; another woman, in long shot in the lower left of frame, sitting glumly beside the door of a residential apartment building; a third dour woman, holding a handbag, standing and waiting at a street corner. Each of these figures, like the man with white hair, is utterly alone. At one point a man and woman leave a bus almost simultaneously through the same door, but they too are strangers who do not acknowledge each other.

Just a few times in this climactic montage do individuals appear to communicate. A nurse pushing a baby carriage at the start of the sequence seems to speak and gesture to the baby. But the action is presented in extreme long shot and no human voice is heard; instead, the main sound is of water shooting from a sprinkler, to which the camera pans from the nurse and child. Later, a bespectacled man and a woman are espied conversing on a roof terrace; but they are even farther away than the nurse and child – and just as inaudible. At least two couples, having emerged with other passengers from a bus at night, seem engaged in conversation. Again, though, as all walk into the distance, only footsteps are heard. Thus, indications of absence and emptiness throughout the closing montage are very much aural as well as visual. As Leonardo Autera and Ettore Mo said to Antonioni, "*Eclipse* ended with the total silence of the human voice, with man reduced to a simple object."[19]

Faint shouts of children playing in the background as a man in the foreground reading a newspaper walks towards them comprise the only exception to human silence in this montage. The man was already reading the paper when, as mentioned earlier, he ignored the female passenger beside him leaving the bus. Particularly in the absence of spoken words, or of human voices other than the children's, the newspaper's headlines warning of an accelerated nuclear arms race take on a chilling, graphic sonority that by itself justifies Chatman's pronouncement that "nothing warm and intimate, perhaps nothing human can happen here".[20] Further, an array of actual sounds in the final montage contributes to the unnerving atmosphere. As the bus conveying the man reading the newspaper turns a corner and comes to a halt, for instance, it swishes and screeches in sync with a menacing close-up of one of its tires. Even the recurrent sound of water shooting from the sprinkler grows ominous. At the start of the montage, this sound underscores the inaudibility of the nurse and child; later, it helps suppress the shouts of the children at play. Moreover, since most natural sounds are suspended during the closing montage, which also includes sudden moments of full silence, the sound merely of footsteps, or of water from the barrel trickling towards the sewer, becomes eerily intrusive. Perhaps still more important to the ending's aural tension and complexity is the music composed by Giovanni Fusco, including the dissonant piano chords that inaugurate and conclude the montage, and the alarming orchestral crescendo that culminates in the film's final image of "an illuminated street light with a glaringly bright halo encircling the lamp".[21]

Conceivably this climactic "light with a glaringly bright halo" suggests an eclipse in reverse, one in which, as Chatman remarks, "a darker body [is] eclipsed by a brighter one".[22] More relevant, though, may be another interpretation mentioned by Chatman, which is that the final image suggests the blast of an atomic bomb.[23] As such, this final image, arising at the dead end of the musical crescendo, renders more conclusive the dread communicated earlier by the newspaper headlines broadcasting the nuclear arms race. One of the numerous anonymous women in the montage prior to this final image resembles Vittoria, until her face turns towards the camera. But the light and halo obviously suggest a deeper terror and disappointment than does the woman who is not Vittoria. The terminal image not only forecloses the return of Vittoria and Piero, but conjures a post-nuclear world largely devoid of human life and love. Yet conceivably such a world – lifeless because loveless – already exists, paving the way for nuclear war; if so, the closing image connoting cosmic void and absence signals how things are rather than solely what is to come. Given this context, it cannot be surprising that the lovers fail either to arrive at the crossing or to trust and act upon their warmer feelings.

Eclipse offers further clues bearing on the lovers' failure to meet and the apparent unreliability of their feelings. Chatman mentions the film's focus on the speed of contemporary life – as indicated, I assume, in the frenzy of the stock exchange where Piero works, the sports cars he prizes, and the bombers and missiles on nuclear alert offscreen. Chatman ascribes the lovers' choice of the crossing as their meeting place to the extreme haste of their universe: "The art of making appointments in congenial places is lost to the hurry-up generation, to their fast sports cars and their breezy approach to life."[24] He adds, "Like celestial bodies (as the title has it), modern lovers converge only for a few moments, since they are traveling at high speeds in different directions."[25] Antonioni himself has blamed money more than speed for the absence or failure of feeling in *Eclipse*. He has called the film a critique both of "the world of money, where feelings have hardly any place"[26] and of "feelings ... filtered through the cobweb money creates around the mind of whoever is involved in it and doesn't see anything else all day long".[27]

Probably it was the absence or failure of feeling itself, however, a theme often central in slow movies, that intrigued Antonioni most fundamentally – more even than money, speed or nuclear confrontation. He later described *Eclipse* as "a modern film in that its protagonists are people who do not believe in feelings – that is, they limit them to certain things".[28] In 1964, just two years after the film's release, he also wrote, "During an eclipse emotions, too, are probably arrested. It was an idea that had vaguely to do with the film I was preparing, a sensation more than an idea, but that already defined the film when the film was still far from being defined."[29] The arrest of emotion and lack of belief in feelings emphasised by Antonioni are especially palpable in *Eclipse*'s closing montage, but these reductive conditions also underlie the lovers' giddy relations throughout the film. Piero and Vittoria, though more expressive than the deadpan strangers who appear in *Eclipse*'s final montage, bear affinity to Deleuze's "being who is absent from the world as much as from himself", to Mekas's people "who don't have anything to communicate", "whose human essence is dying", and to Suner's "emptied" characters.

While both *Distant*'s final scene of Mahmut on the bench and *Eclipse*'s closing montage portray human solitude, silence and emptiness – and perhaps the sense that "nothing human can happen here" – the two renderings diverge immensely, as already indicated. Not the least difference is that *Eclipse* sets the emptiness within a far vaster context than *Distant* does. For instance, *Eclipse*'s ending incorporates more characters, and probably more socioeconomic diversity, though each individual appears just briefly and anonymously. Antonioni's ending also isolates more details of the physical environment, one far more complex and expansive than the locale at the end of Ceylan's *Distant*. Equally relevant to the scope of *Eclipse*'s ending are the headlines that warn of nuclear conflict and thus situate the romantic turns of Vittoria and Piero, not to mention the severe estrangement and emotional dying implicit in the closing montage, within a dire cosmic framework. Events in *Distant* also reflect large issues, such as Turkish migration from the countryside to the city and the tension between the urban and rural milieu,[30] but as no bold headlines summon wide public attention to these issues, Mahmut and Yusuf's drama remains private and contained.

Besides broadening *Eclipse*'s narrative context, the headlines in *Eclipse*'s closing montage deploy words where none are to be heard. The films of both Antonioni and Ceylan are rightly considered to rely on visual more than verbal language. Physical gestures and expressions, and the framing and editing of the human face and body and its material environment, prevail over spoken words. Remarking that dialogue in Antonioni's films is spare, Chatman goes on to contend that Antonioni "virtually returned to the cinema the predominance of the visual that it lost with the advent of sound", and adds that "Antonioni insistently prefers images to dialogue for communicating a character's feelings".[31] In his commentary for the *Distant* DVD, Ceylan subscribes to much the same preferences Chatman finds in Antonioni. Ceylan notes with satisfaction, for example, that most of *Distant* proceeds without dialogue, focusing instead on physical gesture and facial expression. But while both Antonioni and Ceylan prefer images to words, Antonioni uses *more* words – if not always to transform the story, as with the headlines in *Eclipse*, then to advance its expository and expressive course.

This tendency is particularly evident in *L'Avventura*. At the outset, Anna (Lea Massari), who will soon vanish mysteriously and never reappear, quickly voices a sentiment key to both this film and others in the tetralogy (and, incidentally, to Ceylan's *Distant*): "You know, it's terrible to be far away from one another."[32] Her complaint refers to the long intervals she and her lover Sandro (Gabriele Ferzetti) spend physically apart, but also to the vast psychological distance that has developed between them. Her friend Claudia (Monica Vitti), to whom Anna makes this blunt remark, is similarly quick to articulate emotional concerns central both to her life and to the film as a whole: "My God", she says to Sandro as they launch an affair within three days of their first meeting and soon after Anna has disappeared from their yachting party, "is it possible to forget in such a short time, for things to change so quickly?" Then she adds, "It's so sad, so terribly sad ... I have never been so upset in my life."[33] Later she tells Sandro,

"I'm so ashamed of myself ... I tried to hide myself ... I feel so small ... I hate myself."[34] In neither *Distant* nor *Climates* do Ceylan's characters so openly articulate their feelings. In Antonioni's cinema, moreover, such feelings only grow more palpable and emphatic as his characters speak of them. Ceylan's greater resistance to spoken words in both *Distant* and *Climates* coincides with his cinema's more extreme muting, arrest, evasion and de-dramatisation of emotion (a de-dramatisation often influenced by the absence of music, by the way, as well as by the absence of words).

Surprising as it may seem at this distance in time, *Eclipse* was considered a slow film by Antonioni and contemporary reviewers. "The success of ... *Eclipse* in Japan", said Antonioni, "is explained by the very slow rhythm of the film, broken only now and then by 'outbursts', such as the Stock Exchange sequences."[35] Another "outburst" was *Eclipse*'s closing montage, with its average shot length of 7.2 seconds (compared to 32.8 seconds in *Distant*'s final scene) and its disorienting succession of cold, disconnected characters and objects situated in sundry locales related only ambiguously to each other within a large business and residential district. Indeed, by the time *Eclipse* appeared, Antonioni's films overall, not just individual scenes and sequences, had become surprisingly fast-paced. Chatman notes, for example, that there are 473 shots in *L'Avventura* (whereas *Cronaca di un amore*, released nine years earlier, had just 160). The "timing" of *L'Avventura*, Chatman points out, "is not very different from that of Hollywood action footage".[36] His observation parallels James Quandt's (cited in my first chapter) that the average shot length in Bresson's *Pickpocket* "equals the average in concurrent Hollywood films". The same cannot be said, however, of *Distant* or most other slow movies highlighted in this book. Such recent slow movies are distinctly slower paced, as well as more persistently silent and "repressed", to cite Jarmusch's word for *Stranger Than Paradise*, than either present-day Hollywood products or slow foreign classics like *Pickpocket*, *L'Avventura* and *Eclipse*.

Distant's slow, silent, repressed tendencies are quickly evident in the film's opening minutes. With respect to silence, no human voice is heard in the first seven minutes, and no dialogue occurs until almost eleven minutes have elapsed. The first scene, presented in one long take, lasts two minutes and forty-five seconds. Initially in extreme high-angle long shot, the take centres on a lone male figure (Yusuf) trudging slowly through snow across a field and up a hill to a road where he will hitch a ride. The camera is mostly stationary, but when the man exits screen left after ascending the hill and nearing the camera, it moves slowly leftward until the road comes into view for the first time. Then the man re-enters from the left with his back to the camera, and signals to an approaching vehicle to stop. Before it does, the scene ends as the film cuts to opening credits on a black screen.

The look of this initial, one-take scene is not entirely cold and wintry. Behind the flat expanse of snow through which the man makes his way rises a verdant hillside, snow-less and capped with sunlight, cradling a settlement of homes and a church steeple. Yet apart from the call of a rooster and bark of a dog, little if any sign of animal or human life appears. The tiny windows of the homes are either black or silvery voids. It's almost as if the solitary male figure advances through an abandoned though potentially idyllic world. Further, since he is small and unidentifiable in the extreme high-angle long shot at the start of the scene, he is as much a blank as the walls and windows of the distant homes. Even when he nears the camera as he ascends the hill, just a side of his young, rustic face is visible, and then only briefly, before he exits the frame. And since his back is to the camera when he re-enters the frame to hail the ride, he remains a blank, unknown figure.

An indication that he may lack narrative force or agency, moreover, is that the camera reaches the road before he does; and it neither reveals his relation to the road after he exits the frame nor shows the road from his point of view. Indeed, as often is the case in both Ceylan's cinema and Antonioni's, the only viewpoint in this long take is the camera's. When it moves to the left after the man exits, it reveals the road without including him. The camera, not the man, conducts the spectator to the road essential to the man's journey. And in preceding the man, the camera leads *him* to the road much as it does the spectator.

An older individual (Mahmut), also facing away from the camera though partially in profile, sits in the foreground of a dimly lit room at night when the next scene, consisting of a single take like the first, begins after the credits. His motionless face submerged in darkness in the left half of the image, he peers across the room at a blurry female figure (Nazan Kirilmis), more brightly lit than he, slowly disrobing on a bed or couch set against a wall on which hang large, indistinct photographs. His back in sharp focus and more illuminated than his face, Mahmut continues to peer ahead, voyeuristic and perhaps entranced, as the woman, still blurry, billowy and dream-like, removes her reddish shirt or sweater and her lower attire, then wiggles her foot alluringly, beckoning him. Chimes audible since the start of the scene sound in the darkness. Mahmut, after taking a deep breath or two, removes his shoes in a manner suggesting he considers the act a chore rather than a pleasure. Then he stands, steps creakily into the wiggly woman's blurred space, and sits down beside her. He releases in the darkness a heavy sigh that sounds like regret, fatigue or resignation more than relief; then he begins, finally, to touch the woman, whereupon the shot ends, having lasted one minute and eight seconds without a camera movement. No word has been uttered. Nor has either character's face been distinctly revealed.

Distant's avoidance of sustained, frontal, well-lit, sharp-focused views of the human face ends in the next scene. A tense, vigilant stranger (Feridun Koc), his face plainly visible in medium close-up, stands waiting and chewing gum on an urban street at night. Then, from the building behind him, emerges the alluring woman, somewhat furtive but no longer blurred, her face discernible even though in long shot. He turns and sees her glance warily at him, hurriedly walk the opposite way, reach an automobile tightly parked down the block, and drive past his inquisitive gaze. The camera lingers on the man's face in medium shot as he continues to peer screen left, where the car has left the frame. Why does this man merit such exceptional visual attention? Film theorist Béla Balazs described the human face as a crucial window or gateway to the human soul;[37] but why does a gum-chewing, not very soulful character warrant the first sustained close shot of a human face in *Distant*? Has this man been waiting for the woman? Is he related to her in a significant way? Has he been deployed to warn her lest someone witness her presence at the building? More important, will he become a major character, like Mahmut and Yusuf? The brief scene yields no answers; and, like the previous scene inside the dark apartment, it presents minimal action, the barest human contact, and no spoken words.

What follows are seven more minimal scenes, each composed of a single long shot, or at most two. Though the action is scant and slow in each scene, and human contact and speech continue to be withheld, each image reveals, as the following summary indicates, much about the characters and their story.

In the first scene following the cut from the uneasy, vigilant man in the street, Mahmut, observed primarily from the same camera position as before, reappears on the couch in the dark room where he began to touch the woman. Apparently reacting to a sticky sexual or other unwelcome substance his right hand has picked from the couch, he stretches the hand open, exposing it in a pool of light in the darkness. Then he extends his left arm and hand to switch on the lamp and pluck facial tissues from a box, while his right arm reaches in the opposite direction and his right hand stays open and aloft, presumably to avoid further contamination. These symmetrical extensions comically suggest the suffering of a martyr stretched on a cross; and despite the blank look on his face, Mahmut's posture communicates a surfeit of dismay as he applies the tissues to the freighted hand and the couch, and then exits frame right with the soiled material. The next shot finds him in the kitchen, where again he appears to prowl for alien matter. Descending on his hands and knees, he vainly scrutinises the floor and the interior of a cabinet, perhaps for signs of mice that a glue strip at the kitchen entrance is meant to catch. Thus silent, isolate and fastidious, Mahmut moves slowly and cautiously in this pair of scenes to apprehend rodents as well as his sexual remains.

When the ringing of a telephone intrudes on Mahmut's gradual opening of a cabinet door in the kitchen, the film cuts to a phone on the desk in the room where the sexual activity and subsequent clean-up occurred. Before Mahmut can pick up the phone, however, we hear on the answering machine the film's first spoken words: "Mahmut, it's Mom. I called earlier, but you were out. Take care." These words arrive seven minutes and four seconds into *Distant*, but the next moments bring no dialogue. Mahmut switches the desk lamp on and ponders what to do. Slowly and reluctantly, he starts to call his mother, or so we assume, but stops and puts the phone down.

Distant then cuts to this reticent lover and son placing items for a snack along with a half dozen boxes of photographic film on a small kitchen table, where he begins to eat. The film cuts again, this time to a long shot of Mahmut in his studio perfunctorily snapping photographs of nondescript tiles with his tripod-mounted camera. The subsequent shot has him seated outdoors at a waterside cafe with a beverage and newspaper, then rising to leave. In the next long shot, which is also a longer take than either of the two previous shots, the photographer sits impassively in a spacious, wood-panelled office while a man in suit and tie some distance away, with his back to Mahmut, examines a group of photographic negatives. As the man holds them against a large, light-filled window beyond which stand tall office buildings, the negatives appear to fit within a column of windows resembling a celluloid strip in a building across the way. But this visual pun augurs no playful exchange between Mahmut and the man reviewing his photographic work. Just as the man moves from the window to his desk and Mahmut looks up from a magazine, their silent meeting ends abruptly with a shot of Yusuf ambling wearily up the street to Mahmut's residence.

The following shot finds Yusuf at the entrance to Mahmut's building searching for Mahmut's name on a directory beside the door. Then the same man who stood outside when Mahmut's lover left the building enters the frame from the street. He ignores Yusuf at first, unlocks the door to the building, and goes inside, only to emerge a moment later and ask, "Are you looking for someone?" Inquiring whether Mahmut lives in the building, Yusuf identifies himself as "a relative … from back home". The two men then consider whether Mahmut is out or the bell to his apartment is inoperative. However mundane, here at last is the first dialogue in *Distant*, initiated ten minutes and forty-three seconds into the film by the minor character Kamil, evidently an employee at Mahmut's building.

The implications of this brief, unremarkable conversation are considerable. In this film in which people are emotionally remote from one another, Kamil's question to Yusuf could be taken as, "Are you looking for someone so that you will no longer be alone, talking only to yourself?" And Yusuf's mention of being a relative from back home also opens the door to human connection and to being at home in the world, as opposed to feeling estranged in the manner of both Antonioni's characters and Ceylan's. No closeness or sympathy develops between Kamil and Yusuf, however. Though Kamil is far more genial than during his earlier appearance in the street at night, he is quickly distracted by residents who assign him chores. He leaves the scene after a woman, heard but not seen, lowers to him from an upper-story apartment an immense red straw basket containing her shopping list. But if not warm or sustained, the exchange between Kamil and Yusuf is civil, and it implicitly challenges the silence, isolation and impassivity that have thus far reigned in *Distant*.

Asuman Suner considers Yusuf, who is indeed vacuous, the chief example in *Distant* of the type of individual characterised by Deleuze as "absent from the world as much as from himself". Yet Mahmut may warrant this description even more, despite his having established in Istanbul a livelihood and a home (in reality, Ceylan's apartment) containing a studio and a handsome library. While Yusuf may be uncouth and ignorant, he arrives in this metropolis which bridges Europe and Asia eager for travel and exploration as well as money. He tells Mahmut he aims to "see the world as a sailor", adding, "You've been everywhere, so why not me?" But Mahmut no longer has the zest and optimism he may once have had. "Every place ends up looking the same", he replies, sounding like Willie and Eddie in *Stranger Than Paradise*. Disappointed in himself and the world, Mahmut seems to disavow human connection, and perhaps always has: "I did everything on my own here. I came to Istanbul without a cent", he brags. He seems unable to rouse himself even for his mother, not only when she phones but also later, when she falls ill and is hospitalised. By contrast, Yusuf becomes enraged and vows to pummel his mother's long-time dentist when she informs him on the phone that the dentist has refused to care for her because she cannot pay (the factory in their village has laid off her husband along with Yusuf and a thousand other workers).

Mahmut reacts minimally to individuals in addition to his mother, and, as in his response to her, his remoteness is never explained. He responds hardly at all to his lover, either in their first, barely romantic exchange described above, or when he sees her with another man in a restaurant, or still later, when she weeps alone in a bathroom in his apartment while he remains in bed. Perhaps Mahmut was equally cold to his wife, Nazan (Zuhal Gencer), even before he instructed her to abort her pregnancy, arguing that they had been contemplating divorce. Now he seems impassive as she tells him she is moving to Canada with her new husband, who would like to have a child if they can overcome her infertility, which doctors attribute to the abortion. Mahmut responds only by suggesting she seek more medical advice in Canada. Though he occupies the foreground of the image during this exchange, he is visually as well as emotionally remote: his back is to the camera most of the time, his face hidden, his head blurred; whereas Nazan, in sharp focus and fully lit, faces the camera and does most of the talking. Yet it is Nazan who later apologises in a telephone farewell the night before she leaves Turkey: "I was somewhat distant towards you", she tells him, "because of my emotions."

Of course Mahmut also fails to open his arms to Yusuf, his relative from back home. "Sorry, I completely forgot you were coming", he tells the young man when they finally meet as Mahmut enters his building in the evening to find Yusuf asleep. Once inside the apartment, Mahmut welcomes his kin by spraying Yusuf's shoes, presumably ridding them of grime and odour, and tucking them out of view inside a cabinet. Further, as Yusuf in their first lengthy conversation tells Mahmut of his plans following the loss of his factory job, Ceylan again has Mahmut face away from the camera and evince scant sympathy (though he does raise a few practical questions).

Although Mahmut may always have been "absent from the world as much as from himself" in dealing with his lover, his mother, his wife and others, it does seem he once fully embraced film and photography as art. "You used to say ... that you'd make films like Tarkovsky. So why are you trying to forget those days?" asks an old friend during a get-together over drinks and snacks while Yusuf and others look on. "Photography is finished, man", replies Mahmut; but the friend does not relent: "Maybe it's you who's done for. You're announcing your death before it's happened. You don't have the right to bury your ideals or make everything commercial." With these remarks *Distant* comes as close as it ever does to articulating Mahmut's failed ardour and commitment, his remoteness from himself and the world. This predicament seems all the more poignant as more hints surface of his former dedication to cinema, Tarkovsky and photography. On his TV monitor Mahmut still watches Tarkovsky films such as *Solaris* (1972) and *Stalker* (1979), for instance, even though, as J. Hoberman writes, he does so "glumly" and *Distant*'s outlook is far removed from Tarkovsky's "visionary mysticism".[38] Mahmut's faltering is also evident in regard to photography. When, during a photo-taking trip, he and Yusuf come to a lovely natural setting inhabited by a flock of sheep, Mahmut's normally blank, sombre look gives way to wonder for the first and only time in the film, though Yusuf appears unmoved. "Why did we stop?" he asks. Mahmut says, "God, what a place to photograph", and tells Yusuf to open the car window. Then Mahmut points to an ideal spot from which to photograph the scene, and Yusuf declares himself ready to set up the camera. But Mahmut suddenly stops himself: "Fuck it", he says, and after a pause, "Why bother?" Then he drives away.

Just what stops Mahmut? What prevents him from emotionally letting go, except twice late in the film, in anger and fear? In the first case, he berates Yusuf not only for lacking skills and maturity and inconveniencing him, but also for messing up his apartment while Mahmut was away helping to care for his sick mother. "I have lots of worries, and now I have to clean up your shit?" Mahmut exclaims. His second outburst occurs after he receives Nazan's farewell phone call, hides a silver watch he has all but accused Yusuf of stealing, and sees Yusuf mercifully kill a mouse caught on the glue strip in the kitchen. Following this killing, Mahmut sits watching TV as if in a trance in blurry darkness; only static or interference fills the screen on which Mahmut has occasionally viewed pornographic films. Suddenly the lamp next to the TV descends slowly toward him, whereupon the film cuts to a long shot of him bolting awake in his bed, casting off the blanket, sitting on the bed's edge and nearly panting as he shakes off a nightmare. Nowhere else in *Distant* does Mahmut express dread and vulnerability as openly as he does here. Here, more than in his tirade against Yusuf, his unconscious speaks directly.

The intrusion of the unconscious perhaps underscores that in indicting Mahmut at the get-together for burying his artistic aspirations and announcing his death "before it's happened", his old friend probably attributed to the photographer more control over his conduct than he really has. Mahmut indeed may be "trying to forget those days" when he held ideals; yet his effort may be partly instinctive rather than calculated, as he strives to distance or forestall the disappointment and other painful feelings attached to old memories. Similarly, if Mahmut "completely forgot" that Yusuf was about to arrive, the impetus may have been the discomfort he felt in being reminded of the past. In no case is Mahmut's "forgetting" entirely deliberate. He cannot fully understand or control his buried self or the pain he seeks to avoid.

Quite aside from his forgetfulness and his unsettling nightmare, Mahmut's crusty, pent-up style invites speculation as to his inner life and the screened or repressed memories it may harbour. His sexual manner in particular – hesitant, furtive, fastidious, favouring sight over touch – hints at a history of sexual embarrassment and repression. Such a history might account for his extreme reticence in face-to-face encounters with his lover and his wife, his covert addiction to pornographic film, and his spying on his wife at the airport, rather than admitting his physical presence and his caring as she departs for Canada. The focus on Mahmut as repressed does not imply he has been *totally* unaware of what he has been doing and what has been happening to him. He may, in fact, feel blameworthy and ashamed, and consequently seek yet greater cover. "Identity hides behind repression",[39] Richard Kuhns remarks in *Tragedy: Contradiction and Repression*. A man in hiding, Mahmut grows ever more furtive and withdrawn, burying his love, his ideals and his better self more deeply. He remains not only cold and impassive, wary of play and spontaneity, but also absent to himself, virtually annihilated. He mourns his dead self, even while repression, according to Kuhns, functions "to obscure loss and the pain of mourning".[40] Mahmut lives with insurmountable grief that is both hidden and undeniable.

◆

"People always have something to hide in real life", Ceylan remarked in 2004.[41] Somewhat like *Distant*, Ceylan's next major film, *Climates*, awarded best picture by the International Federation of Film Critics at Cannes in 2006, features a character named Isa, a professor of archaeology or architectural history played by Ceylan himself, who has things to hide, and who is hidden from himself and others. Moreover, he never emerges from this condition. "I don't believe in change a lot. I don't think very much changes in a life", remarks Ceylan in his commentary on the *Distant* DVD. He adds that Hollywood makes change seem easier than it really is: "It's not that easy like in Hollywood films." People actually are doomed to repetition, he implies. "For the sake of reality", Ceylan refuses in his films "to change things a lot" – and certainly not for the better. Instead, events in *Distant* and *Climates* suggest that lives spent in hiding only stagnate and perhaps deteriorate. Philip Rieff indicates as much in *Freud: The Mind of the Moralist*: "It is our secrets", Rieff writes, "hidden from ourselves, that fester and infect action."[42]

Consistent with Rieff's claim, Isa's conduct proves corrupt and destructive. He lies to his sweetheart Bahar (Ebru Ceylan), a television art director, about his relationship with Serap (Nazan Kirilmis). And he falsely tells Guven (Can Ozbatur), an old friend who has become Serap's suitor, that he has no time to have a drink with him. Moments later that evening, Isa skulks in the darkness across the street from Serap's apartment as she and Guven pull up in his car and she gets out and enters her apartment (perhaps having spotted Isa's shadowy figure, she leaves the door unlocked; he soon enters, and they jointly betray their lovers). Much as Isa spies on Guven and Serap, he secretly watches and follows Bahar later in the film, after he has travelled to a wintry town in eastern Turkey in hope of finding her and renewing their romance. Moreover, when he reveals himself to her in the falling snow outside a café, he at first intimates that their meeting has occurred by chance, that he has come to photograph architectural ruins for his unfinished dissertation rather than to be with her. Although Isa is physically more imposing than Mahmut, he is no more effective at building emotionally rich, forthright relationships. Nor does he seem able to take pleasure in his work or to complete his dissertation. Instead, like many a slow-movie "hero", he seems dissatisfied and disheartened, restrained or held back, less than fully present and potent.

Yet Isa is probably more outgoing and expressive than Mahmut and other slow-movie characters, including William Blake in *Dead Man*, the son in *The Second Circle* and Alex in *Elephant*. It is Bahar, though, whose passion and expressiveness propel *Climates* beyond the emotive stringency of most slow movies. Whereas in *Distant* the first well-lit, legible and sustained medium close-up of the human face does not occur until a minor character, Kamil, appears five minutes into the film, a close-up of Bahar in daylight appears at the very start of *Climates*. Further, this close-up of her face is the first of four that together consume more than half of the film's first six minutes and fifteen seconds. Still more significant is that in each close-up, Bahar's mute face, somewhat like Joan's (Maria Falconetti) in *The Passion of Joan of Arc* (Carl Theodor Dreyer, 1928), seems fraught with strong, conflicting emotions. And in the fourth close-up, which persists for almost two minutes until the opening credits appear, Bahar at last weeps silently (one tear slips down her cheek, a second from her nose to her lips). Yet another close-up of her teary-eyed face ends the film, after Bahar and Isa's failure to restore their relationship.

Bahar's emotional surge at the start of the film occurs as she observes Isa taking photographs of Roman ruins. Soon the two lovers quarrel during dinner with friends one evening by the sea. Next, a close-up of Bahar's face as she sleeps calmly on a sunlit beach inaugurates a nightmare in which Isa advances from the sea like a gangly ghost in blurred, wobbly silhouette; he kisses Bahar's awakened lips and tells her he loves her; then he slowly buries her in the sand, though both lovers at first laugh softly. Bahar wakes in horror, screaming and perspiring, far more upset than Mahmut after his dream of the falling lamp. But lying beside her, Isa reacts with smug indifference, remarking only that it is dangerous to sleep in the sun, to which Bahar responds with a look of dismay and anger. Then Isa tells her they should break up, at least for a time, which sets the stage for more emotional events. Apparently prepared in the next scene to end both their lives, Bahar places her hands over Isa's eyes as the couple drive on their motor-scooter down a winding road above the sea. Their fall to the ground in a vortex of sunlit dust releases their mutual fury. They shout and struggle. Mocking her eagerness to die, Isa seizes her and threatens to push her off the cliff. Though he relents, she hits him repeatedly, and weeps hysterically.

In such scenes the expression of emotion undoubtedly exceeds the constraints of *Distant* and most other slow movies. Indeed, though film critics and slow-movie makers such as Jarmusch, Van Sant and Ceylan see slow movies as antithetical to melodrama, *Climates* veers towards this disparaged genre. Yet *Climates* stops well short of the hyperbolic melodrama represented, for instance, by *Written on the Wind* (Douglas Sirk, 1956). As if to underscore this difference, the final scene of Ceylan's film, which concludes with the close-up mentioned above of Bahar's sorrowful face, depicts the filming of an extremely melodramatic scene for a television movie. At the start of the scene, which is being shot by the crew on which Bahar serves as art director, a kneeling woman weeps by a grave. When a rifle-toting young man arrives and implies she has been crying too much, she declares she'll not stop until her father's death has been avenged. "I'm going to avenge your father. I'm going to stop those tears", replies the young man. In contrast to the suffering woman in the TV drama, Bahar, who stands among the crew observing the action, does not cry aloud. Nor does she cry at the end of the prior scene in Isa's hotel room when it becomes clear she and Isa will not reunite. After he says flatly that he will take her to breakfast and go on to catch his plane, nearly a minute of silence ensues in which the lovers presumably absorb the fact that the affair has ended. Then, as Bahar faces Isa with her back to the camera, we hear a woman weeping, and attribute the sound to Bahar. But when the film cuts to the weeping daughter kneeling at the grave, we realise we have been hearing *her* in the hotel room rather than Bahar. When the latter finally does shed a tear or two in the concluding close-up in the falling snow after a plane passes overhead, her sorrow is silent; unlike more melodramatic heroines, she appears to be thoughtful and in control of her feelings.

The comments by Ceylan and his wife, Ebru Ceylan, on the *Climates* DVD suggest that both of them were sensitive to the film's divergence from what might be termed emotional minimalism. Ebru Ceylan stresses in her commentary her respect for "small acting", meaning "subtle acting, without emphasis". She worries that "crying scenes can be considered very emotional" and says that by relying on small "facial movements" and, more generally, by acting "as little as possible" she sought to keep the crying scenes from becoming "overly dramatic or extremely melodramatic". Upon viewing the finished film, though, she felt she had overdone some scenes – "that maybe I should have acted less". Her husband also stresses in his commentary the importance of small gestures and movements and "small meanings in the face". He adds that he was determined in *Climates* to communicate something of inner life, of his characters' thoughts and feelings. As a result, he says, he used more close-ups – especially of the human face (primarily Bahar's) – than he had in *Distant*.

Climates diverges stylistically from *Distant* and other slow movies not only in its emphasis on close-ups. It also deploys more point-of-view shots; for instance, the close-up of Bahar that inaugurates the film is succeeded by an image of what she appears to be looking at: a space amid giant columns of the Roman ruins she and Isa are visiting. Soon Isa enters the space in long shot and snaps a photograph; the film cuts back to Bahar looking, then returns to the space containing Isa, which Bahar herself then enters. Further, *Climates* has more shot/reverse-shots than is typical of slow movies, and it differs in other ways as well: it cuts more frequently and abruptly, for instance, and it contains more dialogue, or at least more scenes incorporating dialogue, though probably its characters articulate their feelings no more precisely than is usual in slow movies.

Instances of both frequent cutting and extended dialogue occur within the film's mostly slow and quiet penultimate scene in Isa's hotel room, which ends, after a minute of silence and stillness between Isa and Bahar, with the weeping of the woman who is then observed kneeling at the grave in the closing scene. The hotel scene begins at night as Isa, who has been asleep, rises from bed to answer a knock on the door, a sound that began at the end of the prior scene of Isa alone in a café. He opens the door of his room to find Bahar standing hesitantly in the corridor. Earlier, Isa had asked her to join him after she finished work, but she had indicated she would not. Now she slowly enters, goes to the bed and lies down without removing her white coat; he soon follows, and lets his head and upper body slump onto her leg while he remains grounded on the floor. It is here that *Climates'* visual movement accelerates and grows more complex and indeterminate in a two-and-a-half-minute montage such as occurs nowhere else in the film. The singular montage consists of ten shots, mainly close-ups of portions of Bahar's face and hair, with Isa's hand or part of his face or head entering the frame and touching her intermittently. Besides taking in just fragments of the lovers, the images are often in soft focus, and their temporal connection to each other is unclear. Similarly the lovers, who remain dressed, do not connect or make contact emotionally. Thus the dream-like montage, possibly summarising their disjointed experience until dawn, charts not pleasure and fulfilment, but unrest and detachment – again, perhaps, two people sadly absent from themselves and each other. The gnawing sense of rupture rather than union (and of each lover as fragmented or fractured) grows with each cut to a new shot, each break in the flow of the action.

In a surprising turn of events, though, Bahar emerges from her fitful sleep and promptly asserts her presence rather than absence, and perhaps her potential for wholeness and happiness. Taking a seat opposite Isa at a small table by a window, she smiles radiantly in medium close-up as she tells him of her dream that night of flying gently over rolling meadows in perfect sunshine as her mother below waved to her. "I thought 'Wow! She's still alive!' It was really nice. It made me very happy." Her recital brings to mind bursts of good cheer in Ingmar Bergman's highly verbal and psychological cinema rather than the silent or laconic deadpan of slow movies. Isa cuts Bahar short, however, when he asks, as though eager to restore slow-movie rigour, "What time do you have to be on set?" Then, as the bloom leaves her face, he adds, "You don't want to be late."

Much as Isa's words may be considered a slow-movie riposte to Bahar's rhapsodic report of her dream, *Climates*' reliance on long takes in conjunction with long shots in three earlier scenes stands in sharp contrast to the film's considerable use of cutting, close-ups, point-of-view shots and shot/reverse-shots. The long takes that are also long shots, each lasting four to six minutes with the camera kept stationary, stolidly record the dinner quarrel between Isa and Bahar by the sea, the sexual encounter between Isa and Serap on and off her couch, and Isa's marriage proposal to Bahar in the production crew's van. *Climates* resembles slow movies in other ways as well, as it is slow, quiet and deliberate, encouraging "contemplation rather than distraction", as Manohla Dargis has written.[43]

Somewhat like Antonioni's tetralogy, then, *Climates* is more diverse stylistically than *Distant*, a difference critics have tended to overlook. And while *Climates*, like *Distant* and the tetralogy, thematically involves what Dargis calls "existential solitude"[44] and Suner might term "emptied" characters, thanks chiefly to Bahar the film is more emotionally expressive and inward-looking than *Distant* and most slow movies. In reviewing *Climates*, J. Hoberman hailed Ceylan as "one of the world's most accomplished filmmakers".[45] Perhaps relevant to *Climates*' accomplishment is that it retains slow-movie stringency and tension despite diverging from slow-movie norms; and in probing the boundaries of slow movies, it perhaps casts them into bolder relief than *Distant* does alone.

Wait Time

The Death of Mr. Lazarescu,
4 Months, 3 Weeks and 2 Days and Safe

"Thank you, and I'll be waiting for you."

> – Dante Remus Lazarescu, concluding his second telephone request
> for an ambulance at the start of *The Death of Mr. Lazarescu*

"For the world is silent to us; the silence is merely forever broken."

> – Stanley Cavell, *The World Viewed*[1]

*"Our fingers, our skin and nose and lips and tongue and stomach and all the other parts
of us understand what we see in the film experience."*

> – Vivian Sobchack, *Carnal Thoughts: Embodiment and Moving Image Culture*[2]

The three films examined in this chapter relinquish slow-movie traits to some degree and assume, somewhat like *Climates*, the lineaments of a less stringent type of international art cinema. In all three films, for instance, though especially in Cristian Mungiu's *4 Months, 3 Weeks and 2 Days* (hereafter *432*), major characters evince strong emotions, linked occasionally in Mungiu's film to sharp social insights. Yet strong indications of the emotional restraint and repression typical of slow movies persist, especially in Todd Haynes' *Safe*. Indeed, both Dante Lazarescu (Ion Fiscuteanu) in Cristi Puiu's *The Death of Mr. Lazarescu* (hereafter *Lazarescu*) and Carol White (Julianne Moore) in *Safe* are mostly blank, impassive figures (Todd Haynes rightly regards White as both frightened and "blank",[3] by the way; J. Hoberman aptly describes Lazarescu as "deadpan"[4]). More evident than repression and impassivity in *432*, on the other hand, are the characters' intense efforts to contain their feelings as they undergo a terrifying physical and psychological ordeal. Thus, while emotion in the films examined in this chapter is often more emphatic than is usual in slow movies, the absence, suspension or control of emotion remains a key theme.

Also distinguishing these three films is that the aims of the major characters, and consequently the films' narrative thrust, are more explicit and concrete than is typical in slow movies. Although the life of Dante Lazarescu, for example, a poker-faced retiree without close friends, nearby kin or much to do except tend his cats, seems empty and amorphous, it acquires narrative focus and energy from his need to halt his physical pain and vomiting. In *432*, too, the narrative is driven by a clearly physical dilemma: a student's quest for an illegal abortion without delay. And while emotional and spiritual vacuity underlies Carol White's problems in *Safe*, she regards the causes and effects of her malaise as physical. Impelling the narrative, then, are her concrete efforts to fend off chemical toxins – whether emitted by automotive exhaust, her husband's cologne or a new sofa – so as to end her bleeding, vomiting and convulsive seizures. Thus, all three films addressed in this chapter depict bodily crises deemed to be resolvable, and this goal gives rise to concrete acts. By contrast, the bullet in *Dead Man* lies too close to William Blake's heart to be safely removed; and nothing can be done to remedy the mother's dying of old age in *Mother and Son*.

The concrete efforts to repair the body in *Lazarescu*, *432* and *Safe* defy the notion that nothing happens in these films. Yet true to the standard of slow movies, events in this trio of movies proceed slowly, haltingly and with an air of futility. Further, as indicated above regarding the intensity of emotion in these films, departures from slow-movie traits and tactics are countered, in a sense, by assertions of slow-movie values. Instead of a stationary camera typical of slow movies, for instance, *Lazarescu* deploys an incessantly moving, hand-held camera that brings to mind films by Frederick Wiseman, Richard Leacock and other documentarians. But *Lazarescu*'s camera and characters, confined as they are within an overstuffed apartment, a small medical van (*too* small, complains Lazarescu) and an overcrowded hospital room or corridor, never move far – and these limited movements are anchored to the increasing immobility of Lazarescu's dying body. A further limitation is that the movements are bound or constrained within long takes, which Puiu considered essential to communicating not only "truth" but the inescapable "feeling of time passing".[5]

Like the camera motion in Puiu's film, more dialogue occurs in *Lazarescu*, *432* and perhaps *Safe* than in most slow movies, which tend towards extended silences such as Ebert confronted in *Distant*. Yet silence (figuratively if not always literally) and indifference are conspicuous in the world's response to the desperation of major characters in this chapter's three films. Further, the characters themselves fall silent, or choose silence, as a result of loss, death or an experience of unspeakable horror. "You know what we're going to do", Otilia (Anamaria Marinca) tells her friend Gabriela (Laura Vasiliu) in the final scene of *432*, following the abortion: "We're never going to talk about this." At several moments in *Safe*, Carol becomes physically or psychologically disabled, and finds herself either unable to speak or bereft of words. And in *Lazarescu*, the old man's speech grows more indistinct, confused and infrequent as his physical condition deteriorates, until finally he replies not at all to a physician's queries.

◆

A retired engineer who lives alone on a pension, Mr Lazarescu becomes increasingly still as well as silent over a six-hour period, as he is taken by Mioara Avram (Luminita Gheorghiu), a dedicated, matronly paramedic, from one hospital to another. Avram and sundry doctors and nurses repeatedly enjoin the ailing Lazarescu to be still and quiet. Indeed, they do so about fifteen times during the film. For its depiction of this slowing and silencing, *Lazarescu* won the prestigious Un Certain Regard at Cannes in 2005, and some months later J. Hoberman called it "the great discovery of the last Cannes Film Festival".[6] Yet more important, *Lazarescu*'s success, as A. O. Scott has observed, "turned out to be a sign of things to come".[7] *12:08 East of Bucharest* (Corneliu Porumboiu, 2006), one of two new Romanian films screened the next year at Cannes, won the Camera d'Or for best debut feature. And just a year later, in 2007, *California Dreamin'* (Cristian Nemescu, 2007) won Un Certain Regard, while *4 Months, 3 Weeks and 2 Days* garnered Cannes' highest honour, the Palme d'Or. Thus Puiu's film about a 62-year-old man dying, made on a small budget in a country of slight cinematic and geopolitical significance, inaugurated a series of minimal, realistic films that received unusual international acclaim. "In three years", wrote Scott in the *New York Times*, "four major prizes at the world's pre-eminent film festival went to movies from a country whose place in the history of twentieth-century cinema might charitably be called marginal."[8] Scott heralded the new Romanian films as "reinventing the European art cinema"[9] and constituting "the most exciting development in a European national cinema since Spain in the 1980s".[10]

Upon the release of *Lazarescu*, Puiu seemed to prepare audiences for a slow movie when he issued a statement, widely cited by film critics, in which he contrasted medical practice and life in Romania to the look and pace of the American TV series *ER*: "When you watch [*ER*]", he said, "there's movement in every direction, the choreography of the characters is amazing ... In my country, doctors and everyone else live in slow motion, as if they were on Valium and still had five hundred years to live."[11] Later, Puiu seemed to imply that he liked slow movies when he said that Jarmusch's *Stranger Than Paradise*, perhaps more than any other motion picture, had inspired him as a young painter in Geneva to become a filmmaker.[12] Further, Puiu has spoken of his preference for long takes, often stylistically central to slow movies, in order to render natural continuities of time and space. Citing the remark by Jean-Luc Godard, another filmmaker he admires, that "every cut is a lie", Puiu has said he favours long takes, as already noted, "to get this taste of truth" and "induce the feeling of time passing".[13]

True to his goal, shots lasting two to four-and-a-half minutes are common-place in *Lazarescu* and vital to its verisimilitude; "death is a continuous process here",[14] Puiu said of his film – and its long takes support and underscore this continuity. Moreover, like the slow dying of William Blake in *Dead Man*, which takes up nearly the entire film, Mr Lazarescu's "going out",[15] as Puiu has called it, consumes almost all of *Lazarescu*. Thus the "continuous process" sustained by long takes in this breakthrough Romanian film is not short. Nor is it unchang-ing, since Lazarescu's physical state worsens as time passes. His head, stomach, liver, legs, arms, hands, eyes, skin colour, speech – all "go out" in some way as the weary pensioner, besieged also by abstruse medical terms like "dysarthria", "hemiparesis" and "subdural hematoma", grows more incontinent and helpless. Such entrapment suggests another, though perhaps minor, justification for the long takes: their structure or duration allows no quick or easy exits.

The film's uniformly drab environment and dull available light undoubtedly re-inforce the no-exit atmosphere. Even when a cut to a new shot occurs, the dreary, cramped atmosphere persists, whether in Lazarescu's apartment, the medical van or any of the four hospitals to which the patient is taken. *Lazarescu* represents, then, a return to the stringent mise-en-scène of such slow movies as *The Second Circle*, *Stranger Than Paradise*, *Elephant* and, to some extent, *Dead Man*. As in these films, the persistent bleakness of the locales signals a closed world rather than openness and release.

Lazarescu's efforts to secure medical treatment are blocked at each of the first three hospitals to which Avram and her driver Leo (Gabriel Spahieu) take him. Even before Lazarescu sets out, his next-door neighbour predicts that since it is Saturday the ambulance will never come; a bit later the neighbour partially relents: "Don't you know it takes them forever to get here?" On arriving at each hospital, Lazarescu, Avram and Leo are challenged by diverse employees such as orderlies, nurses and senior physicians to justify why they have chosen this hospi-tal rather than another. In one instance well into Lazarescu's quest, the ostensible reason for the query is that a different hospital is known for the neurosurgery he is thought to require. But the reason typically given is that the hospital's employ-ees and facilities are overwhelmed by the needs of twenty-nine victims of a bus crash and related accidents previously announced on the television in Lazarescu's apartment. As the hospital employees try to turn Lazarescu away, moreover, they evince anger and resentment more than sympathy. They appear almost too eager to reject his plea for care. He meets such resistance repeatedly, both when he arrives at a hospital and when he manages to reach departments or stations within it. Perhaps most important from a slow-movie standpoint is that as a result of roadblocks and impasses he faces, the flow of action slows, stops or backs up, somewhat as in Van Sant's *Elephant*, though without *Elephant*'s temporal shifts and ambiguity.

At times the resistance encountered by Lazarescu becomes personally abusive and humiliating, further obstructing his care and the flow of the action. His heavy drinking contributes to his degradation even before he reaches the first hospital. The same neighbour who doubts that the ambulance will come also exclaims, "Gee, you stink. Have you been drinking rat poison?" At the first hospital the senior physician is both repelled and misled by Lazarescu's awful smell. While Avram suspects Lazarescu has colon cancer, and Lazarescu himself suspects ulcers, for which he underwent surgery fourteen years earlier, the harried physician dismisses Lazarescu's pain – both his headache and his abdominal discomfort – as due only to his drinking: "Stop drinking and it won't hurt." Besides relieving the doctor of responsibility for Lazarescu, the assessment furnishes an excuse to further criticise and insult him. The doctor accuses Lazarescu of basely displacing those "who have real emergency needs". He also threatens Lazarescu – "I'll blow you and your ulcer to bits"; calls him "a pig"; and orders his staff to get him "out of my sight". Lazarescu interjects that it is the physician's duty, for which he is paid, to help him. Finally the doctor recommends a CT scan of Lazarescu's liver, though he remains convinced that the patient's drinking is the main problem.

Though Lazarescu manages to see this physician and other medical personnel at the first hospital, he is ordered to find a less crowded institution for the scan. But at the next hospital he along with Avram and Leo face obstacles resembling those at the first. Finally the pensioner is admitted, however, and perhaps because he has grown weaker and more incontinent and his speech has become more confused and indistinct, the medical staff at this hospital aims fewer barbs at him. An exception arises when Lazarescu, about to be X-rayed, says that he's cold and a youthful doctor replies, "What can I do about it? Jump up and down and warm up." Clearly too feeble to comply, Lazarescu proceeds to "wet himself", which a nurse announces to all present. The patient then demands to change into clean clothes before resuming his slow glide into the scanner. The professionals say nothing to aggravate his embarrassment; but Puiu's camera underscores his delinquency by panning from him being changed like a baby to his urine being wiped off the scanner bed.

Even as the barbs directed at Lazarescu subside, those aimed at Avram mount; she in fact displaces Lazarescu as the "piñata" of stressed, resentful hospital employees of both sexes who are determined to assert their authority. Her difficulties become evident at the first hospital when she voices her opinion that Lazarescu suffers from a tumour in his colon and a male physician asks, "Since when do you make the diagnosis? Are you using bio-energy?" Avram also reports that when Lazarescu threw up in his apartment the vomit included threads of blood, to which another physician archly replies, "Define threads of blood … could be tomato skins", later adding, "I'd say you better stop playing doctor." Avram runs into more roadblocks inside a third hospital. When she insists that Lazarescu needs surgery immediately, a female nurse responds, "Let me do my job", and then condescendingly asks Avram if she is familiar with medical terminology. When Avram seems undaunted, the nurse warns, "Don't patronise me." A male doctor steps in, asserting that only a specialist like him can decide about surgery and that Avram should not presume to know very much. Finally he says incredulously, "You really don't respect us." When she replies, "I only said we needed to hurry up", a female physician advises, "You should start by learning your place." In search of common ground, Avram then says that each of them is a medical professional striving to help the patient; but the male doctor only reaffirms the nurse's earlier point about difference and authority, noting that a medical hierarchy exists in which Avram is distinctly inferior.

Seeking care for Lazarescu, Avram is belittled and made to wait by medical personnel who seem more concerned to safeguard their dignity and authority than to heal her patient. In discussing the slow motion of medical care and of life in general in Romania, and in citing the "case around 2000 when an ambulance drove a patient around to lots of hospitals which refused him" until eventually his nurse "left him on a street to die",[16] Puiu has emphasised *Lazarescu*'s basis in fact. Indeed, its spare, low-budget realism bears resemblance to Italian Neorealism. At the same time, the obsession with authority which distracts *Lazarescu*'s medical professionals brings to mind the concerns with authority, as symbolised by the hotel porter's uniform, in *The Last Laugh* (F. W. Murnau, 1924), a film notable for its expressionistic as much as its realistic elements. Although *Lazarescu* looks very different from Murnau's film and makes very different use of long takes and the moving camera, thematically it often feels like the German film. But whereas the latter reflects, according to Siegfried Kracauer, psychological tendencies in the German soul which facilitated Hitler's rise,[17] *Lazarescu* perhaps suggests the lingering effects of the totalitarian order, spearheaded by German Nazism and Soviet Communism, that prevailed in Romania from the late 1930s until 1989. In any case, the issue of authority in *Lazarescu* involves not only social, economic and political differences between people, but also their emotional and psychological distance from one another, and ultimately from themselves.

In a *Cinema Scope* interview in 2006, Puiu discusses emotional distance in *Lazarescu* in ways that seem to me relevant to the workings of both authority and dehumanisation in his film. Puiu asserts in the interview that doctors, even at the risk of being rude and abusive to their patients, must protect themselves from excesses of compassion. "There is this distance they must keep", he says. "They should not get emotionally involved. I think it's the way it has to be. They have to act as machines. They first have to protect themselves to protect others."

He adds, "When, as a patient, you're going to a doctor, you're expecting to be cured, not to find him crying on your shoulder because of his diagnosis."[18] Yet as I have suggested, the mechanistic coldness and rigidity of the medical personnel in *Lazarescu* often seem to *over*-distance them from their patients and to slow and hinder medical care rather than advance it. Such mechanical rigidity seems not merely distinct from, but opposed to, the humaneness and organic mutability of Avram and Lazarescu; and this opposition defines the film's central dramatic conflict and sense of deadlock.

Curiously, Puiu recalls in the *Cinema Scope* interview instructing his actors in *Lazarescu* to function as he felt doctors must. Although he overlooks the parallel, he describes telling his actors to keep their distance, to curtail both their emotional involvement and their expressiveness. The actors required such advice, he explains, because having been trained for the stage in Romania, which lacked a sizable film industry, they tended to "overact" when placed in front of a motion-picture camera. Puiu had to restrain them, he says: "I really had to fight with them!"[19] He also felt obliged to restrain and "cure", he explains, "their understandable desire to be loved". He advised them to overcome such desire by thinking of other people as objects or machines (and perhaps by becoming more machine-like themselves). His actors were to behave "not as if a human being were in front of them", he said, "but rather a car they have to repair".[20] Notable also is that he apparently sought to impose this emotion-arresting "mechanic viewpoint", as he calls it, on all his actors, not just those portraying medical professionals.[21]

Lastly, Puiu invokes the "mechanic viewpoint" in the *Cinema Scope* interview to praise long takes – in particular the long take that captures much of the neurologist's examination of Lazarescu in the second hospital: "When the neurologist is testing Lazarescu", says Puiu, "the duration of the shot is six to seven minutes. This is very important, because it's so mechanical. It marks the time passing."[22] Although by my count the long take cited by Puiu lasts less than five minutes rather than six or seven, the unblinking mechanism of the take does underscore the passing of time – continuous, prolonged, inexorable – as the neurologist gauges the incontrovertible decline of Lazarescu's reflexes, speech, cognition and strength.

Obviously Puiu is not the first director of film or theatre to invoke the "mechanical" in describing his thematic interests and directing methods. Robert Bresson, too, sought revelations of mechanism and automatism in his actors' performances, as noted in this book's first chapter. Another well-known advocate of the "mechanic viewpoint" was Sergei Eisenstein, inspired by biomechanical acting and experiments in set and costume design by theatre director Vsevolod Meyerhold. Both Meyerhold and Eisenstein, in turn, were influenced by Constructivism in Russia following the 1917 Communist revolution, and particularly by Constructivist views of the artist as an engineer helping to build a new industrial society and of the actor as a machine-like body conveying emotion through precise physical movements. But in the course of emphasising such physical and mechanical bases of emotion in an era already drawn to melodramatic excess and simplification, Eisenstein gravitated in his films of the 1920s towards emotional and moral exaggeration. Thus his engagement with the mechanical yielded emotional expression quite different from that found in slow movies.

Puiu, on the other hand, obviously shares with recent slow-movie makers a minimalist's impulse to pare down emotion as well as action and motion. Though he is not a fan of Bresson's work,[23] he shares the Frenchman's inclination to explore mechanical features of human behaviour in order to achieve emotive stringency rather than Eisenstein's effusiveness. Yet the emotional spareness of characters in *Lazarescu* differs from the leanness in Bresson's cinema. Whereas Bresson's characters are surprisingly ethereal, those in *Lazarescu* are conspicuously physical, and the film's medical professionals are particularly hard and opaque.

As I have indicated, Puiu suggests that such hardness and opacity joined to an authoritarian style are qualities that medical professionals must develop in order to protect themselves from feelings that could hamper their treatment of patients. Yet as I have also noted, all this armour in *Lazarescu* encumbers not only medical care but the flow of action, which persistently seems to stop and even to back up. This pattern resembles, in addition to the retarded and uncertain narrative in Van Sant's *Elephant*, the historical trajectory of Romania itself as portrayed by E. M. Cioran. A well-known Romanian author who spent much of his life in France, Cioran characterised Romania as one of those countries "for whom nothing succeeds and whose very triumphs are but failures. When they try to assert themselves and take a step forward, some external fate intervenes to break their momentum and return them to their starting point."[24]

"Romania: Bottom of the Heap", an essay by historian Tony Judt that ends with this statement by Cioran, appeared in the *New York Review of Books* in 2001, and again in Judt's *Reappraisals: Reflections on the Twentieth Century* (2008) under the less pessimistic title "Romania Between History and Europe". Judt's data and observations support Cioran's gloom:

The Romanian economy, defined by per capital gross domestic product, ranked eighty-seventh in the world in 1998, below Namibia and just above Paraguay (Hungary ranked fifty-eighth). Life expectancy is lower in Romania than anywhere else in Central or Southeastern Europe ... It is estimated that two out of five Romanians live on less than $30 per month (contrast, e.g., Peru, where the minimum monthly wage today is $40) ... According to *The Economist*'s survey for the year 2000, the 'quality of life' in Romania ranks somewhere between Libya and Lebanon ... The Foreign Affairs Committee of the European Parliament lists Romania as last among the EU-candidate countries, and slipping fast.[25]

Judt also notes that "Romanians were for many centuries ruled variously by the three great empires of Eastern Europe: the Russian, the Austro-Hungarian, and the Ottoman."[26] Although the defeat of these empires in World War I resulted in a vast increase in Romania's territory, population and aspirations, World War II again subjected Romanians to the yoke of foreign powers: initially Nazi Germany, which drew sympathisers from the Iron Guard and other Romanian Far Right groups, and then the Soviet Union. Romania's communist government eventually secured a measure of freedom from Moscow, but brutally repressed its own people, bequeathing them, when the Iron Curtain and dictator Nicolae Ceausescu fell in 1989, the dismal conditions sketched above. The nation drew closer to the West as it sought to establish a more democratic society and a capitalist market economy. But though Romania's economy grew after 2000, in the 1990s the nation remained mired in economic depression and political unrest. It applied for admission to the European Union in 1993, but had to wait until 2007 to be accepted.

Summing up Romania's subjection to foreign powers for much of its history, its exploitation by its own leaders, and its sense of economic and political inferiority, Judt describes it as "a nation that has suffered serial historical humiliation".[27] His remark perhaps points to a broader explanation, beyond the goal of providing adequate medical care, for the rigid insistence by *Lazarescu*'s medical professionals on their status and authority: intent on emerging from their nightmarish past, Romanians have become perhaps too quick to perceive and counter spectres of defeat and humiliation. Further, in their view not just status and authority may forestall humiliation, but also machine-like force and impersonality, or what Puiu calls the "mechanic viewpoint". Romanians (and others of us) seeking relief from historical subjugation may be drawn to the unfeeling, mechanistic power of military and political strongmen, both past and present, foreign and domestic: "Don't give yourselves to these unnatural men – machine men with machine minds and machine hearts. You are men", warns Charlie Chaplin as the barber mistaken for Hynkel in *The Great Dictator* (1940). Yet the temptation to embrace mechanistic power may prove irresistible.

The postures of rigid, machine-like authority in *Lazarescu* are perhaps designed to keep medical practitioners from faltering not only in the face of their patients' woes but also under the weight of their national pain. Possibly another reality these practitioners seek more or less consciously to stave off is suggested by Kracauer in a comment about *The Last Laugh*:[28] "Thus the film advances, however ironically, the authoritarian credo that the magic spell of authority protects society from decomposition."[29] The decomposition feared in Murnau's film is primarily social, political and economic; at stake is the survival of the Weimar Republic's fragile democratic experiment. The decomposition in *Lazarescu*, on the other hand, bears immediately on the human body. Its breakdown and rotting are not merely feared, but really occur, and are witnessed in some detail. As noted above, multiple organs and limbs of Lazarescu's failing body are repeatedly touched, probed, tested and scanned amid the stench of his whiskey, vomit and incontinence. Not inconceivable is that prolonged exposure to such deterioration prompts in caregivers anxieties about their own health, and consequently provokes defensive postures such as those in *Lazarescu*.

In discussing his film, Puiu has presented his views concerning the psychological attitudes of doctors and actors. He has also stressed the film's relevance to life in general in his nation following Ceausescu's execution. In addition, though, he has argued that the film's primary import is metaphysical, transcending time and place: "Firstly it is about this disappearance, the extinction of a human being, of a soul";[30] it's about medical care, of course, "but not just that: it's more about a man who is dying;"[31] "*Lazarescu* for me is not so much about the social level, but the metaphysical level. We are somehow doomed."[32]

Yet if *Lazarescu* achieves metaphysical import, it does so by focusing on the disintegration of a human body more relentlessly than have most films, including those by Vittorio De Sica and other Neorealists to whom the Romanian New Wave of Puiu, Mungiu and others has been compared. Quite simply, Puiu's film never leaves its central, mortal subject – Lazarescu appears in virtually every shot. His daughter and sister evidently avoid him, and the film never cuts to reveal either of them. Nor does it digress to show the massive bus accident that churns out the victims whose needs pre-empt Lazarescu's in the city's hospitals. Lazarescu mutters something late in the film about a World War II bombardment, but his muffled words yield no flashback of an attack such as appears in *California Dreamin'*. No music (either diegetic or non-diegetic) such as reinforces emotion in *Bicycle Thieves* (1948) and *Umberto D* (1951) enters *Lazarescu*. Nor does the film include dreams, imaginings or even subjective point-of-view shots and shot/reverse-shots, any of which might distract Puiu's objective, clinical eye from the physical immediacy of Lazarescu's body and the cramped negotiations surrounding it.

Puiu has mentioned that he relied on a hand-held camera rather than one fixed to a tripod because this produced a more "carnal, fleshy" sensation.[33] The result, of course, is not the least erotic. Lazarescu underscores the absence of sensual and sexual pleasure in Puiu's film when, flat on a gurney in a hospital elevator, he flirts with Avram ("There's a certain something about you that's attractive"), prompting a new admonition from her to "stay put and be quiet". Probably the darkly comic moment is one of many that moved one film critic to say of *Lazarescu*, "it's as funny as Beckett".[34] While Puiu depicts no carnal satisfaction in *Lazarescu*, he does stress what Vivian Sobchack, in *Carnal Thoughts: Embodiment and Moving Image Culture*, describes as "the embodied and radically material nature of human existence".[35] She urges film theorists and spectators to acknowledge more deeply than in the past that "we matter and we mean through processes and logics of sense-making that owe as much to our carnal existence as they do to our conscious thought".[36] Sobchack's view illuminates how the fuzzy-voiced Lazarescu and the film bearing his name matter and mean – and how Puiu attains "the metaphysical level" he seeks by steadfastly focusing on Lazarescu's material decline.

◆

Consistent with Puiu's intent, Manohla Dargis observes that "Lazarescu's body becomes a field of meaning, a landscape of despair and a site of brutal exchange among other, more robust bodies".[37] The body is similarly crucial in Mungiu's *432*, says Dargis. Both films explore, in her view, "the intersection of the social and the personal on the human body, and the incalculable trivial and monumental ways our bodies are at once situated in the world as objects and subjects".[38] The central crisis in both films, then, is not only physical, but moral, spiritual and sociopolitical as well.

First of all it is physical or "embodied", however. In *432*, Gabita, an attractive, anxious and confused young college student, seeks to terminate her pregnancy. But Ceausescu's communist regime, in its campaign to build a more populous and powerful nation, has made abortion illegal. Gabita risks physical injury as well as imprisonment. Minor physical discomforts distract her in the film's opening scene, which takes place in the dormitory room she shares with Otilia, her fellow student. As Gabita collects a few belongings for her stay in a hotel room where the abortion will begin a half hour later in the film, she suffers from a toothache, headache and stomachache. Once in the hotel, she learns of more physical dangers from the abortionist, Mr Viarel 'Domnu' Bebe (Vlad Ivanov), who comes to the hotel room she and Otilia have secured. After inquiring whether Gabita suffers from allergies and high blood pressure, Bebe tells her to expect pain and bleeding, and perhaps infection and fever. He also acknowledges, in response to a question from Otilia, that the fetus may not emerge and that Gabita may lose consciousness, but adds that both outcomes are unlikely. After examining Gabita and prodding her to admit she is nearly five months pregnant rather than two, as she had claimed on the phone, Bebe stresses the extended prison sentence he could receive for performing the late abortion, and then he and the women discuss inconclusively how much they can afford to pay him. Finally, with deadpan, insidious indirectness, Bebe conveys a final requirement: if he is to insert the probe for the abortion, both women must first have sex with him. Gabita, horrified, says softly, "I feel sick. I can't believe this is happening." Much as disease ravages Lazarescu, Gabita's sick feeling engulfs her body and spirit. Otilia appears equally repelled, and nearly as stricken.

For reasons cited at the start of this chapter, *432*, *Lazarescu* and *Safe* are not slow movies in every respect; moreover, dialogue and suspense are even more prominent in Mungiu's film than in the other two. Further, in much of *432*, Otilia's breathless movements, whether tracked by the hand-held camera through city streets or dormitory corridors, are anything but slow. Yet the tension and horror of the conversation in the hotel room between Bebe and the two beleaguered young women gains force from the film's increased emphasis in this scene on aspects of slow-movie form. For instance, though 432 deploys long takes throughout the half hour of the film preceding the confrontation in the hotel room, the takes are significantly longer in the room, and the movements of characters are far more constrained. James Naremore has observed that the long-take style that "has become a hallmark of contemporary art movies, particularly those of the Romanian new wave", is capable of sustaining "different rhythms and moods".[39] Certainly motion, rhythm and mood in the hotel room diverge sharply from what has come before. Except for Gabita's "I can't believe this is happening", which comes at the start of a new shot, the confrontation between Bebe and the young women as described thus far consumes just two shots, the first lasting six minutes and the second, seven minutes. In addition, the span and speed of characters' movements are severely curtailed. Bebe and Otilia sit for the most part in chairs on either side of a table against the wall, while Gabita sits opposite them on the edge of the bed until she lies down to be examined and remains still. Only once does the camera move quickly – to track Bebe's few steps from the bed back to the table after he examines Gabita. The feeling of immobility and entrapment in this scene resembles the sense of constriction maintained throughout *Lazarescu*. Supporting the immobility in the hotel room is the camera's fixed stare, which brings to mind a comment by minimalist sculptor Carl Andre: "Art is about seizing and holding space."[40] Bebe underscores both the enclosure of the space in the hotel room and the suspension of action within it by thrice warning Gabita to remain "absolutely still" after the probe has been inserted and to keep the door locked, admitting no one.

Each character in the prison-like hotel refers to time. Bebe insists that Gabita estimate how much time has passed since her last period, and warns in a prosecutorial tone that the abortion procedure, like the legal penalty if they are caught, depends on her answer. Otilia also is mindful of time – and of money. She asks Bebe how long it will take for the fetus to emerge and reminds him that she and Gabita have paid for just a three-night stay in the hotel. Obviously such questions related to time are fraught with tension and suspense, as are the two long takes, totalling thirteen minutes, in which they occur. Citing the long-take "style" in *Police, Adjective* (Corneliu Porumboiu, 2009), another well-regarded Romanian film, James Naremore writes of "long takes viewed from a distance and filled with dead time".[41] But time in the hotel room in 432, charged as it is with urgent dangers and desires, cannot be considered dead, empty, aimless or formless. Despite the scene's strong slow-movie elements, it presents neither the empty time, space or stillness of a slow movie like *Stranger Than Paradise*.

Critics and scholars besides Naremore have commented on uses of the long take in Romanian cinema, and in 432 in particular. Richard Porton admires that the stationary, long-take camera in Mungiu's film "maintains a distance" and "an impassivity" resembling "the stare of a peculiarly empathetic surveillance camera",[42] while Ben Walters in *Sight & Sound* zeroes in on a particular image in which the long take, combined with a fixed, not very distant camera, achieves its "greatest triumph". This image "comes with the dinner Otilia attends for her boyfriend's mother's birthday ... Otilia is fixed at the end of the table, mute, in a tightly framed shot around whose edge buzzes facile chatter."[43] Anthony Lane in the *New Yorker* seizes on the same shot: "hands reach in from the side [actually, from both sides of the image] for pickles and wine but the camera holds steady, minute upon minute, and we gaze at her [Otilia] face to face."[44] What has happened is that after the insertion of the probe, Otilia has left Gabita alone in order to keep her promise to her boyfriend Adi (Alexandru Potocean) to visit his parents' home on his mother's birthday. But a dinner party is underway and she finds herself obliged to join his parents and their boisterous friends at the table. Otilia sits crunched between Adi's parents, wanting to rejoin Gabita but unable to either move or speak up when some of the guests criticise her generation as having life too easy. Here again, then, is a scene of confinement and immobility as in the hotel room. Despite the chatter, the dinner scene also depicts the muting of the human voice, Otilia's voice, a circumstance unusual neither in slow movies generally nor in the specific films explored in this chapter. As in the hotel room, moreover, the stare of the unmoving camera accentuates Otilia's confinement and her inability to state the full truth of her situation. The take, which lasts seven minutes and thirty seconds, is among the longest in *432*.

Perhaps in order to stress Otilia's entrapment in this scene, Ben Walters overstates her silence. She is not totally mute during the long take at the dinner table, since she briefly answers questions concerning her parents' occupations, her main field of study in college, and whether she would like a cigarette. But of course she dares not speak of Gabita's abortion or of the price Bebe has exacted. There is another shot, though, prior to this scene and immediately following Otilia's off-screen sex with Bebe, in which both she and the camera are fully still, and in which she is entirely silent. Indeed, the universe itself seems to fall silent in this shot. The context is as follows. First, in a seventeen-second medium long shot, Otilia, naked from the waist down but wearing the same green top as throughout the film, quickly enters the bathroom and, with the camera behind her, sits down in the tub, turns on the water, and starts scrubbing herself. The film then cuts to a seven-second medium shot of her in profile as she continues to wash herself. Then comes the fourteen-second close shot devoid of all motion and sound: no scrubbing, running water, talking, breathing or ambient noise. The stationary camera simply fastens on the stricken stillness of Otilia's upper back and shoulders, covered tightly by her green top, and on the back of her blonde head, slightly bowed towards the blue-and-white tiled wall that surrounds her. Following this image, which suggests both death in life and a suspension of time, motion and sound resume in a new shot of Otilia, suddenly upright at the bathroom sink, observing herself in the mirror as she washes her hands and face.

Mungiu as well as film critics rightly attest to the realism of 432. In his commentary on the DVD, Mungiu emphasises that his film (like *Lazarescu*) is based on an actual event which wasn't "that unusual" in Ceausescu's Romania. Mungiu adds that in shooting the film he preferred real locations, available light, unobtrusive editing, a camera that "simply witnesses the action"[45] and naturalistic sound without music. Richard Porton cites in *Cineaste* the film's "startlingly naturalistic style".[46] Manohla Dargis praises its rendering of "a painstakingly real world of worn-out rooms and worn-out lives" and its "naturalistic conversations that ... seem artless, more like real life than aesthetic choices ... The verisimilitude can be startling."[47] Roger Ebert values the absence of "fancy shots" and "effects".[48] J. Hoberman observes that "with virtually every scene shot in a single setup, the movie feels like it is unfolding in real time".[49] Obviously the still, silent image of Otilia's upper back contrasts to the film's prevailing realism. Though neither a freeze frame nor a still photograph, it takes leave of a world that is too much for the heroines of 432.

Simultaneously the shot confirms a disposition in Mungiu's film to restrain emotion as well as motion. "I wanted to keep a proper distance from the subject",[50] Mungiu has said of his approach throughout 432. The shot of Otilia is immensely forceful, which is perhaps why one might remember it as a long take,[51] even though it is rather brief as well as close. Enhancing the shot's impact is that Otilia – viewed from the back, unnaturally still and silent – seems emotionally distanced and perhaps detached from the viewer as well as from the world. Mungiu advised Marinca to restrain Otilia's emotions, which she did brilliantly. At times, moreover, Mungiu's long shots also serve, literally and figuratively, to distance the subject matter, or to contain what he has termed his story's "great emotional intensity"[52] and Manohla Dargis has referred to as its potential for melodrama and sentimentality.[53] Mungiu employed other distancing tactics as well. He has told Richard Porton, for instance: "If you watch the film carefully, you'll notice that, when [Otilia] walks ... we only see her from the back."[54] The link Mungiu suggests between limits on emotional display and the camera's avoidance of Otilia's face applies, if not to every moment of her walking, certainly to the still, silent image we have been addressing of her in the bathtub. Mungiu's suggestion applies also to a later image of her, after she has carried the aborted fetus in a bag through urban streets at night for almost six minutes of film time, ascended the metal staircase of an apartment structure, raised the lid of a garbage chute atop the structure, and inserted the bag. Here again her face is not visible, as darkness shrouds her entire body and Mungiu's unsteady, almost quivering camera records her immobile profile in extreme long shot. Moonlight falls on the cover of the chute and outlines the top and back of Otilia's motionless blonde head, which is angled towards the chute in silence except for the tremulous sound of her breathing.

The avoidance of point-of-view shots and shot/reverse-shots in *432*, as in *Lazarescu*, is another tactic that tends to limit the expression of emotion. When, for example, the aborted fetus is revealed in the bathroom of the hotel room following Otilia's return from the dinner party for Adi's mother, the point of view is not Otilia's nor that of another character, but purely the camera's. "I got rid of it. It's in the bathroom", Gabita says after Otilia has awakened her. Otilia proceeds to the bathroom to look and kneels beside the fetus that lies outside the frame. She looks stunned. Only after she stands again and walks out of frame does the camera, which has been stationary, descend with brutal, intrusive speed to reveal the fetus lying on a bloodied towel on the bathroom floor. Thus conducted to the fetus directly by the camera rather than a person's gaze, the spectator experiences his or her own horror unencumbered for the moment by the feelings of a character. The spectator experiences horror alone.

Such grave, distancing moments possibly contribute to the impression of "cool devastation" and "calmly observed melodrama" that Stuart Klawans and other critics derive from *432*.[55] Klawans notes traditional melodramatic elements in the film such as an "overbearing villain", time pressures and "a heroine [or two] who might as well be tied to the railroad tracks". He cites as well, however, "the formal restraint that Mungiu exercises … a restraint that extends to Marinca's inward-looking, furiously controlled performance and to the deep, steady gaze of Oleg Matu's cinematography".[56] In the horrific long take we have been discussing, the camera continues calmly and coolly to hold on the fetus as Otilia returns to the frame, though her face remains outside the frame, perhaps in keeping with Mungiu's determination to maintain "a proper distance". With only her lower body and her hands and arms in view, Otilia wraps the fetus in the towel and empties personal items from her bag, making room for the fetus. Finally the camera tilts up, briefly taking in Otilia's face joined by Gabita's before Otilia exits to dispose of the body. Eighty-seven seconds have elapsed without a cut since Otilia first knelt by the fetus; as in the rest of the film, no shot/reverse-shot or point-of-view shot – either of which might magnify emotion – has occurred.

Before turning to *Safe*, I would like to linger on the relevance of "the overbearing villain" mentioned by Klawans to the mix of horror and emotional restraint in Mungiu's film. Rather than conveying sympathy when he asks Gabita about the duration of her pregnancy, Bebe virtually taunts her, either for not knowing the answer or for lying to him about it, just as he taunts both young women in regard to how little they can afford to pay him. Indeed, during most of his engagement with the women, he is not merely domineering and unfeeling but sadistic and prosecutorial. When he tells Gabita how "absolutely still" she will have to remain once the probe is inserted, he coldly savours his ascendancy. "Bebe is a tyrant, clinical in attitude, even when demanding sex from both women for his services. He'll freeze your blood",[57] observes Peter Travers in *Rolling Stone*; and the *New Yorker*'s Anthony Lane likens Bebe to "a predatory machine".[58]

In the absence of Romania's totalitarian rulers, Bebe reigns as the chief oppressor in this film, a machine-like tyrant and criminal counterpart to *Lazarescu*'s medical personnel who deride and suppress the terminally ill pensioner. As with those barbed professionals, Bebe's conduct suggests a personal if not national past of political, economic and social failure. His climactic emotional outburst, as Gabita and Otilia resist the sexual demands he makes to perform the abortion, seems mired in fears and memories of painful humiliation: "What do you take me for, a fucking prick? I could eat you for breakfast! Smarter people have tried to fuck me, think you'll do it? Two foxes versus a moron! Fuck this bullshit ... I'm risking my freedom ... Did you think I'd risk ten years for 3,000 lei? What did you take me for, a beggar? Did you see me begging? ... Think I was born yesterday?" As Bebe spits out these lines, the camera moves towards him, culminating in one of the rare close-ups of a human face in *432*.

◆

Bebe's unlikely counterpart in Todd Haynes' *Safe*, a film also set in 1987 but in affluent Southern California and picturesque New Mexico rather than in Romania, is Peter Dunning (Peter Friedman), founder of Wrenwood, the desert retreat in the foothills of Albuquerque where Carol White, convinced that she suffers from environmental illness, and that she is allergic to the twentieth century, undertakes what she and other guests call the "healing process". Dunning dictates the often humiliating physical and emotional steps in this process, at times through Claire (Kate McGregor-Stewart), Wrenwood's director, and an assistant, Susan (April Grace), both of whom are as persistently genial, and possibly as fatuous, as he is. Claire explains in a welcoming speech to Carol and other patients that total silence must be observed at breakfast and lunch, "with a side of the room for men, and a side for women". "Moderation in dress and restraint in sexual interaction" are among other requirements. "We ask that you try and focus these kinds of feelings inward", she adds, "toward your personal healing and self-realisation." Claire introduces Dunning, whose most evident passion is to further specify which inward feelings are permissible and which are not. He insists that patients allow only good, warm feelings, only love and forgiveness, from which must ensue only sunny views of the external world, since what we see, he says, merely reflects our inward disposition. "Remember your affirmations", he adjures Wrenwood's staff and patients. His regime is an extreme instance of America's commitment – in Robert Warshow's words, cited in this book's introduction – to "a cheerful view of life" – and to the creed of positive thinking analysed recently in Barbara Ehrenreich's *Bright-Sided: How the Relentless Promotion of Positive Thinking Has Undermined America*.[59] Like other rigidly positive outlooks, Dunning's precludes vast realms of thought, feeling and social exchange, and tends as a result to reduce rather than enhance the well being of those in Wrenwood's care.

Although Carol goes to Wrenwood to rebuild her body's resistance to the chemical toxicity of the modern world, she grows more frail, fearful and withdrawn under Dunning's influence. She becomes, as Murray Pomerance has noted, even more of "a paralyzed wraith" than before,[60] and finally retreats within Wrenwood to sleep in what the screenplay aptly describes as the "clean, white emptiness" of a miniscule "safe room" suggestive of "an antiseptic space capsule".[61] Roger Ebert describes the room as "a kind of igloo that is completely sterile";[62] Janet Maslin calls it a "porcelain-lined igloo".[63] In this barren enclosure as the film ends, Carol turns on the green oxygen tank that has become her most constant companion, breathes in deeply, puts the oxygen mask down, and approaches a small mirror on the wall that occupies a position coincident with the camera's. Her face very close to the mirror, the camera, and in a sense the film's spectator, she clears her throat and repeats meekly and hesitantly, "I love you. I really love you."

Dunning too has a retreat within Wrenwood – a mansion atop a hill overlooking his creation, and he eventually announces a further retreat: "I've stopped reading the papers", he tells patients and staff while Carol's husband Greg (Xander Berkeley) and his son Rory (Chauncey Leopardi) are visiting Carol at Wrenwood. "I've [also] stopped watching the news on TV. I've heard the media doom and gloom and I've seen their fatalistic attitude ... if I really believe life is that devastating, that destructive, I'm afraid my immune system will believe it, too. And I can't afford to take that risk. Neither can you." Even as he distances himself further from the world, Dunning, described by Susan as "a chemically sensitive person with AIDS", whose "perspective" as a result is "incredibly vast", acts to control knowledge and emotion at Wrenwood. In any case he signals doubt that the external world will continue to reflect his inward love, or that his inward love will suffice to parry the world's destructiveness. Although perhaps less removed from society than Carol and other slow-movie characters like Mahmut and William Blake, he remains decidedly apart, and his conduct, awareness and feelings are sharply circumscribed.

Carol's apartness, besides being more extreme than Dunning's, is more central to *Safe*'s narrative. "She's not connected to anybody", Christine Vachon, the film's producer and once a college classmate of Haynes, remarks to him and Julianne Moore in their three-way commentary on the *Safe* DVD.[64] One recurring manifestation of Carol's disconnectedness is her resistance to touching or being touched by another person. Just before her avowal of self-love at the mirror at the film's end, for instance, she walks back to her safe room in the night accompanied by Chris (James LeGros), a male patient who has shown interest in her. Moments earlier he surprised her with a birthday cake that capped off a successful meal they jointly prepared for several Wrenwood patients, staff members and Dunning. The published screenplay describes Chris and Carol as walking "hand in hand". But in fact, though romance is in the air, they do not touch. Chris keeps his hand that is near Carol locked in his trouser pocket; and on reaching the safe room's closed door, they exchange kindly looks and wave goodbye; but again, contrary to the screenplay, they do not touch, though Chris looks inclined to.

Carol's coolness if not aversion to touching is evident as early as the film's third shot, an overhead close-up of her face in bed looking up and away, dutiful but detached, as Greg assiduously thrusts and attains orgasm. In the same bedroom thirty minutes later in film time, Carol, saying she has a headache ("I still have this head thing"), rejects sex with Greg, who frustratedly indicates that her refusal is not new. The next morning, dressed for work, he stands near the bed, where Carol, sitting up, tells him she's sorry. He says he is too, and steps towards her; she stands before him, and they embrace. Or rather, he cradles her head and body while she nestles into his chest. Then Carol's body starts to throb, as though weeping, but draws back, vomiting, which of course startles Greg, who moments earlier completed his ablutions. The film quickly cuts to Carol being examined by her physician in his office.

She again withdraws from physical contact with Greg towards the end of the film, a few scenes before her touch-free farewell to Chris. Greg and Rory have been moving her belongings into the safe room. As Rory hauls a piece of luggage to the entrance, Greg and Carol, who carries the oxygen tank, slowly walk some distance away. Ever more frail, Carol trips and totters; Greg holds her up, and then lowers his face, apparently intending to kiss her. She quickly pulls away, however, and the shunned husband, who has spent the entire film vainly soliciting her ardour and embraces, asks timidly if he can at least give her a hug. She agrees, but her sexless stance in his arms resembles her earlier posture when she threw up.

Carol's resistance to physical contact, so different from the attitudes of the mother and son in Sokurov's film discussed in the second chapter, may be an inevitable reaction to environmental threats, human callousness and the proliferating ailments – almost as numerous and unnerving as Lazarescu's – from which she suffers. Radio and television inundate her with reports and predictions of environmental disaster, unstoppable viruses, the end of the world, crashes on the freeway, removals of life support from ill patients. Friends and family also dwell on dangers and woes. Seven minutes into the film, Carol's friend Linda (Susan Norman) tells her of her unmarried brother's death, and Carol suspects AIDS is the cause. Later Linda invites Carol to join her on a fruit diet to cleanse their bodies of toxins. At dinner with Greg and two other couples at an upscale restaurant, Carol falls asleep as her companions savour a joke about a "beautiful blonde" with a vibrator stuck inside her that no one seems able to remove. At dinner at home with Greg and Rory, Carol hears Rory read his report for school about gang violence in Los Angeles – shootings, knifings, "legs being dissected". Carol asks, "Why does it have to be so gory?" Meanwhile she endures a growing assortment of physical disorders herself, including extreme fatigue, rashes, vomiting, headaches, nose bleeds, seizures, panic attacks, uncontrollable coughing and inability to breathe or speak. At times a problem seems provoked by a physical occurrence, such as exhaust billowing from a truck in front of her car that coincides with her coughing. But in most instances the cause is indeterminate. Carol's physician repeatedly tells her and Greg he can find nothing physically wrong, and finally he recommends a psychiatrist.

When her meeting with the psychiatrist begins haltingly, Carol says, "Aren't you supposed to ask more questions?" to which he replies, "We really need to be hearing from you. What's going on in you?" Haynes interjects in the DVD commentary that this exchange "means Carol has to figure out that there's something inside". But Carol discovers, or in any case reveals, nothing inside. "Life of a Hollow Woman", the title of Janet Maslin's review of the film, suggests as much. Maslin regards Carol's privileged suburban life as "a dead world under glass" and sees her receding at Wrenwood into a "weak, sickly specter".[65] Roger Ebert agrees that Carol's "life and world are portrayed as ... empty ... pointless";[66] and Edward Guthmann, another film critic, says "she seems to gradually disappear".[67] Indeed, even before Carol's ailments set in – for instance, when she looks up absently from beneath Greg in bed in the film's third shot – she seems to enact Deleuze's "lost gaze of the being who is absent from the world as much as from himself".[68] Put another way, Carol is "not connected to anybody", as Christine Vachon says, because she is not connected to herself. The emptiness "inside" is vast, nothing is going on, all has ground to a halt.

Two further accounts of the film from the distinct perspectives of actress Julianne Moore and scholar James Morrison address both Carol's insubstantiality and her disconnectedness. "I ... tried to keep my voice unconnected to my body by just talking like above my chords", says Moore on the *Safe* DVD, "so I wasn't actually ever making any contact with my vocal chords, so it gave it a kind of breathy, bodiless quality ... I wanted to be that disconnected, ephemeral ... I wanted her body to disappear too."[69] Morrison's essay, "Todd Haynes in Theory and Practice", lends historical and cultural perspective to the forlorn character played by Moore before addressing physical contact and touching in Haynes' cinema. Morrison considers Carol one of many "pathetic nonentities" in Haynes' films "unwittingly enduring the benumbed death-in-life of late capitalism via Fredric Jameson by way of Theodor Adorno". He adds: "The split self, the alienated subject, the interpellated body, the evacuated being, even the literal zombie – these are the figures that populate the post-structuralist landscape and, in turn, make up the casts of Todd Haynes' movies."[70]

But among the alienated figures of diminished thought and feeling who populate Haynes' films, the post-structuralist landscape and, one might add, recent slow movies, Carol looms as unusually spectral and constrained. Morrison's analysis of the juncture of physical touch and emotion in Haynes' oeuvre bears on the void and disconnection both within Carol and between her and others: "The image of the touching hand is a familiar trope in art ... to objectify the encounter of self and other, self and world, with all the residual emotion that encounter entails. Haynes uses this image to suggest that meaningful emotion inheres in contact, *between* subject and object, rather than simply *within* subjects."[71] If Haynes' films imply that meaningful emotion inheres in touching, that the two are deeply interlinked and perhaps engender one another, such interaction breaks down in the universe of Carol White. Here the complex circuitry of human connection fails and the self loses all moorings. For "if we cannot know our touch makes true contact", states Morrison, "how can we know our feelings are real – or that they are what we can count on to evidence or legitimate our own subjectivities?"[72]

As Morrison also notes, Carol is not totally devoid of emotion. If nothing else, she is immensely fearful, much like Lester (Rio Hackford), the isolate, plaintive figure she espies in the distance at Wrenwood who looks towards her but never approaches. "Reed-thin", as the screenplay states, and "completely covered, wrapped tightly in a variety of knit clothing", the figure "walks as if it were out of an Egyptian painting, stepping sideways while facing front."[73] Dunning informs Carol that Lester is "very, very afraid. Afraid to eat. Afraid to breathe", and she seems riveted by his appearance far more than other patients are, perhaps because she is new to the community, or because Lester is virtually her double – too frightened to think, talk, walk or feel anything except fear. Rarely in slow movies, though they gravitate towards emptiness, stillness, silence and death, does existence seem as blank, mute and inert as it does when Carol and Lester observe each other from afar.

Carol's husband, Greg, cannot fail to recognize Carol's vacuity and incapacity; nor can he help her. A laconic, inexpressive businessman of imperceptible interests, Greg sees Carol continuing to shrink and totter during his visit to Wrenwood. Earlier in the film, as he witnessed her decline at home in California, he evinced a combination of patience, annoyance and bafflement. "What's going on, Carol?" was perhaps his commonest refrain. Now, given Carol's further deterioration at the New Mexico retreat, Greg is a bit more engaged and articulate, but nonetheless tentative, as he questions her decision to remain at Wrenwood: "So you really feel like it's ... still the right choice. I mean..." he says, to which Carol replies unhesitatingly that it is. "I just think it's really true what they say", she concludes, "that it's up to the individual, that it takes time." Greg's "wait time" in *Safe* proves every bit as long and futile as his wife's.

Whatever is "going on" in Carol is never clarified. Ebert opines that Carol "has grown allergic as a form of protest" against an unbearably "empty" and "pointless" existence,[74] whereas Guthmann points out that "Haynes ... never makes clear if Carol's symptoms are psychosomatic, imagined or a real biochemical reaction to an unsafe world."[75] Guthmann's alternatives echo a cultural puzzle cited by Deleuze in *The Time Image*: "We run ... into a principle of indeterminability, of indiscernibility: we no longer know what is imaginary or real, physical or mental."[76] The indeterminacy of the causes of Carol's symptoms underscores that limitations of understanding and awareness concern Haynes as much as do absences or failures of emotion. He has said that *Safe* is about "restraint" and "keeping things tucked in",[77] a comment reminiscent of Jarmusch's remark that *Stranger Than Paradise* is about "repression".[78] Not very different is Sokurov's stress on "reticence" as key to his cinema: "A limitation of what we can actually see and feel. There has to be mystery."[79] Such linkage of mystery to limitation (and to restraint, repression and reticence) seems compatible, moreover, with Lyotard's notion that a central task of art, or at least of avant-garde art, is "to bear witness to the indeterminate".[80] Junctures of limitation and indeterminacy, such as strongly influence style, theme and character in slow movies generally, are especially prominent in *Safe*.

As indicated early in this chapter, while many of *Safe*'s cinematic traits fit the slow-movie mould, the film does not conform in every respect. Citing Akerman's *Jeanne Dielman...* as a major influence, Haynes has described his film's style as "pared down",[81] and critics seem to agree. Guthmann praises *Safe* for its "eerie austerity" of style,[82] Desson Howe admires the actors' "hypnotically restrained performances",[83] and Jonathan Rosenbaum tells his readers that *Safe* will likely remind them of films by Akerman or Antonioni.[84] In addition, Guthmann singles out specific aspects of *Safe* that bear on the importance of emotional distance and detachment in slow movies: Haynes "films Carol's world from a cool distance", he observes, "using master shots and slow, stately camera moves". Yet one could also argue that *Safe* diverges from slow-movie norms, particularly in its uses of sound and editing. For example, Carol endures constant intrusions of non-diegetic music, plus a mysterious, non-diegetic hum or buzz (noted in Ebert's review of *Safe*[85]). Silence in her world is further disrupted by radios and televisions, onscreen and off, blaring reports of contemporary anxiety and distress. While this barrage seems less unusual than the non-diegetic music and the buzz, it becomes so incessant and repetitive as to seem like an extreme manipulation by the filmmaker rather than just an everyday assault. Further, while the editing of the image track in *Safe* feels far less intrusive than the manipulations of sound, the former reflects mainstream rather than slow-movie practice. Guthmann compliments Haynes for avoiding "nervous, jumpy editing"[86] and Haynes himself describes the cutting in *Safe* as "minimal".[87] Yet the film contains far more cuts than most slow movies do; the shots comprising *Safe*'s first thirty minutes, for example, last on average just 17.7 seconds. Further, as the truck exhaust causing Carol to cough forces her to drive her car off the road and into a parking garage, the cuts come more quickly. By the time her vehicle reaches the garage's empty upper levels, there appear alternating shots of her, the back of the truck and the interior of the garage lasting just two, three or four seconds. Such rapid cutting occurs nowhere in *Lazarescu* or *432*. Both Romanian films, moreover, contain numerous shots several minutes longer than any in *Safe*.

While *Safe* tends to forgo natural continuities of time and space afforded by long takes, it deploys long shots in which Carol, situated in large spaces often devoid of people, appears remote, isolate, diminutive and inert. An instance of this slow-movie practice occurs early in the film as she stands waiting for twenty-seven seconds at the door to her friend Linda's home at the end of a long walkway dividing the home's immense front lawn. In this extreme long shot Carol appears almost stranded as well as remote, but she does occupy a central point in the image. In other long shots, her body is radically de-centred as well as remote; indeed, when she returns home following the visit to Linda, she at first appears nowhere on screen. There is simply the sound of her disembodied voice calling out, informing the maid of her return (and hearing in reply the distant whir of a vacuum cleaner). Instead of Carol, a large living room looms, its plush chairs, lamps, tables, columns and beams symmetrically arranged before a dark fireplace set in a wide wall in the background. Then, as the camera remains stationary, Carol appears in the kitchen, in the rearmost part of the image on the upper right. Through a small vertical opening, barely more than a slit between the edge of the fireplace wall and a wet bar to the right of it, we get a glimpse of her pouring a glass of milk.

When the phone on the wet bar rings, she walks a short distance towards the camera to take the call (from her mother, a character who never actually appears). But even at the bar Carol remains in extreme long shot. Eventually she proceeds along the right of the image through the living room to a large threshold opening onto another room. Here, located in the foreground at last, she stands horrified, as she observes two new sofas offscreen that are black rather than the colour she ordered. The film cuts to a new shot from within the room that reveals the wrong sofas, and in this shot, which encompasses Carol as well as the sofas, she stands even more to the right than previously. Indeed, as the shot begins, a portion of her body is cut off by the vertical frame line. "She's on the margins" or "literally squished out of frame",[88] says Haynes of Carol's position in this shot and others. The sympathetic viewer may want Carol to be more central, to fit more comfortably into the spaces she inhabits, and perhaps even to dominate them. But whether in long or close shot, Carol rarely if ever moves or shifts position in a manner that eases her estrangement or lodges her more securely in the world.

Haynes also points out that "you don't get shots from Carol's point of view", an observation borne out in the new shot which reveals Carol and the sofas from a position quite separate from hers. Shots from her point-of-view might impute to her greater focus and agency than she possesses. She remains instead a meagre figure gripped by emotional and bodily crisis. Her voice disconnected from her body, a body pierced by the frame line, she remains cut off from herself and the world.

Drift and Resistance

Liverpool and *Ossos*

"The viewer is freed to read calmly and with distantiation [sic] and with time to ponder … There are times that I will see films I'm very interested in, and I can 'leave' them and escape into my own world … But it's something that comes from the film itself, otherwise I would not have arrived at the place I did."

– Lisandro Alonso, interviewed in 2011[1]

"Sometimes in the cinema, it's just as important not to see, to hide, as it is to show … one of the cornerstones of filmmaking is resistance … The spectator can see a film if something on the screen resists him."

– Pedro Costa, at the Tokyo Film School in 2004[2]

If *Safe*, *4 Months, 3 Weeks and 2 Days*, *The Death of Mr. Lazarescu* and *Climates* adhere imperfectly to slow-movie norms outlined in the introduction, Lisandro Alonso's *Liverpool* (2008) represents perhaps the purest instance of slow cinema explored in this book. Both the Argentine filmmaker's remark in *Cineaste* that "not much happens"[3] in his films and his interlocutors' characterisation of his work – especially the trilogy *La libertad* (2001), *Los muertos* (2004) and *Liverpool* – as a "stylistically rigorous, minimalist exercise in 'slow cinema'"[4] hardly overstate *Liverpool*'s emotional stringency, its slow pace and sustained focus on emptiness, inaction, silence and stillness, its attention to the mystery and indeterminacy of human experience, and its steely, surprising force.

The film's plot could not be leaner: Farrel (Juan Fernández), a taciturn merchant sailor, obtains permission from the captain of his freighter to take two days of leave when the vessel docks at Ushuaia in Tierra del Fuego so he can visit his mother in a remote village. He explains he has not seen her for a long time and that she may be dead. Almost an hour of this 84-minute film elapses before Farrel completes his slow journey and steps at last into the room of the bedridden woman we assume to be his mother. But when he tells her his name without saying he is her son, she fails to recognise him: "I see so many people that I don't know or recognise", she remarks before proceeding to mistake their connection: "I was still a child when you were already a big boy." As Farrel sits on a narrow bed across from the old woman, a single medium-long shot without a camera move renders their entire encounter, which lasts nearly three minutes. Farrel then rises and leaves the room; four minutes later he leaves his mother's village and the film itself. Before departing, with a terse "I'm off", he hands a small object, later shown to bear the word "Liverpool", to Analia (Giselle Irrazabal), a girl who resides with his mother. Alonso describes Analia in the *Cineaste* interview both as Farrel's daughter and as "suffering from a mental disability";[5] J. Hoberman in the *Village Voice* judges her "young enough to be his daughter" and "apparently simple-minded".[6] The film does not make explicit Analia's relation to Farrel, but her mental impairment is evident. After his departure, it is she who appears in most of *Liverpool*'s remaining eighteen minutes, which focus on life in and around the village. These remaining scenes, as low-key yet also as piercing as the rest of the film, culminate in *Liverpool*'s final shot: Analia, leaning against the wall of a barn, contemplates the small object bearing the word "Liverpool" that she accepted with indifference more than nineteen minutes earlier in the film.

Particularly in regard to the question of emotion in slow movies, this concluding shot featuring the solitary Analia bears comparison to the final image in *Safe*: an unusual close shot of Carol White's face as she looks into a mirror and tentatively declares her love for herself. As in most of the film, Carol's facial expression is timid and blank, lacking "the 'polyphonic' play of features", the revelation of "emotions, thoughts and ideas",[7] which captivated Béla Balazs in close-ups of the human face in *Broken Blossoms* (D. W. Griffith, 1918), *The Passion of Joan of Arc* and other classic films. Close-ups of faces revealing inner life are even rarer in *Liverpool* than in *Safe*. One reason is that Alonso's film has few close-ups of any sort, whether of natural or man-made objects or of people's faces. The film relies instead on long shots and medium shots in which the environment is more imposing and riveting than the human characters. Further, even when close-ups of the face occur in *Liverpool*, the result is opaque: the film's characters, as well as the non-actors who portray them, seem programmed to hide or deny rather than reveal emotion. "I always tell my actors, don't look into the camera and don't express anything", Alonso has said.[8]

Analia does not look into the camera in *Liverpool*'s final shot, a long take lasting two minutes and twenty seconds, but her appearance is not entirely devoid of emotion. As the take begins, she is observed in long shot feeding sheep with her back to the camera; eventually she turns, approaches the camera and leans against the barn wall. At this point she is closer to the camera and in a sense to the spectator than ever before in the film, though most of her body, rather than just her face, continues to be in view. After hesitating for about fourteen seconds, she draws from her pocket the object Farrel gave her before he left. Both Alonso and film critics refer to the object as a souvenir keychain. But until this moment its nature or identity has been obscure. For it was shown only in extreme long shot when Farrel – after detaching it from what in hindsight must have been a key – gave it to Analia without saying a word about it. Now the camera tilts down a bit to centre on the object as Analia's fingers turn it over and over. With this slight camera move, most of Analia's face rises out of frame – only her mouth and chin remain visible. These too are excised, though, as she takes one more half-step forward. Then, in the absence of her face, the strange, rotating souvenir, observed against the backdrop of her immobile and suddenly anonymous body, dominates the long take's remaining fifty-five seconds. But while the shot substitutes a trinket's blankness for a human face's potential richness, humanness and human feeling are not eradicated. Rather, as in *Safe*'s closing shot and slow movies generally, the emotion is severely constrained; and at this moment in *Liverpool* it is also rendered indirectly.

The final long take of Analia charts not a simple feeling, but a complex if muted emotional journey all the more noteworthy because even modest emotional change and expression is unusual in the film. Although Analia is a droopy, passive individual who ordinarily averts her eyes when addressed, eager if wary desire flashes on her face, particularly on her lips and in her eyes, as she nears the barn wall, having fed the sheep and peered furtively ahead and back, apparently making sure no one is watching. Her less vital and wakeful look returns, however, as she hesitates before drawing Farrel's gift from her pocket. Then the camera descends, and, in a moment reminiscent of Bresson's *Pickpocket*, indications of Analia's feelings shift from her face to her fingers as they brace the gift at both ends. Besides spinning the keychain, the fingers repeatedly angle or dangle it or hold it still, as if pondering its nature and the mystery of the man who gave it to Analia. Implicit in the busyness of her fingers is not only her puzzlement but also her glimmering desire for friendship and access to a larger world. More than once as her fingers manipulate the keychain, the word "Liverpool" carved within it is revealed to the spectator. But it is unlikely that Analia can read, or that she can recognise "Liverpool" as a famous port emblematic of Farrel's seafaring life; moreover, keys may be uncommon in her village. Such considerations perhaps underlie Alonso's assertion in the *Cineaste* interview that the souvenir means "absolutely nothing" to her.[9] Like the singular encounter between Farrel and his mother, this final moment in *Liverpool* yields little recognition, connection or understanding. Like the viewer, Analia is simply left hanging.

Which is how she was left earlier as well, though her indifference masked her vulnerability, as Farrel sped off after pressing upon her the metallic souvenir instead of the warmth of a loving hand. Despite his haste to depart in that shot, a long take just four seconds shorter than *Liverpool*'s concluding shot of Analia alone, his departure was protracted, as he marched through snow for some ninety seconds at the end of the take before disappearing in extreme long shot over the distant border between the snow and the dark forest. Rarely, indeed, does Farrel proceed quickly and dynamically in *Liverpool*. On his way to visit his mother, for instance, he generally appears idle – whether sitting, standing, reclining, eating, smoking or gulping from a liquor bottle he carries everywhere. After leaving the freighter, he delays entering Ushuaia, both the world's southernmost city and the launching point for his trip. Even though a two-minute-seventeen-second long take in his cabin on the freighter was devoted to his packing for the trip, he stops at the edge of the city to re-pack in an empty alley on a rainy night, recorded in another take more than two minutes in duration. Warily looking around and setting his big black bag on a barrel, Farrel shifts a few belongings from the big bag into a small red one he has removed from it, then hides the black one behind planks angled to a wall. Next, a brief shot of him standing on a glittery urban street is succeeded by yet another two-minute take, with the camera stationary as usual, in which Farrel eats and drinks alone in a restaurant with no other patrons in sight. Also lacking human presence are the quiet lake and autumnal forest in the huge *trompe l'oeil* behind him.

Farrel's slow, idle manner persists after the long take in the restaurant. The subsequent two shots find him immobile again in a new space, a strip club featuring voluptuous hostesses, strobe-lit and barely clad. Once more seated alone, this time at a smaller table, he smokes and drinks a beer spiked with contents from his private bottle while a woman's shadow dances on the wall where he rests his head. Presumably observing the woman dance, Farrel appears weary and empty rather than aroused. After weeks or months at sea, he finds no release or satisfaction in this locale, by far the most gaudily sensual in *Liverpool*. The scene shifts in just thirty-four seconds to a lengthier two-shot scene of Farrel sleeping and then waking, scarcely invigorated, on an empty, dilapidated ferryboat. The first image, an unusually tight shot of his face that soon widens a bit, has him sitting asleep at the back of the vacant passenger zone, which includes windows looking onto the sea; eventually he wakes, looks to his right and left, and lights a cigarette. After ninety seconds the film cuts to the scene's second shot, one perhaps more typical of *Liverpool*'s slow-movie style. Both a long shot and a long take lasting more than two minutes, the new composition reveals litter, torn seats and a gouged foam-rubber block, all of which contribute to the site's ravaged, abandoned air. Farrel stands, lifts his bottle from his bag, peers through windows on either side, sits down again, puffs on his cigarette, gulps from his bottle, checks his wallet. As in earlier scenes, not much happens. Rather than seeking high drama and action, Alonso remains low-key, lingering on dormant moments and narrative lacunae such as most filmmakers avoid.

Further, in support of his emphasis on inaction, Alonso adopts a common slow-movie tactic, which is to underscore his protagonist's lack of dynamism and narrative agency by excluding images that reflect the protagonist's point of view. As Shigehiko Hasumi has said of Pedro Costa, Alonso does not "connect the eyes, which are the origin of sight, to the objects captured by their gaze".[10] When Farrel peers in one direction, then another, what he sees is not shown from his perspective – and often it is not shown at all. Hence the spectator does not see what Farrel sees when he furtively scans the back alley at night before he rearranges his belongings, or looks around in the restaurant featuring the huge *trompe l'oeil*, or wearily contemplates the dancer in the strip club. Besides supporting the spectator's impression that the protagonist's perceptions, like his thoughts and feelings, are limited, the elisions of Farrel's perspective tend to restrict the spectator's access to the external world. They also diminish the spectator's intimacy and identification with Farrel, as they impede visual alignment with him and narrow the sights shared with him. The spectator remains detached as well from other characters in *Liverpool*, who like Farrel are denied point-of-view shots and often seem distanced, if not absent, from themselves and the world.

An odd moment that possibly underscores Alonso's resolve to disengage the spectator from Farrel's point-of-view occurs during the ride Farrel hitches on the back of a logging truck as he nears the end of his journey to his mother's village. At the start of the ride, Farrel hoists himself up following another passenger, and the two men simultaneously take seats on thick logs on the truck bed. The first passenger sits closer to the cab than Farrel does and faces screen left; Farrel sits closer to the camera, in a medium shot, and faces screen right; a chain over the logs separates the two men. The ride including a brief stop occurs in a single take that lasts two minutes and fifty-three seconds, during all of which Farrel remains seated. The truck slows and halts after thirty-four seconds, allowing the first passenger to hop off, towards screen right – the same direction Farrel faces. Then the truck resumes its motion past leafless trees in the snow on the right side of the road. While the image of the gliding trees and snow does not reflect Farrel's point-of-view exactly, the match-up seems close enough for the spectator to imagine that he or she is sharing Farrel's view. But at the end of a fifty-two-second interval following the first passenger's departure, the camera pans back towards screen left, away from the trees on the right, to find Farrel in a sharply altered position, one virtually identical to the first passenger's before he stood and hopped off: close to the cab, on the far side of the chain, and facing screen left rather than right. Thus, instead of underscoring a congruence between Farrel's viewpoint and that of the camera and spectator, the pan exposes an extreme disparity. After the pan ends, the long take continues for about eighty-seven seconds, focusing on Farrel sitting, taking a swallow from his bottle, and briefly looking back towards the side of the road he faced earlier – as if to remind the spectator of expectations when the pan began. As always, though, what Farrel sees when he looks back towards the side of the road is not shown.

Not only Farrel but also lesser characters, as mentioned earlier, are denied point-of-view shots in *Liverpool*. A mildly amusing example occurs in the village's canteen close to Farrel's mother's home. Sometime after Farrel exits the film, Torres, who seems to operate the canteen by himself, sits drinking and conversing in a rare leisurely moment with a younger man across the table who inquires about conditions at the sawmill (probably the village's economic mainstay) and the health of "Nazarena", who may well be Farrel's mother, the only infirm female character in the film. Suddenly the two men turn their heads sharply towards the upper right of the frame. Possibly their attention has been drawn by an image on television just beyond the frame; but neither a television nor light from a television appears, and one wonders whether this remote, poor village receives television. (As for the musical backdrop to the men's conversation, the film generally excludes all but diegetic music and other sounds. The likely source of the music accompanying the conversation is a radio, though a radio is no more visible in the canteen than a television.) In any case, what the two men see when they resolutely and simultaneously look up is not shown. Instead, *Liverpool* cuts to black for five seconds, as it does at no other point in its eighty-four minutes, before proceeding to a shot of Analia at night entering the bedroom she shares with Farrel's mother.

In presenting a blank screen reminiscent of the repeated "blackouts" in *Stranger Than Paradise*, Alonso again elides his characters' points of view and restricts the space and world of the film. Such stringency brings to mind not only Jarmusch but other makers of slow movies including Sokurov[11] and Pedro Costa, who also cautions that "it's just as important ... to hide ... as it is to show" and thereby to "resist" the spectator.[12] James Quandt's characterisation of Alonso's films as a "withholding cinema"[13] undoubtedly reflects their adherence to notions like Costa's and Sokurov's. More specifically, Quandt cites *Liverpool*'s "antidramatic ways, attenuating narrative through empty time and withheld information".[14] J. Hoberman, in a review published some months after Quandt's essay, describes *Liverpool* similarly: "The tone ranges between withholding and enigmatic."[15] Alonso suggests that not merely individual viewpoints and visions of a wider world are limited or withheld in his films, but also freedom itself. It's important to communicate, he tells *Cineaste*, "a situation of very few options, not much freedom".[16]

This "withholding" pattern entails a refusal to track either promptly or closely the actions of characters as well as their shifts of attention or points of view. As previously indicated, the film's workings, including its uses of camera and editing, seem almost detached from the characters as well as indifferent to the spectator's curiosity. When Farrel in long shot, soon after dismounting the flatbed truck at the edge of his mother's village, kneels by a wooden post and scrapes ice off it with his knife, or when, later, he peers at a photograph on a shelf in his mother's home, his actions provoke no camera move or cut to a closer shot such as might address the spectator's curiosity about the focus or object of Farrel's actions. Similarly, when Farrel exits a space he has been occupying, such as his tiny cabin on the freighter or the main room of his mother's home where he has espied the photograph (and where, though I have not mentioned it, he has given Analia money in response to her entreaties), *Liverpool* tends to linger on the vacated space rather than promptly pursue Farrel. After the latter, following Analia, exits the aforementioned room (having finally placed the mysterious photograph in his bag), Alonso's stationary camera lingers for twenty-nine seconds, even though the shot – a long take as well as a long shot – has already lasted one minute and twenty-one seconds. The resulting emphasis on both empty space and what Quandt terms "empty time" is hardly uncommon in *Liverpool*. Also brought to mind by the camera's lingering on the vacated room – and, for that matter, by the ninety seconds of Farrel disappearing in the snow at the end of the subsequent shot – is James Naremore's phrase: "long takes viewed from a distance and filled with dead time", cited in regard to Romanian cinema in the previous chapter. No doubt empty or dead time and space are intrinsic to *Liverpool*'s distant, "withholding" style.

Alonso clearly considers this style consistent with slow-movie values. Moreover, Farrel's personality is no more dynamic than either the plot or the style. The combination of such minimalist features may well provoke the viewer to leave *Liverpool* entirely rather than ponder and meditate on the film. Recognising this danger in her review of *Liverpool*, Manohla Dargis remarks that "Alonso's style … seems calculated to bring him as modest an audience as possible."[18] The Argentine filmmaker nonetheless reaffirms in his *Cineaste* interview his commitment to a sort of minimalism, detachment and indeterminacy resembling that of other makers of slow movies including Van Sant and Sokurov.

No doubt the cinemas of Sokurov, Van Sant and Alonso differ greatly from one another; and both Van Sant and Sokurov have made films in various styles and genres. Sokurov's films have ranged from "baroque" and "kaleidoscopic" to "minimalist" and "ascetic", for example, as Edwin Carels and Nancy Condee have noted;[19] and Van Sant himself has distinguished between his films of "very specific intentions"[20] – meaning that they eschew ambiguity – and his far less determinate works. Like Sokurov and Van Sant in *some* of their movies, Alonso, who is more than twenty years their junior, embraces what Van Sant (as discussed in my second chapter) has called the "open film"[21]: a film of deliberately indeterminate meaning that invites multiple interpretations from diverse spectators who thus contribute to "the creation", as Sokurov would say, of the film's artistic world.[22] The open film, moreover, not only resists offering the spectator unequivocal information, perhaps what Sokurov terms "the overly sharp quality of screen reality",[23] but also rejects what Van Sant calls Hollywood busyness, the plethora of fast-paced action and scene changes typical of commercial cinema. Though not necessarily Brechtian or Marxist in its approach, the open film favors distance and detachment; it would sooner forgo a large audience than emulate mass entertainment packed with action, motion and melodrama.

Noteworthy are some close resemblances between Alonso's remarks about his aesthetic outlook and statements by Van Sant about the open film. While Alonso cautions that in his films "the spectator is not spoon-fed one piece of information after the other" and "I'm not the one guiding the spectator",[24] as already noted, Van Sant says regarding *Elephant*: "Modern-day cinema takes the form of a sermon. You don't get to think, you only get to receive information. This film is not a sermon. The point of the film is not being delivered to you from the voice of the filmmaker. Hopefully, there are as many interpretations as there are viewers."[25] Alonso acknowledges that his refusal to guide viewers may encourage them to wander – or to "leave" the film; and rather than expect them to stay riveted, he endorses their straying: "the spectator can be looking at something, he or she can think about it, and can even 'leave' the film and then come back into it."[26] Much as Alonso touts leaving the film, Van Sant, in discussing *Gerry*, praises drifting off and getting lost: "A lot of movies don't want you to have space to drift off and reflect on what you are thinking. Or for you to get lost, which is what this film is about…"[27]

Although Farrel doesn't lose his way as *Gerry*'s two hikers do, he perhaps fits James Quandt's description of Alonso's protagonists as existing "at a remove from humanity" and as "lost even to themselves".[28] Alonso has regarded Misael (Misael Saavedra), the protagonist of his first major film, *La libertad*, as anything but lost: "To me he's a sage", said the filmmaker. "Someone who isn't interested in society, who creates his own world."[29] But Alonso thinks differently of Farrel, observing that the sailor is lost – even to himself. Alonso details this lostness as an "inability to communicate or have a relationship, this tendency to marginalize himself, to punish himself, or to exclude himself from any kind of human life, any kind of emotional contact with others, such as his mother or his daughter".[30] Similarly, Dennis and Joan West, Alonso's interlocutors in the *Cineaste* interview, speak of Vargas (Argentino Vargas), Alonso's protagonist in *Los muertos*, as lacking "a sense of meaning or community" and consequently as leading "a sort of death in life".[31] This last phrase brings to mind James Morrison's description of Carol White and other characters in Todd Haynes's cinema as "enduring the benumbed death-in-life" which Morrison considers endemic to "late capitalism" and "the post-structuralist landscape".[32] Thus slow-movie characters as diverse as those of Van Sant, Alonso and Haynes (not to mention Jarmusch, Sokurov and Ceylan) seem fatefully aligned.

As noted in the previous chapter, from within her benumbed state Carol White exudes an air of unease and estrangement even in her own home. Indeed, feeling at home, whether in one's home, one's skin or the larger world, eludes not just Carol but virtually every slow-movie character we have considered, starting with Willie in *Stranger Than Paradise*, the son in *The Second Circle* and William Blake and Nobody in *Dead Man*. Farrel, the "world-wandering sailor",[33] proves to be no different. While his addled mother fails – or perhaps refuses – to recognise him when he returns home, her caregiver Trujillo (Nieves Cabrera), who also patiently teaches Analia how to trap foxes, tend sheep and step safely across ice, makes clear to Farrel that the place to which he has come cannot be his home: "What are you doing here?" the older man sternly asks the sailor. "Not long after you left, Analia was born. Nobody here knows you now. Not even your mother. She's sick. I don't know why you came back. You left me one heck of a legacy. What are you hoping to find? I know you can hear me." The reply is silence. Withdrawn and taciturn even when awake, Farrel has been carried asleep from an outdoor latrine where he spent the night, and he remains unconscious during Trujillo's speech, perhaps the longest in the film. Consonant with Alonso's description of his protagonist, Trujillo implies that Farrel, though presumably innocent of heinous misdeeds such as the double fratricide ascribed to Vargas in *Los muertos*, has wronged and perhaps disavowed the community, and has forfeited his right to a home there.

Trujillo's indictment seems all the more telling since it succeeds Farrel's night in the door-less latrine. Apropos of Quandt's view that Alonso's protagonists subsist "at a remove from humanity", the sailor's choices of sleeping quarters are often unseemly and antisocial. Even aboard the freighter, which perforce is Farrel's home as well as his workplace, he is shown sleeping not in his private if cramped cabin, but in a large, clangorous boiler area off-limits to him and most other members of the crew. "Are you crazy?" shouts a shipmate upon discovering him there. "You can't sleep in here! Get out!" By sleeping in the latrine, the decrepit ferryboat and the prohibited area in the freighter, Farrel comes to resemble a homeless person, or a person who prefers homelessness to conventional shelter and community.

"Home is the normal – whatever place you happen to start from, and can return to without having to answer questions", remarks Susan Neiman in *Evil in Modern Thought*.[34] Although Farrel spends most of *Liverpool* journeying to his mother's home, he is met only by Trujillo's angry questions and his mother's failure to recognise him. The sailor soon leaves, and, given his preference for temporary shelters and trappings of homelessness, might have done so even had he been warmly received. A primitive man largely divorced from modernity, Farrel nonetheless reflects the incapacity or indisposition to have a home – or to feel at home – often considered a particularly modern dilemma. Neiman relates this dilemma to various oft-cited historical developments: the loss of belief in God (as chronicled by Nietzsche, for example); the rise of technology; and the genocide of European Jews and other groups by the Nazis in World War II. Neiman invokes a passage from Theodor Adorno's "Homeless Shelter" in *Minima Moralia*: "The house is gone. The destruction of European cities and the concentration camps merely continued the processes that the immanent development of technology decided for the houses long ago. 'It is part of my happiness not to be a homeowner', wrote Nietzsche in *The Gay Science*. One must add today: it is part of morality not to be at home with oneself."[35] Neiman, too, sees the concentration camps and the Holocaust as bound up with historical processes that were already under way: "Auschwitz was the completion of a process inherent in the modern, not a departure from it. Through that process we lost something too deep to be entirely fathomed."[36] Such profound loss requires, in Neiman's view as in Adorno's, revision of our sense of "home" in relation to "the normal": "What remains is only the moral imperative not to deceive ourselves about the magnitude of the modern catastrophe", states Neiman. "Decency demands that we refuse to feel at home in any particular structure the world provides to domesticate us. It also requires that we refuse to feel at home in our own skins."[37]

Alonso found circumstances akin to homelessness in the village he selected to be Farrel's mother's home. "It's a very isolated place," said the director, "filled with people who are hiding from something or someone. And I like that, people who are escaping, watching through the window for ten years."[38] Alonso's words, "watching through the window", bring to mind Farrel's stealing up to the window of his mother's house soon after he has reached her village, and his earlier stealth, in the empty alley at the edge of Ushuaia, as he peered into a window and then into the rainy night before repacking his possessions. Alonso's stress on hiding, and on furtive, fugitive and perhaps guilty conduct, brings also to mind both Nuri Bilge Ceylan's remark that "people always have something to hide in real life" and the wary, repressed bearing of Ceylan's protagonists, Mahmut and Yusuf in *Distant* and Isa in *Climates*. Whether in Alonso's cinema or Ceylan's, hiding or hidden characters are rarely secure or at home in the world.

Despite Alonso's initial impression, however, the characters in the village in *Liverpool* do not appear to be hiding; nor do they seem to lack a sense of home and community. For instance, in a radio communication to Torres in the canteen, a higher-up addresses workaday matters such as the village's fuel needs, road conditions and care for the sheep; but he also evinces personal warmth and neighbourly concern, inquiring how "everyone" is and whether "Nazarena" (probably Farrel's mother) is "any better". Later, Torres drinks rum in the canteen with a young patron whose communal interests range from activity at the sawmill to Trujillo's well being. Trujillo himself assists in the canteen, in addition to caring for Nazarena and Analia. On the whole, then, the villagers portrayed in the film do not quite mirror Farrel's cold, wary detachment and inscrutability.

Yet they remain somewhat undefined and remote. One major reason is that

Alonso's actors follow his orders not to "express anything" or "look into the camera" or "try to be an actor". Such dictates reflect the Argentine filmmaker's regard for "the Kuleshov Effect"[39] (an effect cited in relation to Sokurov's *The Second Circle* in the first chapter), whereby the spectator comes to ascribe diverse meanings to an actor's neutral, unchanging expression as it is juxtaposed to various images – of a corpse in a coffin, for example, a child playing and a piping-hot bowl of soup. In addition to looking blank or expressionless, Alonso's actors generally appear in static long shots, far removed from the spectator; and, as in the canteen, they often face away from the camera. Further, his characters are predominately silent; not only does nothing much happen in his films, but since the characters say very little, nothing much is revealed or explained. In *New Argentine Film: Other Worlds*, Gonzalo Aguilar praises the result, hailing the "indeterminacy of meanings" and "the poetics of indeterminacy" in Alonso's cinema.[40] Manohla Dargis is less enthusiastic, judging Alonso's approach in *Liverpool* "bloodless" and decrying his attempt "to wring feeling and meaning from characters whose silences I'm not sure he even hears".[41]

Whether one sides with Aguilar or Dargis, instances of uncertainty and puzzlement in descriptions of *Liverpool* attest to the film's sparseness and indeterminacy. One elusive matter, as indicated previously, concerns Analia's relation to Farrel. Although in interviews Alonso has unequivocally described her as Farrel's daughter,[42] critics have hesitated: J. Hoberman refers to her as "a woman in the household young enough to be his [Farrel's] daughter".[43] James Quandt describes her as "the damaged girl we take to be Farrel's daughter".[44] Dargis identifies her simply as "a young woman" who lives with Farrel's bedridden mother.[45] Hoberman adds that Farrel "is solicited" by Analia.[46] But while she asks him for money more than once, she offers no sexual favour in return. Another challenge is to learn more about Trujillo's identity and connection to Farrel. Hoberman regards the old man as "some crusty local, old enough to be [Farrel's] father", but does not weigh or interpret the past intimacy between the two men implicit in Trujillo's bitter claim: "You left me one heck of a legacy." Nor do Hoberman and other critics ponder the origins of Trujillo's devotion to both Farrel's mother and Analia. Might Trujillo be Farrel's father? And what of the woman who gave birth to Analia – where is she? Aside from "the damaged" Analia, Farrel's mother appears to be the only female in the village.

Such questions of identity and connection go unanswered, since *Liverpool* poses an informational void, spiced with intimations of dark or unnatural circumstances. Regarding such intimations, we may ask, for example, how if at all we are to understand Farrel's mother's suggestion that she was a "child" when Farrel was a "big boy". Further, when *Liverpool*'s indeterminacy and unanswered questions do not prompt the spectator to "leave" or "drift off", as discussed above, they perhaps provoke suspicions and conjectures that the viewer then projects onto the film's void. Consider, for instance, Hoberman's parenthetical question regarding Farrel's departure, "Before heading back over the snow (to his freighter, to his death?)",[47] or Quandt's speculation about Farrel's mother: "the old woman, who may be feigning nonrecognition of her son".[48] While films less stringent and indeterminate than *Liverpool* may prompt comparable conjectures, *Liverpool* stays unusually aloof from its provocative riddles, troubling neither to acknowledge nor to resolve them.

◆

Much the same can be said of Portuguese filmmaker Pedro Costa's *Ossos* (*Bones*). Indeed, in ways suggested by photographer and art critic Jeff Wall, whose work like Costa's frequently involves a conjoining of documentary and fiction, *Ossos* may be even more indeterminate, strange and distant than *Liverpool*. In his praise of *Ossos*, a film about depressed parents of an unwanted baby who are neighbours of Clotilde (Vanda Duarte) and her family in the Lisbon slum called Fontainhas, Wall underscores the "consistent enigmatic quality maintained throughout the film".[49] He admires the scenario for not being "too clear or organized", as indicated, for example, by its inclusion of "characters who do nothing, who almost do not participate in the story at all". Such characters just observe and listen and then disappear; he calls one of them "the watcher". "They're not background figures," notes Wall, "they're not extras; they seem to be very important, yet they don't have any material effect on the course of the action." Further, Wall finds the central characters just as puzzling as the narrative's watchful non-participants. "All the characters are enigmatic ... we don't really get to know much about them ... we don't really feel that we've entered into their consciousness or ... their personality ... They remain strange to us ... strangers ... a real mystery."

Tag Gallagher, Cyril Neyrat and Shigehiko Hasumi are among several critics who agree with Wall. Gallagher writes that "Costa denies us entry to his characters",[50] Neyrat remarks that the characters "preserve their mysterious density until the end",[51] and Hasumi notes that their "identity" and "interrelations" are "difficult to know".[52] Wall hints that like the whirl of offscreen, though diegetic, animal and human sounds that penetrate almost every image in *Ossos*, the characters' mysteriousness indicates that life is too vast and complex to be encompassed and explained in this or any other film. Possibly even more relevant to Costa's aesthetic, however, is that the mystery and indeterminacy of *Ossos*, its withholding of information and its underscoring of lack and emptiness, are central to "the resistance" Costa mounts to prevent spectators from entering the film too easily.

While both mainstream and art films often invite spectators to identify with movie characters and to enter into, as Wall says, the consciousness and personality of these characters, slow movies generally discourage such intimacy. Costa gives his particular reasons for denying the spectator easy entry or an open door:

"I believe that today, in the cinema, when we open a door, it's always quite false, because it says to the spectator: 'Enter this film and you're going to be fine, you're going to have a good time', and finally what you see in this genre of film is nothing other than yourself, a projection of yourself."[53] Costa seeks to block such projections and good times, even if doing so makes the spectator "uncomfortable" and turns him or her "against the film".[54] The spectator will truly see the film, claims Costa, only "when the film doesn't let him enter, when there's a door that says to him: 'Don't come in.' That's when he can enter. The spectator can see a film if something on the screen resists him."[55]

In Costa's ideal cinema, such "resistance" exists not only between a film and its spectator, but also within a film: "the material itself ... resists ... one image resists another, one sound resists another",[56] says Costa, perhaps reprising Sergei Eisenstein's stress on formal conflict or discord within a film. Costa's maxim, "it's just as important ... to hide, as it is to show", further affirms his belief in resistance, especially in regard to the film's relationship to its spectator, but also regarding relations among its characters. The intention to hide or resist, in any case, informs events throughout *Ossos*. The film ends, for example, as Tina (Mariya Lipkina), the unwanted infant's listless young mother, bars the camera's view by closing a door. Similarly, her initial act upon arriving home from the hospital with her baby early in *Ossos* is to close windows, curtains and shutters in the apartment, presumably to prevent pedestrians on the narrow walkways outside from observing the lives within. As if to make these closures more emphatic, the shutters, curtains and windows nearly fill the screen in each of three successive shots.

Further, Tina broaches the topic of seeing and showing just moments prior to these closures when she asks (as she and Clotilde, having travelled by bus from the hospital, enter the slum with Tina's newborn son), "You think he can see yet?" Enervated and dejected, Tina has ignored the baby; first the nurse in the hospital and then Clotilde have carried him and shown him affection. The question – can he see? – is the young mother's first indication of interest in him. "He knows you already, Tina", replies Clotilde, who is older than Tina. "Go on. Everyone wants to see him." The two women stand with their backs to the camera as Clotilde speaks. Then Tina slowly walks off, and, though we have not seen Clotilde transfer the baby, he is suddenly – for the first and only time in *Ossos* – in Tina's arms. When she blocks visual access to the apartment a few seconds later, however, he is nowhere to be seen and has been shown to nobody. He reappears a minute after the closures on a couch to which his mother drags a propane canister; she seats herself not far from his face and outstretched hand and turns the gas on.

Tension over the extent of inner and outer life to be either hidden or revealed in *Ossos* is palpable also in the film's initial image, a medium shot of a silent, isolate young woman Wall calls "the watcher", who looks contemplatively towards – but rarely into – the camera for forty-five seconds, until the film's opening title appears. No hint is given of her identity, her potential role in the narrative, or what she might be thinking or observing. Such puzzles persist seven minutes later in the film when she abruptly reappears for thirty seconds, wordlessly dispensing food in a mostly offscreen public eatery and looking surprisingly cheerier than before. A bit later she appears yet again, for just fifteen seconds, soberly standing and watching along one of the slum's narrow lanes; the prior shot has revealed Nina, Clotilde and the newborn returning from the hospital, but it is hardly clear that the watcher is observing them. As Shigehiko Hasumi says of characters featured at the start of Costa's *Casa de Lava* (1994), "It is unclear what their eyes are seeing or what their blank faces are trying to say."[57]

More than eight minutes after the fifteen-second shot of the watcher on the narrow lane, she watches intently again in a medium close-up that lasts eighty-one seconds. This shot connects a grim image of the infant's estranged parents to a long shot of a convivial but unidentified man viewed through a doorway from a pocket of darkness. The watcher may be transfixed either by the parents or by the unidentified man, who, incidentally, is featured nowhere else in the film. But the indeterminate space the watcher inhabits appears contiguous with neither the parents' abode nor the man's. So once again the watcher's place in the film and the object of her attention remain hidden or mysterious. Similarly enigmatic is the young woman who earlier joined the watcher in dispensing food, and who later, when Tina collapses on the floor at a party, helps Tina get up with the portentous words, "The evil eye is upon you. It's over now. You must pass it on to me." Like the watcher, this strange figure who tends Tina appears rarely in the film and remains silent except here.

Although major characters like Clotilde have more time on screen and become more familiar to us, they too retain, as Wall, Neyrat and others stress, a "mysterious density". Aspects of such opacity and mystery are already evident in the eleven-shot sequence centred on Clotilde and the baby's boyish father (Nuno Vaz) that connects the title shot to Clotilde's arrival at the hospital to meet Tina and the baby. The second shot in this sequence reveals Clotilde in a bathrobe in her kitchen, smiling momentarily as she savours coffee, drags on a cigarette and ruminates for forty-three seconds. But just as *Ossos* does not disclose what Wall's watcher sees, whether in the film's initial shot or thereafter, it does not divulge the object or nature of Clotilde's thoughts and feelings. Subsequent images are equally unrevealing. In the shot following Clotilde's appearance in the kitchen, she stands outdoors fully dressed, her face pressed into the shoulder of the boyish figure who will turn out to be the baby's father and who looks away – towards the street with its moving vehicles. The couple's silence and seeming intimacy persist in the next image, in which they face the camera and one another, she with an almost imploring look, and in the subsequent shot, which frames their lower bodies as they ride on a bus and she comfortingly takes his hand as it rests above his knee. But why does the young man need comforting? Why does he look dazed, empty and dejected? Why does Clotilde, who appeared mildly upbeat and self-sufficient in the kitchen, look grave and imploring as she presses against him on the street? More fundamentally, who are these individuals and what is their connection to each other?

Following the shot of the twosome on the bus, Clotilde enters an apartment and cautiously announces herself by name; then she roughly pulls the young man in by the edge of his jacket, in effect ending the tender if doleful amity of the prior three shots. In the sequence's five remaining shots, Clotilde sets about cleaning the apartment, and she and the young man remain physically apart and avoid looking at each other. Apparently oblivious to Clotilde vacuuming in front of him, the downcast fellow sits dazed for a while on the edge of a soft chair in the living room. Perhaps she has brought him along to help her clean, or in order to look after him – we never know. The man seems disposed, as Luc Sante suggests, "to make himself invisible ... to make everything go away".[58] Shortly he exits the apartment without a word, and Clotilde, hearing the door close, mutters "... bastard".

The next shot, at the hospital, raises an important question as Clotilde, her back to the camera, tells Tina, "I came alone": has Clotilde intended to bring the depleted young man to the hospital? Is he the father of Tina's baby? Our curiosity is stoked when seconds later a shot of him picking through trash at a produce market is intercut with Tina and Clotilde preparing to leave the hospital with the baby. But ten more minutes of film, or twenty-six shots, must pass before the question of his relation to Tina and the baby is somewhat more fully joined. Only then does he enter what we have assumed to be Tina's apartment and encounter the mother and newborn lying asleep or dead on the couch – though gas no longer hisses from the canister. Wobbly and bleary-eyed, the young man seems scarcely to take note of their presence as he wordlessly steps past them from the kitchen to the bedroom, where he falls unconscious onto the bed.

Ossos obviously teems with unanswered questions as to plot and character, beyond those already indicated. Tina and the baby survive Tina's release of gas from the canister, but we do not learn how. Nor do we learn the father's fate after Clotilde, having threatened to kill him for upsetting Tina, discovers him asleep towards the end of the film in nurse Eduarda's (Isabel Ruth) apartment, turns on the gas in the kitchen and departs. We do behold unusual levity between Tina and Clotilde following Clotilde's murderous act: at home just six shots after Eduarda's apartment door shuts tightly behind Clotilde, the two friends burst out laughing when they bump into each other and Tina drops a pot. Nonetheless, one cannot be sure the father is dead; also unknown at the film's end is the condition of the baby, whom the father has been trying to sell, to either his prostitute friend (Inês de Medeiros) or Eduarda.

Adding to *Ossos*'s uncertainties or indeterminacy, Eduarda's claims of deep affection for Clotilde, Tina and the father are made suddenly and with little or no basis – these characters are almost strangers to her. Clotilde begins to work for Eduarda late in the film, cleaning her middle-class apartment while the nurse is at work; the two women intersect briefly once or twice, scarcely enough to foster a significant bond. Eduarda meets Tina just once before declaring her affection. Having been assigned by Clotilde to clean Eduarda's apartment, Tina chooses instead to asphyxiate herself in the nurse's kitchen. Eduarda "meets" her only upon arriving at the apartment to find her unconscious; she revives and feeds Tina, who after some sleep heads home. While this encounter is more touching than any between Eduarda and Clotilde, Tina's sheer helplessness rather than her minimal, often cold response to the nurse must suffice to explain Eduarda's deep caring. One-sided and suspect as well is Eduarda's affection for the baby's father. Probably they meet for the first time at the entrance to the upscale grocery where he begs for food for himself and his son. Yet they soon address each other with enough familiarity, possibly tinged with erotic interest, to suggest prior involvement; and soon we find him residing – or at least resting and sleeping from time to time – in her apartment, both with and without his infant son. Early on she tells him she expects her husband to return home shortly, but no such person arrives.

As we have seen, critical opinion does not ignore Costa's disposition in *Ossos* to hide or elide information that could illuminate the film's plot and spatiotemporal context as well as its characters. Cyril Neyrat describes the film's plot as "elliptical",[59] while Luc Sante finds *Ossos* "reminiscent of the late movies of Robert Bresson in its ellipses and silences".[60] Sante adds that *Ossos* relegates "pivotal occurrences behind an unseen curtain between shots".[61] Tag Gallagher remarks that Costa challenges the spectator "to find the connection between one shot and the next. Are we in the same place? The same year?"[62] Much like Wall's "watcher" and the spaces she occupies and observes, events as well as characters in *Ossos* exist in an indeterminate realm or context subject to Costa's elliptical manoeuvres. Barbara Barroso remarks on the "denial of context"[63] in *Ossos*, while Shigehiko Hasumi states that in "Pedro Costa's editing, the story's context is rarely explained through sequences of shots".[64] Yet *Ossos* does not come apart as a result of its lack or "denial of context" – its omissions of pivotal events and its refusals of explanation, connection, causality and resolution. Instead such emblems of Costa's strategy of resistance become integral to the film's strange, riveting coherence – and to the peculiar welcome it grants the spectator.

As mentioned earlier, Costa defines resistance as arising not only between a film and its spectator but also *within* a film ("the material itself ... resists ... one image resists another, one sound resists another"). Within *Ossos* elliptical manoeuvres and the denial of context resist or impede what Wall refers to as the "onward movement" of the film's narrative.[65] In other words, the pace or momentum of the film as a whole is slowed. Moreover, the ellipses distance or "divert" the spectator, notes Wall,[66] prompting the viewer to ponder the film's meaning, as Alonso advocates, rather than become unthinkingly absorbed in the action. A further effect is that the individual image or moment acquires independent standing or distinction, apart from its narrative function. Echoing André Bazin's precepts, Shigehiko Hasumi celebrates that in *Ossos* the present moment "is made visually absolute"[67] rather than being subordinated to either "narrative flow" or "human psychology".[68]

Not only the narrative's elusiveness and impenetrability allow images in *Ossos* to emerge in their own right, but also the indisputable beauty of these images, which, as Hasumi states, "grab hold of our gaze".[69] Although the Fontainhas slum portends a mise-en-scène as deprived and unglamorous as any in slow movies, Costa's way with light, colour, texture and composition transforms the environment, including the slum's weathered walls and pocked shutters and doors. Indeed, this convergence of aesthetic richness and physical decrepitude comprises yet another tension or resistance within the film. No less riveting than *Ossos*'s scarred inanimate surfaces are its human physiognomies. Luc Sante describes *Ossos* as "a beautifully painterly play of faces and hands";[70] a *Manchester Guardian* blog calls the faces "compelling";[71] Tag Gallagher testifies that "Costa's portraits are stunning, conjuring Jan Vermeer in light, colour ... conjuring [Danièle] Huillet-[Jean-Marie] Straub in sheer sensuality".[72] *Ossos*'s portraits stand out also because the film's characters, particularly Tina and the baby's father, look ghostly or zombie-like, "suffused with death".[73] Finally, Thom Anderson's remarks about close-ups of faces in Costa's subsequent film, *In Vanda's Room* (2000), pertain to the faces in *Ossos* as well: "almost all of these close-ups stand by themselves as separate scenes. They appear as privileged moments, outside any chain of action, almost like commentaries providing a reading of the whole film. These images can be a critique, even a repudiation, of the cinema of action."[74]

Like close-ups in *In Vanda's Room* as described by Anderson, characters in *Ossos*, while enigmatic and unknowable as Wall says, provide "a reading of the whole film". Their faces reflect pervasive tensions in *Ossos* between showing and hiding, presence and absence, emotion and its disavowal, expressiveness and blankness, life and death. The faces especially of Tina and the baby's father suggest untold need and suffering but also a refusal of engagement such as one might associate with Costa's closed door ("Don't come in"). Costa's faces in *Ossos* – blank, passive, immobile, inured to inaction, yet also intense and haunted – both resist feeling and mutely cry out.

Indeed, one might say that the film veritably brims with emotion: "At times [Costa's] scenes sting our eyes with their piercing pain", writes Hasumi, "and at times they wrap our eyes in ineffable tenderness."[75] Conceivably *Ossos*'s undeniable emotion derives from its resistance to emotion, reprising Robert Bresson's slightly paradoxical maxim, "Production of emotion determined by a resistance to emotion."[76] Like Bresson, Costa insists on filtering the excess and impurity from emotion, but not on abolishing it. A story of an unwanted, starving baby whose father carries him in a trash bag through city streets and tries to sell him while his mother attempts suicide can hardly be devoid of emotion. Even though Costa's commitment to de-dramatising the action and resisting excesses of feeling keeps melodrama in check, *Ossos* suggests that emotion is as central to his aesthetic as resistance: "The cinema is made above all with feelings", he stresses in the Tokyo lectures. "To understand is to feel and to feel is to understand ... All the feelings of life must pass through your shot."[77]

In *Ossos* stillness pervades both the feelings of life and the resistance to feeling. Again a maxim of Bresson's seems relevant: "Be sure of having used to the full all that is communicated by immobility and silence."[78] Wall and other critics stress *Ossos*'s stillness as exemplified by the film's first shot in which the watcher just sits on a bed, the camera remains stationary and nothing happens. The film's slow pace prompts Wall and others to imply that *Ossos* makes heavy use of long takes,[79] as slow movies usually do. But the average shot duration in *Ossos* is just 32.3 seconds, far less than in *Liverpool* and several other slow movies, which partly explains why eighty-one seconds or even forty-five seconds of the silent watcher feels exceptionally long. *Ossos* also diverges from slow-movie practice by using numerous close-ups and medium shots. On the other hand, it adheres to slow-movie norms such as fixity of the camera, immobile or slow-moving characters, emotive stringency, sparse and enigmatic plot, distancing of the spectator, and emphasis on human isolation, finiteness and mortality.

Another slow-movie trait, paucity of dialogue, also contributes to the stillness and silence of Costa's film as well as to its mystery and opacity. Barely thirty words are uttered in the film's first twenty-five minutes. Costa's resistance to the spoken word in *Ossos* seems consistent with his commitment to economy as well as to cinema as "an art of absence",[80] a notion he attributes first of all to D. W. Griffith. He cites as well the inspiration of Charlie Chaplin – and more generally of silent comedy and melodrama, arts distinguished by the absence, or at least inaudibility, of spoken words. *Ossos* "comes from Chaplin", Costa states, "from the melodramas of the beginning of cinema, a boy with a baby who has nothing to eat, the street, speeding cars, bread, a prostitute, a kitchen, all of that is the beginning of cinema".[81] Alonso also invokes an earlier era as he accounts for his resistance to the spoken word, which perhaps exceeds Costa's: "I just don't have any confidence in words. I do have confidence in what I see", states the director of *Liverpool*.[82] "Previously in the history of cinema image was everything, or almost everything. So I don't believe that I need to have recourse to words in order to explain how my characters feel."[83] Thus the creators of both *Liverpool* and *Ossos* draw inspiration from silent cinema as they rely on images and resist spoken words in their quest for truth.

Death-Drive, Life-Drive

A Talking Picture, Taste of Cherry, Five Dedicated to Ozu and *Still Life*

"Somebody said that the present is eternal, but the present is immobile. It's just like the images in celluloid, every single one is still and we only see movement with a succession of them."

– Manoel de Oliveira[1]

"In the cinema organic movement is transformed into its inorganic replica, a series of static, inanimate images, which, once projected … become animated … The homologies extend: on the one hand, the inanimate, inorganic, still, dead; on the other, organic, animate, moving, alive."

– Laura Mulvey, *Death 24x a Second: Stillness and the Moving Image*[2]

"What lives, wants to die again. Originating in dust, it wants to be dust again. Not only the life-drive is in them, but the death-drive as well."

– Fritz Wittels, explaining Freud's post-World War I thinking
in *Beyond the Pleasure Principle* and other writings[3]

With the exception of *Five Dedicated to Ozu*, which contains no dialogue (and purports in its title to consist of just five long takes), this chapter's films do not resist the spoken word in the manner of Lisandro Alonso's *Liverpool* and Pedro Costa's *Ossos*. Indeed, the title of Oliveira's film, *A Talking Picture*, signals an embrace of speech impossible during the silent era when Oliveira's filmmaking career began. Yet the talk in *A Talking Picture*, as in *Taste of Cherry* and *Still Life*, often focuses on loss, absence and death; it suggests, as do other aspects of this trio of films, a waning of the principal characters' capacity for action and movement.

Besides containing more dialogue, however dispirited and banal, than occurs in *Liverpool* or *Ossos*, *A Talking Picture*, *Taste of Cherry* and *Still Life* contain more cutting. For example, though certain shots in *A Talking Picture* last up to five minutes, most are far shorter, and the average duration is just 18.8 seconds. Probably the film's long takes, because they are infrequent, contribute modestly to the sense of time passing slowly and to the film's ability to prompt thoughtfulness in the spectator. The relative brevity of most of the shots, on the other hand, does not prevent the film from feeling slow and even static. More consequential than either cutting or long takes in the achievement of slowness in *Taste of Cherry* and *Still Life* as well as in *A Talking Picture* are other aspects of style, theme and plot that I have linked to slow movies and now wish to examine in relation to the films at hand. The respective directors come from diverse cultural backgrounds and were born at least thirty years apart – Oliveira in 1908, Kiarostami in 1940 and Jia Zhang-ke in 1970 – but they share major thematic as well as stylistic interests fundamental to the slow-movie aesthetic.

Perhaps the most decisive of these interests was expressed by Oliveira in a 2008 interview: "The present is immobile ... just like the images in celluloid, every single one is still and we only see movement with a succession of them." He also affirmed, regarding his film *Christopher Columbus, the Enigma* (2007), the importance of giving the spectator "time to think, bit by bit", and added that "movement is distracting".[4] Such privileging – even within relatively brief shots – of stillness and opportunity for contemplation rather than motion and action is hardly unusual among slow-movie makers, including Kiarostami and Jia Zhang-ke. In *A Talking Picture*, Oliveira keeps his camera stationary, and restricts as well the movements of his main characters. Further, as Randal Johnson has noted, the Portuguese director generally bans "the spectacular" from his films and "studiously avoids melodrama"[5] and emotional agitation. He in fact calls himself "a resistance filmmaker" as opposed to an action director.[6] Moreover, Oliveira for the most part avoids drawing attention to his directorial presence or to the filmmaking process. He cultivates instead a self-effacing cinema, a simple style marked by civility and dispassion. "I'm always looking for the greatest simplicity", he says, "to render ... deep things clearer, to be simple, not to rush, ... to represent reality such as it is."[7]

Oliveira's regard for stillness and related qualities as pivotal to life and film seems consistent with Deleuze's account of the displacement of the "movement-image" by the "time-image" in European cinema after World War II. This shift away from action and movement has been attributed by cultural analysts to altered perceptions of human nature, and particularly to the moral horror and scepticism heightened by the war and genocide. As mentioned previously concerning Alonso's *Liverpool*, Adorno and Neiman are among the cultural observers who have addressed this change in human consciousness. More recently, Thomas Elsaesser has underscored the link between the reduction of action and movement in the "time-image" and the increased sense of human displacement, homelessness and disorientation following World War II: "Deleuze's theory of the 'time-image'", writes Elsaesser, "responds to the crisis of the 'movement-image' when European cinema realized the impossibility after Auschwitz of telling stories or inhabiting a world, of aligning body and mind (perception, sensation and action) in a coherent continuum."[8] This impossibility seems as formidable today as it was then.

But despite the ongoing cogency of the "time-image" and the human predicament it reflects, assertions by Oliveira and like-minded filmmakers of the importance of stillness in life and film are anomalous. The dominant view remains that in today's cinema – as perhaps in our fast-changing lives – action and movement count most. Hence the remark by Agnès Varda, scarcely a director of action films, cited in this book's introduction: "In all film there's the desire to capture the motion of life, to refuse immobility." Scott Bukatman puts the matter more sweepingly: "The cinema ... is a medium dedicated to the recording of action, of movement, whether the movement of the objects of the world, the movement of the camera, or even the movement of the film through camera and projector."[9] In *Film: A Very Short Introduction*, Michael Wood also emphasises motion: "Since very ancient times – there were experiments in Egypt and Rome around the time of the birth of Christ – people have been interested in making and seeing images of movement."[10]

The belief of Varda, Bukatman and Wood in motion's cinematic primacy is shared by critics as well as filmmakers and theorists. Terrence Rafferty, for instance, in praising William Wellman's films dwells on their rendering of motion: "What's constant in Wellman's work, for all its radical variations in style and tone, is a fascination with pure movement: how people get from one place to another ... Even when Wellman's people are at rest", Rafferty adds, "they look about to burst into motion ... He's an action director even when nothing's happening on the screen ... Wellman worked best with actors who could give him the brisk tempo he needed."[11]

By contrast, motion in *A Talking Picture*, *Taste of Cherry* and *Still Life* remains, as indicated above, slow and confined, even when characters do get from one place to another. While these films are not devoid of action, their grave stillness and sense of emptiness outweigh the action. One could say that if Wellman is an action director, Oliveira, Kiarostami and Jia Zhang-ke direct stillness. And they align themselves with classic slow-movie makers whose work has rejected the supremacy of action and motion: Oliveira cites Carl Theodor Dreyer,[12] Jia

Zhang-ke embraces Bresson for revealing in *A Man Escaped* (1956) "the charm of time itself",[13] and Kiarostami's most minimal and experimental film bears the title *Five Dedicated to Ozu*.

In such writings as *Death 24x a Second: Stillness and the Moving Image*, Laura Mulvey challenges the "obsession with movement", which she states "has dominated cinema from its origins".[14] Rather than movement, she stresses "the halt and stillness inherent in the structure of celluloid itself".[15] Such stillness may be considered to inhere not only in the intermittent motion and illumination of celluloid passing through the projector, but also in the empty spaces between the still photographs on the celluloid roll. In a meditation on stillness related to Mulvey's, and based like Mulvey's on celluloid rather than digital materials, Mary Ann Doane stresses "the division between frames" and the fact that "during the projection of a film, the spectator is sitting in an unperceived darkness for almost forty percent of the running time".[16] Moreover, the repeated halting and the recurrent darkness as celluloid passes through the projector probably ensure the clarity of what appears on the screen; if not for the suitably paced lacunae or interruptions, in other words, action and motion on the screen would appear unnatural and illegible. Hence stillness may be considered the foundation "on which", as Mulvey writes, "cinema's illusion of movement depends".[17]

Stillness and emptiness are perhaps magnified when the motion-picture screen remains blank after a film ends. More important, stillness may stand out *during* a motion picture, in the form of freeze frames, for example, or frames of sheer light or darkness, such as signal death and dying towards the end of *A Talking Picture* and *Taste of Cherry*. Yet stillness need not always signal death. As noted above, Oliveira associates immobility primarily with the present moment rather than with death, whether in the cinema or in everyday life. Wood considers motion rather than stillness most important in the cinema, but he does not identify stillness with death. Indeed, he apparently sees stillness as allied to motion when he concludes from the studies conducted by Étienne Jules-Marey and Eadweard Muybridge in the 1880s "that an extreme expertise in stopping motion was an essential prelude to starting plausible pictures of it".[18] Then again, Wood views Doane's darkness as "the invisible reality [that] haunts the world of the visible";[19] and since this darkness seems to me coincident with Mulvey's stillness, I take him to imply that stillness may threaten instead of support motion and life on the screen. Regarding the interaction of stillness, life and motion, Mulvey seems to me unequivocal: drawing perhaps on Roland Barthes' view of still photographs, she sees stillness not primarily as either haunting or requisite to motion, but as akin to death: "on the one hand, the inanimate, inorganic, still, dead; on the other, organic, animate, moving, alive".[20] She indicates that death, and not merely stillness, inheres in motion pictures. Hence the stillness signalling the death of characters towards the end of *A Talking Picture* and *Taste of Cherry* may be taken as a reminder of the death integral to celluloid cinema. Mulvey further suggests that any movie, whether celluloid or digital, drives towards death, or towards its original state of stillness prior to projection. This drive combined with dying characters and techniques like freeze frames used to signal death may occasionally foster a sense not just that life must end, but that it longs for an end, both to its own existence and to that of others. To cite Wittels: "Not only the life-drive is in them, but the *death-drive* as well."[21]

Only in *Taste of Cherry* does the main character, driving his car up and down winding roads on mostly barren hillsides near Tehran, claim to want to die. But though the central characters in *A Talking Picture* and *Still Life* do not proclaim such a desire, death precedes, awaits or surrounds them, which may explain their wistful, inhibited manner and restricted movements. Although not benumbed, the leading characters in all three films endure something of the "death-in-life" James Morrison finds in Todd Haynes' cinema.[22] In *Still Life*, amid the vast upheaval and devastation linked to the construction of the gigantic Three Gorges dam, two forlorn individuals, a man and a young woman unknown to each other, search for loved ones who have ceased to communicate with them. The man seeks his wife, the woman her husband, both of whom – in search of economic opportunity years earlier – journeyed to this region on the Yangtze River now redolent of death. In *A Talking Picture*, a Portuguese mother and daughter perish when time bombs presumably installed at the seaport of Aden explode on the ship that has been conveying them on a grand tour of the remnants of once great civilisations.

The repetition of themes and images in *A Talking Picture* contributes as much as the sparse, inhibited movements of its camera and main characters to its static, confined quality, a quality that brings to mind Oliveira's remark that "we are not as free as we think".[23] One recurring image is a close shot of the ship's prow moving through water, which could be anywhere. No camera movement is detected, and the prow's position in the frame does not change. The result is an impression of static rather than dynamic motion – or of stillness in motion. Another repeated image, also executed with the camera stationary, reveals the mother, Rosa Maria (Leonor Silveira), and her daughter, Maria Joana (Filipa de Almeida), standing relatively still on deck and either looking towards the pier below prior to their ship's departure or facing the camera in front of them. Another recurrent shot, usually taken from a high angle indicating the mother and daughter's viewpoint, reveals people looking up from a pier and waving farewell. Further, in three instances a taxi enters the shot of the pier, and a female passenger emerges and heads towards the ship. The film then cuts to the mother and daughter on deck as they vaguely recognise the new passenger to be a media celebrity.

Superposed on the sea in the film's third shot is a printed statement that seems to anticipate considerable physical and intellectual activity: "In July 2001, a little girl crosses thousands of years of civilization along with her mother, a distinguished history professor, while on their way to meet her father." But even though thousands of years are to be bridged in a short time, the little girl and her mother, both of whom have been introduced on the ship's deck under some of the film's opening credits in the prior shot, appear less than animated. Indeed, whereas almost all the passengers around them wave cheerfully to the small crowd of well-wishers on the pier below, Rosa Maria and Maria Joana wave to no one. Nor at the end of the shot do they walk out of frame, screen left, as their fellow passengers do. Instead, essentially unmoved and unmoving, though Rosa Maria does stroke her daughter's hair, the two remain fixed in the central foreground.

Thus they remain as the ship moves slowly out of the harbour, past statues of early Portuguese adventurers. The mother tells her daughter that the adventurers sailed "hitherto unexplored waters", "found new lands" and waged wars. Yet the fixed, lifeless remoteness of the sculptures, as viewed in long shot by Rosa Maria and Maria Joana, undercuts Rosa Maria's account of the adventurers and underscores the rigidity of these two observers, who, as Dennis Lim has written, are "poised to the point of stiltedness".[24] The mother and daughter remain so throughout *A Talking Picture*, which is to say they look stiff and awkward, as if posed for a travelogue or a photograph that will freeze them in the moment. Not surprisingly, their location frequently seems as manipulated as their posture and manner. In Egypt, for instance, Rosa Maria and Maria Joana sit on either side of a small table in the foreground of the image, while the huge Pyramid of Khafre and Great Sphinx of Giza conveniently loom in the background. Rosa Maria's body intersects the very centre of the pyramid's base, and the sphinx presides exactly between the mother and daughter.

An extreme instance of the stilted stance of the two travellers, or at least of Rosa Maria, occurs in a hotel near the Suez Canal later in the Egyptian sequence. Escorted by a well-known Portuguese film actor (Luís Miguel Cintra, playing himself), Rosa Maria and Maria Joana reach the hotel, and, observed in a low-angle long shot, proceed down the entry corridor towards the camera. The long shot becomes a close shot when they enter the foreground and halt, presumably just in front of the low stationary camera. Here Maria Joana, peering into the camera, is fully visible, but the faces of the two adults are out of frame; just the middle of their bodies are visible, on either side of Maria Joana. Cintra, in voice-over, says, "Have you noticed the jeweller's shop windows? As you can see here in the hotel there are many pieces in the shape of a beetle. They're to be found everywhere." At this point Rosa Maria bends into frame on screen right, angling her face and body towards Maria Joana, who remains at the centre, still peering into the camera. A slow pan of mostly bluish, beetle-shaped objects follows, during which Rosa Maria, in voice-over, remarks on their great popularity in Egypt. Oliveira cuts back to Rosa Maria and Maria Joana as before, both of them looking into the camera. Cintra then bends into frame on screen left as Rosa Maria had on the right, and gently places his hand on Maria Joana's shoulder. Simultaneously his angled head and Rosa Maria's almost meet near the top of the composition above Maria Joana, virtually ensconcing the little girl in a triangular frame within the motion-picture frame. As Rosa Maria and Cintra continue to press their bent bodies into the rectangle of the motion-picture frame, Cintra explains to Rosa Maria as well as Maria Joana, who still stands erect, that beetles in Egypt "used to be worshipped as gods. They were the symbol of the sun." Then Oliveira finally cuts to a medium long shot from behind the trio as Rosa Maria and Cintra resume their normal, upright stance.

The new shot reveals for the first time, beyond them in the background, a portion of the interior of the store as well as the display in the jeweller's window that presumably the observers have been scrutinising. Yet the row of beetle pieces is not discernible in this medium long shot, and the window appears more distant from the observers than was suggested in the previous tight shots. Both the apparent absence of the beetle pieces and the window's distance make it more difficult for the movie spectator to believe that the three of them have been looking into the window. Adding to this difficulty, of course, is that the window was not shown prior to the tight shots of the trio looking. Hence the medium long shot belatedly picturing Rosa Maria, Maria Joana and Cintra in relation to the window does not reverse the spectator's impression that the three – especially the oddly bent and squeezed adults – have been looking into, and stiffly posing in front of, a camera rather than the window.

As already indicated, the often stilted poise and calculated positioning of the mother, daughter, Cintra and other characters, including the ship's captain (John Malkovich), prime them to be seen, pictured, photographed, commemorated. But it is also evident, as Rosa Maria and Maria Joana journey from Portugal to France, Italy, Greece, Turkey and Egypt, that the two are primed to (sight) see. In neither case, of course, are they figures of action and movement like the Portuguese adventurers and warriors memorialised in the harbour. Cintra addresses Rosa Maria and Maria Joana as passive viewers: "Have you noticed the jeweller's shop windows? As you can see ..." he says. His words underscore a salient objective shared by Rosa Maria and her daughter. At least five times in *A Talking Picture*'s initial three minutes, Rosa Maria urges Maria Joana to "look", and expresses anxiety about her daughter being able to "see". In the film's first spoken words, Rosa Maria tells Maria Joana, "Look at this mist. What a pity. If it gets worse, you won't be able to see the monument to the Discoveries." For the remainder of *A Talking Picture*, much of the dialogue between mother and daughter concerns their effort to see or discern monuments of human achievement, or what remains of such monuments and achievement, while reflecting on "thousands of years of civilization".

A recurrent theme in Rosa Maria's reflections is the near impossibility of seeing and comprehending the past, of penetrating what Rosa Maria calls "the mists of time", which appear more intractable than the vapour shrouding monuments in the Portuguese harbour. At the Acropolis and elsewhere, "distinguished history professor" Rosa Maria often seems obliged to confront the vanishing or absence of the past and even its unknowability. She refers to "the mists of time" soon after a Greek priest whom she and her daughter have met near the Temple of Erechtheum on the Acropolis relates a complicated tale involving two statues of the goddess Athena, one of which he says was real, while the other, thought to be much larger, was imaginary. The real statue was removed to Constantinople, he says, whereas the imagined statue vanished, and the story surrounding it was lost. At this moment Rosa Maria and Maria Joana stand amid physical emptiness and decay. Like Pompeii's central square, which Rosa Maria and her daughter visited earlier, the sacred temples of the Acropolis are in ruins, deserted except for tourists, and severed from their original beauty ("See how beautiful it must have been", says the mother, after the film has presented a close shot of human forms sculpted in a frieze). As history seems to dissipate before their eyes, Rosa Maria, in reply to Maria Joana, concedes that the goddess Athena did "not really" exist – there was "just" a statue. And "the story of the statue", she says, "is an ancient legend that was lost in the mists of time".

Furthermore, her remarks earlier in the film have suggested that even were the legend recovered or at hand, it would yield no sure vision of the past. For legends exist, she has indicated, at a remove from actual historical events: "Legends are like fables. They're invented stories like the muses who inspired poets ... or mermaids ... Muses or mermaids are imaginary beings, invented to explain certain events." Her tone, as much as her words, implies that the legends and imaginary beings fail to render historical reality accurately and ought not be taken too seriously. Indeed, they may obscure the past rather than illuminate it, in which case history is inaccessible owing to mists of fantasy as well as of time.

Motifs of loss and absence are taken up midway through the film by the three female celebrities we have seen approach the ship at various ports of call. We encounter the women together for the first time when the American captain ushers them into the ship's dining room and then to his personal round table within view of Rosa Maria and Maria Joana, who as they dine alone are intercut observing them. Perhaps surprisingly, the shift in the film from the mother and daughter to the captain and these celebrities shifts the film's focus, at least for a time, from the public to the private realm. During the first half of *A Talking Picture*, Rosa Maria and Maria Joana's visits to historic sites yield little evidence that either character possesses an inner or private life. Rosa Maria repeatedly tells the men they meet on their journey, including the Portuguese actor with whom she and Maria Joana eventually converge in a familial pose at the jeweller's window, that they are bound for Bombay to join the airline pilot who is Rosa Maria's husband and Maria Joana's father. But there is no indication of the absent father's personality, of their life together as a family, or of why Rosa Maria and Maria Joana are so conspicuously alone. By contrast, the trio of celebrities and the captain enter immediately into a lengthy exchange – partially rendered in one of the film's longest takes, almost six minutes – about their personal lives. Whether a

French entrepreneur, an Italian fashion model or a Greek stage actress and singer, the celebrities have enjoyed outstanding success, and two of them, Helena (Irene Papas) and Delphine (Catherine Deneuve), remain content in their respective careers in theatre and business. But the captain's dinner partners also experience deep sorrow. Each of them, including the unsentimental Delphine, misses love and companionship in her private life, as does the captain. At the same time, he and the women fear domestic discord and threats to their personal freedom, which may be why none of the four currently has a spouse or a child. No longer young, set in their ways, all four individuals at the captain's table are vulnerable to pangs of loss, isolation, confinement and declining vitality. Francesca (Stefania Sandrelli) speaks of her "lost happiness". Helena's song, which she performs at the captain's request, laments the loss of beauty: "Little orange tree, thick with leaves, where are your flowers? Where has your beauty gone? Where is your loveliness of old?"

Once an internationally acclaimed fashion model, Francesca is the celebrity who complains most poignantly of confinement and solitude; the others chime in, and together they give voice to concerns relevant also to Rosa Maria and her daughter. "They called me Aphrodite", Francesca announces. "I, who was never free ... I was never free even in my work, which forced me to keep to strict timetables and had very rigid rules. I didn't even stop working when I got married." Further, she found love imprisoning; marriage failed to augment her sense of personal freedom. "Love is a tyrant", she tells her companions, who echo her sentiments: Delphine says that "passion makes prisoners of women", and Helena adds that "love is a prison of desire". Then Francesca laments that she is childless and no longer has a husband: "I've gone from a kind of prison of love to a nostalgic solitude." Such references by Helena and Delphine as well as Francesca to bondage and imprisonment bring to mind signs of comparable if less conscious constraints endured by Rosa Maria and Maria Joana. The fixity of the mother and daughter, who while stiffly poised to view historic monuments are disinclined to look inward, parallels the immobility of the celebrities, who undertake in the film no activity more strenuous than sitting and talking and who find a bit of consolation but no cure for their sorrows. Hence all the major characters – Rosa Maria as well as the captain and the celebrities – seem a bit wistful, even mournful. Whether owing to the inaccessibility of both history and the self or to failure to fill the vacancy of their lives with love and trust, they are at a standstill psychologically even more than physically.

As part of the film's web of repetition, Maria Joana follows almost every statement of her mother's with a question: "Why?" "What is a legend?" "What's a volcano?" "What is a sinful life?" "Was there really such a goddess?" "What are the Middle Ages?" "Who are the Arabs?" "What does civilisation mean?" Repeatedly the questions prod Rosa Maria to acknowledge not only that much of history is hidden or lost, but that what is known is riven by absences of love and freedom echoed in the laments of the characters at the captain's table. An example of the historical absences and failures emerges when Rosa Maria tells her daughter that the pyramids were built because the Egyptians were civilised (the "greatest civilisation of antiquity") and defines civilisation as "what man creates over time using his intelligence". But then she concedes that the pyramids were built by forced labour of the "twelve tribes of Israel", enslaved in Egypt as they fled drought and hunger. "Is that why they [i.e., the Egyptians] were civilised?" asks Maria Joana. "No," responds Rosa Maria, "the history of civilisation is made up of these contradictions. Man is not perfect, and he makes mistakes."

Another mistake, in Maria Joana's opinion if not her mother's, is war. As early as the first scene, as their ship leaves the Portuguese harbour, Rosa Maria cites various wars waged throughout history, often between Christians and Muslims vying for religious and economic dominance. The topic of killing and destruction arises again later in the sea voyage during a five-minute long take of Rosa Maria and Maria Joana at night, standing on deck in their usual spot as the ship crosses the Red Sea to Arabia. Rosa Maria mentions that Arabs have had to fight many wars, in which many people have died, ever since Abraham expelled Ishmael from his home. Prompted by this reminder of so much killing, Maria Joana asks, "Why were men so wicked?" Rosa Maria replies with her usual poise and emotional distance: "They weren't really wicked. They were people like us. Lust for power leads to war. That's our nature." Maria Joana asks, "What do you mean, nature?" Her mother's reply, though rendered from a victim's standpoint rather than an aggressor's, bears on the theme of material and emotional loss or lack that courses through the film: "It's like being hungry or wanting something very much", she says. "Suppose you had a doll and someone tried to take it away. You'd hold it tight to keep it." Why Rosa Maria thus positions her daughter to ward off aggression is unclear. Perhaps the mother means that if necessary she herself would hold her daughter tight and fight to keep her. But perhaps she cannot say this openly without jeopardising her cool composure. In any case, her grim hypothesis evokes keen anxiety in Maria Joana: "But if I had a doll, would they try and take it?" It is perhaps the first time in *A Talking Picture* that the daughter evinces inner concerns – and that the threat of physical assault becomes intensely personal.

Whereas the focus of Rosa Maria and Maria Joana thus shifts from the public realm to the private, the celebrities at the captain's table veer in the opposite direction. From loss and vacancy in their personal lives they segue to the decline of civilisations and the failure to preserve humanity's achievements. Expressing a view comparable to Rosa Maria's, though with greater emotion, Helena says, "No civilisation lasts forever. Time will tell how best to preserve the memory of the past." She cites Alexander the Great's effort to preserve the past by building the largest library in the ancient world in Alexandria and the destruction of that library when Muslims conquered Egypt. She considers it "most curious [that] the Arabs, who ... spread Greek culture in Europe and beyond, were the ones to destroy it, burning all the books in the blindness of their religious fervour." Yet the Arabs themselves "founded a great culture", notes Francesca, though it too, adds Helena, "is in decline".

Eventually Delphine is moved to remark on "the sad history of humanity", which the captain quickly seconds: "Yes, the sad history of humanity. Absolutely." Indeed, the lengthy conversation at the captain's table underscores several perhaps regrettable aspects of human existence: great cultures rise only to fall. Humanity fails to sustain or build on its achievements, partly because it cannot agree on what is valuable or worth preserving. Language differences worsen the disharmony and confusion, and possibly make them inevitable. In any case, as Rosa Maria tells her daughter, people are not just creative but also destructive: it's their nature to kill and to wage war. The mother's view bears on the sad frustration of the celebrities and the captain as well as on the static quality of the film's plot. Contrary to psychologist Steven Pinker's claim that violence declines as humanity grows more rational and civilised,[25] Rosa Maria, like Delphine and the captain, sees virtually no prospect of change. She implies that humanity will remain as it is regardless of action or education that seeks to alter it; perhaps this is why Rosa Maria has withdrawn into her poised, distant passivity.

The theme of immobility, of life and action trumped by lethal stillness, swells in the film's final scenes. The ship's captain enters the stationary long take of Rosa Maria and her daughter on deck as they conclude their exchange about the doll and human bellicosity. In Aden, the next port of call, he acquires an Arab doll that he presents to Maria Joana after the ship has moved on and she and her mother have joined the celebrities at his table. Unfortunately, the daughter's instant attachment to the doll soon contributes to her death as well as to her mother's. Apprised of time bombs about to explode, the captain commands everyone on board to escape in lifeboats; but Maria Joana instead runs to retrieve the doll, and Rosa Maria races to find her. The search ends in the cabin they have shared as Maria Joana kneels, holds the doll firmly, and says, "Don't be afraid. I'll look after you." By the time Rosa Maria and Maria Joana emerge on deck, all lifeboats have departed. Espying them in extreme long shot from one of these boats, the captain tries to take action. But when he orders a boat to turn back to save the stranded mother and daughter, he's told it's too late. Then he shouts to Rosa Maria and Maria Joana, urging them to jump into the sea. When they do not, he starts removing his clothes, evidently intending to swim to their rescue. But the sound and light of explosions offscreen cause him to stop. A freeze frame then arrests his stricken, incredulous look for the film's remaining two minutes – as in the stillness of night credits ascend on screen right and Helena's earlier song is heard, imploring the north wind to blow gently.

In his description of alterations in European cinema after World War II, Deleuze writes in *The Time Image* that "the post-war period ... greatly increased the situations which we no longer know how to react to" and featured "a new race of characters" who "saw rather than acted, they were seers".[26] Such situations and characters figure prominently in *A Talking Picture*. The Portuguese mother and daughter, the American captain of Polish descent, the French, Greek and Italian celebrities all for the most part see rather than act. Eventually, however, they are acted upon by terrorists offscreen who plant bombs containing timing devices too complicated to be disarmed, explains the captain. Rather than the bombs, it is the central characters, the subjects onscreen, who in some sense are deactivated. Whereas the offscreen explosions signal what Deleuze might term "a movement of world",[27] the onscreen subjects, devoid of narrative agency, are stymied and still.

◆

Taste of Cherry almost ends, somewhat as *A Talking Picture* does, in stillness and death. Mr Badii (Homayoun Ershadi), having spent most of *Taste of Cherry* driving in Tehran and outside the city searching for strangers who will help him attempt suicide, at last swallows a few pills and arrives by taxi one night at the grave he has dug in the hills far above the city's lights. Thunder and lightning punctuate the taxi's approach but abate as Badii sits on a slope below a tree by the grave which will soon be revealed. In long shot, the fixed camera behind Badii observes his still, seated body in the lower half of the image for a full two minutes. Then Badii stands and exits the bottom of the frame, whereupon a medium close-up of his face shows him tucked in his shallow grave with his eyes open and his body girded for whatever will come. A new long shot shows clouds darkening and drifting across the moon. Next, the close-up of Badii returns; but in the course of ninety seconds, the blackness of night, at first interrupted by renewed lightning, consumes his face, while silence displaces earlier sounds of thunder, birds and rain. Whether Badii is dead or alive, an almost voluptuous sensation of nothingness and stillness settles over the movie.

Suddenly, though, a military cheer is heard rising in the blackness. A splotchy, hand-held video image fades in, revealing roughly the same physical environment as before, but in day rather than night, as a troop of soldiers trots slowly on the winding road in the lower left of the image. Twelve more shots appear before *Taste of Cherry* ends, each of which bears on what Gilberto Perez has called Kiarostami's "modernism". As early as the 1970s, in films the director made for Iran's Institute for the Intellectual Development of Children and Young Adults, Kiarostami "was laying bare the device," writes Perez, "drawing attention to the medium, like a teacher making clear to children how things work".[28] Perhaps in keeping with this modernism, *Taste of Cherry*'s twelve-shot coda begins by focusing on two members of the film crew, one of whom holds a film camera while the other walks towards him with a tripod. Then Ershadi, the actor who has portrayed Badii, casually brings Kiarostami a lit cigarette, which the director starts to smoke. The film cuts to an individual holding sound equipment amid green and yellow vegetation in a high-angle long shot. The next image begins with distant soldiers crossing the centre of the screen, then pulls back to reveal observers in the foreground, apparently including Kiarostami, whose voice is heard: "Tell your men [i.e., the soldiers] to stay near the tree to rest. The shoot is over. We're here for a sound take." Louis Armstrong's "St. James Infirmary" follows immediately on the audio track, while onscreen the men attired as soldiers loll and stroll beside the road and smile and greet the camera, which suddenly moves more spontaneously and extensively than at any time prior to the coda. Indeed, though "St. James Infirmary" is a kind of dirge, the camera takes on new life as it roams free of both a tripod and Badii's drive towards death.

The reflexive turn taken in the twelve-shot coda is unusual in a slow movie, and it probably surprises and distances the spectator; yet it does not greatly complicate the film. A major reason is that Kiarostami's "laying bare the device" follows rather than interrupts the film's minimal action. *Taste of Cherry* may seem unfinished because Badii's fate remains unclear. Yet the passage into total darkness, silence and stillness just prior to the coda does mark an endpoint. Further, key aspects of Badii's motivation and circumstances have been unknown since the start of the film, which, like other slow movies, generally prefers indeterminacy to clear disclosure and definition. Does Badii have a family or friends? What does he do for a living? Why is he hell-bent on suicide? Or *is* he? If so, can he find no more direct path than engaging strangers to visit his grave the morning after he has taken the suicide pills, and there bury him if he is dead? Does Badii truly want to die, or simply to meet people? The coda's intent seems more clear and simple than the film, including Badii's motives and fate, has been so far: we have come to an end, and here are a few individuals and implements responsible for the fiction we have been watching. Further, as if to indicate the fellowship among these individuals who have been engaged in making *Taste of Cherry*, they are pictured together in most of the coda's images, unlike Badii and other characters who in the fiction have usually appeared alone in the frame. The unhurried coda thus comprises an antidote to Badii's isolation and destructive mania, and sends the spectator off on a positive note, perhaps to enjoy the warm, life-affirming company of family and friends.

Like other slow-movie makers, Kiarostami often stresses the virtue of simplicity. Much as Oliveira declares, "I'm always looking for the greatest simplicity ... to be simple, not to rush",[29] the Iranian director remarks (regarding *Shirin* [2008]), "I love simplicity."[30] Elsewhere he tells students that "making something simple requires a great deal of experience. And, first of all, you need to understand that simplicity isn't the same as facility."[31] Slow movies, I have suggested, comprise a relatively simple cinema – structurally uncomplicated though richly nuanced. Their reflexive gestures are usually minimal, avoiding the intricate intrusiveness, say, of Godard's cinema; and they rarely if ever conjoin sharply divergent aesthetic styles, generic allusions or planes of reality. Such conjunctions, including blends of the real and the fantastic, are more evident in the complex slow cinema of such directors as Apichatpong Weerasethakul and Tsai Ming-Liang.[32] Slow movies I have been exploring, on the other hand, render a world that is less surreal, shifting and fluid, one perhaps closer to that of Italian Neorealism, though more resistant to emotion and melodrama and less determined to win the spectator's sympathy. The nonchalant, pared-down reflexivity of *Taste of Cherry*'s coda reflects, in any case, Kiarostami's love of simplicity and directness and the minimalist disposition of slow-movie makers generally.

Perhaps reflexivity, like beauty, lies in the eye of the beholder, though, and cinematic gestures yet more restrained than Kiarostami's coda may function reflexively. Hence Lisandro Alonso regards as reflexive his stationary camera's lingering on spaces vacated by major characters in *Liverpool*. Dennis and Joan West describe one such lingering (or instance of dead time): "Farrel leaves definitively the scene of his shipboard cabin; and then we are left for X number of seconds simply contemplating the setting."[33] Another instance occurs when Farrel, about to depart his mother's village, leaves her home after Analia does, whereupon the camera lingers on the large entry room he has vacated for twenty-nine seconds. Alonso claims to include such pauses "in order to raise the question of what happens if after a given sequence, in which not very much has happened, we nevertheless give the spectator time to think about what it is that is happening ... During that pause", he adds, the spectator "comes to realize that cinematographic language exists – because he is made to feel the presence of the camera. And if the viewer feels the presence of the camera, he is also feeling the presence of the director." Simultaneously, the viewer recognises that "over and beyond what is happening to the fictional character, there is always someone else who is narrating the story."[34]

The effects of a camera rigidly observing a space in which little happens obviously intrigue not just Alonso but also Kiarostami, Oliveira and other slow-movie makers as well as their commentators. Jared Rapfogel cites the frequently "prolonged, unadorned, and steady gaze" of Oliveira's camera,[35] while the elderly filmmaker himself remarks that "the steady shot brings us to another state".[36] Oliveira's suggestion that the fixed camera, usually focused on spaces with little or no action, alters the spectator's awareness seems borne out by Kiarostami's *Five Dedicated to Ozu*. The title refers to the five long takes that apparently comprise the film, with the camera stationary in each. While *Taste of Cherry* also deploys a fixed camera, its spatiotemporal continuity is interrupted more than is typical in slow movies as Kiarostami intercuts between Badii driving his car and the various passengers he tries to engage in his suicide attempt. Spatiotemporal continuity in *Five...*, on the other hand, obviously exceeds the norm in slow movies: as the entire film runs for seventy-four minutes, each shot on average lasts nearly fifteen minutes. One complication, however, is that the fifth shot actually consists of some twenty shots executed over many months in several places, though the shots are joined seamlessly and appear as one.[37] In any case, each of the five segments presents for a relatively long time a distinct, natural and peaceful scene in which not much happens. In each scene, the sea or a swamp appears, occasionally with people, ducks, dogs, clouds, the moon or a piece of driftwood. Free of dialogue and conventional action, *Five...* has been termed a film of "contemplative rhythms".[38] It is also a work of unusual stillness, which like Alonso's pauses and Oliveira's "steady shot" stimulates reflection about the nature of movies. Indeed, *Five...* may launch the viewer into Oliveira's "another state", a place of wonder, one might hope, in which the viewer finds time and reason to reflect on cinematic language. Here, too, the viewer may reflect on his or her expectations and habits of seeing – or as Jean-François Lyotard has written, on "the ways in which the subject is affected, its ways of receiving and experiencing feelings, its ways of judging works".[39]

In addition, *Five...* may heighten the viewer's sense of the centrality of chance in human and natural affairs. Kiarostami has described switching his camera on at the start of one or more segments in *Five...* when almost "nothing could be seen on the shore", then going to sleep, leaving the device to record whatever might enter its sight.[40] Through such acts (or gimmicks, a detractor might say), the director avers that he fully opens his film to chance and accident, the importance of which he believes people tend to overlook in their daily existence. There are "other factors contributing to one's destiny than skill, intelligence and experience, factors that many of us are unaware of", says Kiarostami. Perhaps salient among these factors is chance – "a wise person" is one who "allows for these accidents in the game". But the viewer is left to do more than behold the spectacle of chance (and reflect on film language and reception) when the director goes to sleep. The director's departure, says Kiarostami, bequeaths to the audience immense creative freedom and opportunity to "build their own film based on their experience or even their momentary need". Alfred Hitchcock often spoke of manipulating the viewer, of "processes through which we take the audience ... to create this audience emotion".[41] But Kiarostami echoes the notion of the "open film"[42] voiced by Gus Van Sant and other filmmakers reluctant to "take the audience" to fixed and predetermined destinations. Kiarostami himself calls *Five...* an "open film or half-made film", to be created or completed by the spectator. His goal brings to mind, in addition to Van Sant, Alexander Sokurov, as when the latter describes the viewer as "never a passive contemplator, but someone who participates in the creation of [the film's] artistic world".[43]

It seems fitting that Kiarostami, having withdrawn from making *Five...* – having relinquished his movie to chance, to the camera's automatism, and to the viewer's creativity – often sounds like a spectator, and not simply a director, in discussing his readings of *Five...*, his creations or discoveries while viewing the film. Such is the case, for instance, as he marvels at the camera's ability – without human guidance or direction – to "extract and expose" multiple "values hidden in objects" like the piece of driftwood, carried by the shifting tide, that becomes the focal point, virtually a central character, in *Five...*'s first segment. He speaks of having "met" this piece of wood and of having regarded it (as it appeared in actuality, in the film, or both) as "a person" and then as "a sea creature". He marvels at the narrative tension that arises when the wood breaks in two, the larger piece drifts away from the smaller, then towards it, back again, and at last out of the static frame without reconnecting. Moreover, not just driftwood in the first segment, but also waves at various moments in *Five...* are transformed in Kiarostami's view into "sea creatures" venturing in and out of the frame. "Everything", he then states, "moves toward a total non-existence ... and a new existence will appear from the heart of this non-existence".

In charting Badii's world as he moves towards killing himself, *Taste of Cherry* conducts what Hamid Dabashi calls "an examination of being-unto-death".[44] But the film's coda, emerging from the darkness and stillness of Badii's grave, posits an existence where death yields to the life of creating cinematic art. Similarly, in *Five...* the viewer may discern as Kiarostami does – in the waves, or the waves as sea creatures – "a new existence", the life drive counterpoised to death. Kiarostami also hints at a dualism of life and death in his account of filming *Five....* For by going to sleep after setting up the camera, he not only absented himself from both the shooting and what he terms the "obligation of narration", but also rehearsed his own death as *auteur*. Simultaneously, though, he saw himself as granting the spectator new life to "build" the film and "furnish the meaning" of events.[45]

Such respect for the spectator's creativity, incidentally, has long been characteristic of Kiarostami. He remarked about an earlier film: "When the woman stops walking in the last sequence of *Through the Olive Trees* [1994], audiences invent their own close-ups without me providing any because of their own attentiveness to what's happening."[46] Finally, in regard to the absence of the filmmaker as well as of clear narrative direction in *Five...*, we should note that Kiarostami has spoken not just of the viewer's opportunity to build his or her own film, but also of the freedom *not* to build or attend, freedom simply to drift within stillness and silence and to carry away a "relaxing feeling".[47] In either case, though, *Five...*'s static camera, extreme long takes and narrative vacancy, partly by declining to "take the audience" anywhere, alter the viewer's relationship to cinema, to the self, and even to life and death.

◆

Commentators describe Jia Zhang-ke's cinema as slow, though usually it is more eventful than Kiarostami's or Oliveira's. "Slow and gradual", writes A. O. Scott in his review of *Platform* (2000), "describe Jia Zhang-ke's approach to storytelling."[48] "The movie is long and slow", Roger Ebert says of *The World*

(2004).[49] And Manohla Dargis writes of Jia's documentary, *Dong* (2006), and *Still Life*, which won the Golden Lion for best picture at the Venice Film Festival, "it's striking how much slower and more calmly paced these films are, compared with much of mainstream cinema, both American and foreign-made".[50] But as becomes evident in *Still Life*'s first three shots (which together take up three minutes), this film's slowness is more supple and sensuous than that of *A Talking Picture*, *Taste of Cherry* or *Five*…. In these initial shots, the camera is not static, but pans slowly over bodies and faces of passengers on a moving boat, finally coming to rest on the figure of Sanming (Han Sanming), the film's unhappy hero. Besides the pans, such as persistently open or enlarge space throughout *Still Life*, slow dissolves connecting the first three images, along with soft focus inaugurating each image, yield lush, fleeting moments of abstract light and colour. This film of rubble and desolation resulting from the destruction of long-established communities to make way for the Three Gorges hydroelectric dam can hardly be called sumptuous, despite the inspirational landscapes that often rise in the background. Yet in diverging from the stylistic stringency and immobility of *A Talking Picture*, *Taste of Cherry* and *Five Dedicated to Ozu*, *Still Life* attains a warmth and plastic beauty which engage rather than distance the viewer.

Nonetheless, Jia's film engages viewers in dilemmas of absence and loss much as *A Talking Picture* does. One reason is that the coal miner Sanming has been separated from his wife and daughter for sixteen years, while the second major character, nurse Shen Hong (Zhao Tao), has neither seen her husband nor known how to contact him for two years. After travelling from her home in Shanxi province, she finds him in Fengjie, a town in the Three Gorges area, and at the end of their lengthy meeting informs him she has fallen in love with another man and wants a divorce. Similarly, Sanming, having made the same journey, locates his wife, who apparently has been indentured to settle a debt incurred by her brother, and arranges to buy her back. But despite their respective victories in locating their mates and settling on future courses of action, both Sanming and Shen Hong seem locked for the entirety of *Still Life* in inexpressible sadness, as if irremediably hurt by the prolonged absences of their loved ones – as well as by the arduousness of life in their country.

The cold reception Sanming and Shen Hong encounter in Fengjie as they search for their mates and even as they stand before them scarcely improves their morale. When Sanming tracks down Old Ma (Luo Mingwang), his wife's older brother, the gruff fellow resists Sanming's questions about the missing wife and daughter, warns Sanming against stirring up the past, and even denies he is Sanming's brother-in-law. Of no help either is a bandaged youth on the boat Old Ma commands who, apparently influenced by Old Ma's surliness, attacks and wounds Sanming. When at last Sanming and his wife (Ma Lizhen) meet, both of them are quietly suspicious and accusatory (why did she leave him? why did he wait until now to pursue her?), though eventually they agree, with no evident joy, to reunite. Yet more dispiriting is Shen Hong's meeting with her husband Guo Bing (Li Zhubing), a businessman of dubious virtue who is prospering in the shifting economy surrounding the new dam, and who evinces no love for his wife, nor regret for having abandoned her. Indeed, while Guo Bing reacts with mild vexation and puzzlement to Shen Hong's muted signs of suffering as a result of his absence and indifference, he seems for the most part hollow, devoid of feeling.

Besides confronting in Fengjie the vacancy and wreckage of their personal lives, Sanming and Shen Hong face the hideous destruction of the city. Workers armed with sledgehammers (whom Sanming soon joins to earn money) pound buildings into hills of rubble, which multiply alongside jagged remains of old structures and newly vacated spaces suggestive of Deleuze's "world of any-space-whatevers".[51] On walls and buildings that still stand hang announcements of imminent flooding, and much of the city, including Sanming's wife's old residence, is already submerged. "That little island out there, that was your street", a young motor-biker who transports Sanming tells him shortly after the miner arrives in Fengjie. "And the people?" asks Sanming. "Gone. Everyone moved out", the youth replies.

When Jia visited Fengjie to make *Dong*, his documentary about artist Liu Xiaodong, the devastation stunned him. It was "like after a nuclear war or alien attack", he has said. "I felt the disappearance of substance."[52] Further, the film-maker learned (and Sanming and Shen Hong surely know) that Fengjie's fate was not singular. "Dozens of 2,000-year-old towns", states Jia, were falling victim to the dam, or to the ambitions of political leaders determined to construct it; and well over one million people were losing their homes – in many cases their birthplace – and being forced to relocate to other parts of the country. Hardly mitigating the anguish and disillusion was the lack of time and provision to mourn or memorialise, respect or preserve, treasured aspects of the history and culture being swept away. Mindful that famous painters and poets had found inspiration in Fengjie, as in other parts of the Three Gorges area, Jia set about commemorating in *Still Life* both Fengjie's demise and "the space, the buildings, the culture, the interpersonal relations, the heavy history this town carries".[53] Taking a cue regarding cinema's embalming function from André Bazin, a film theorist he admires,[54] Jia set about creating, before all substance disappeared, a lasting image of "things [and] their duration, change mummified as it were".[55]

Still Life's slow panning shots, such as those inaugurating the film as discussed above, were valued by Jia and his cinematographer, Yu Lik-wai, for evoking "the horizontal expanse of Chinese scroll paintings",[56] which represented in their eyes the broader cultural heritage threatened by the construction of the dam. "In classic Chinese landscape painting", states Jia, "we can see a lot of foggy mountains and rivers; they were all inspired by the views in the Three Gorges area."[57] One or two thousand years earlier, he adds, painters "were facing the same hill, the same brook". By rendering such views in a style evoking scroll painting's "horizontal expanse" and "unfolding", Jia sought to ensure that Chinese history and identity visually resonated throughout *Still Life* and to affirm that despite the upheaval and discontinuity entailed in the demolition, "we are actually very close to our ancestors".[58]

He remarks that in attempting in *Still Life* to "embalm time", as Bazin might say, he raced against time: "I felt like I was racing against the vanishing of the city." Indeed, scholar Jiwei Xiao writes that the attempt "to keep up with the pace and speed of actuality" is a salient theme in most of Jia's documentary and fiction films.[59] Like the director, Jia's characters feel pressured by the rapidity of contemporary change, the vanishing of old ways as well as of old cities. The stress may be one reason Jia has turned in *Still Life* and later projects to digital technology for speed and convenience in filming and editing. But digital technology makes it no easier for Jia's characters to adjust. "To varying degrees", states Jiwei, "all of Jia's films reveal a 'time lag' between the fast and furious economic transformations [in contemporary China] and the slower-moving changes in people's behavior and mentality".[60] Such people in Jia's films are simply "ordinary folks who try to grow with the changing world but are unable to keep up with it".[61] Consequently time in their personal lives "seems to slow down and tarry".[62]

Probably the sadness fixed on the faces of Sanming and Shen Hong betokens a slowdown in response to "fast and furious" change as well as to loss of loved ones. Further, like major characters in *A Talking Picture*, Sanming and Shen Hong know they are unable to influence the waves of change and the vanishing of the past. "It seems that to see through Jia's camera-eye", writes Kevin B. Lee, "is to become a spectator to one's own ineffectuality in the face of global forces that seem well beyond one's own control."[63] While contending with their loneliness and ineffectuality, Sanming and Shen Hong confront the brutality and corruption of change in their personal lives as well as in the public sphere. Sanming, for instance, finds his young friend Mark (Zhou Lin) dead, buried in a mound of rubble, after Mark has embarked with a truckload of thugs, all apparently in Buo Ding's employ, to maul employees of one of Buo Ding's rivals. Earlier, Mark cautioned Sanming, "You know, in our world, it's dog eat dog ... We're not suited for this modern world", adding that rather than wax nostalgic they must adapt, perhaps become more savage. Sanming simply replied, "We can't forget who we are."

At least once in *Still Life* a character calls for slowing the process of change. In a relocation centre following the scene in which Sanming discovers a lake in place of his wife's residence, he overhears a government official telling a group of displaced Fengjie citizens who angrily seek compensation, "A city with two thousand years of history was demolished in just two years ... We need to slow down a bit to solve the problems." But whereas the demolition does not slow down, *Still Life* does – especially at key moments related to human loss and dying. Sanming's painful discovery of his wife's submerged street, for instance, occasions the film's first long take, lasting almost three minutes; not only is editing suspended in this interval, but also, for the most part, the motion of both Jia's camera and Sanming himself. Similarly, it is in one of the film's longest takes, almost four and a half minutes, that Shen Hong and Guo Bing halt their forlorn dance by the sea under a bridge occupied by romantic couples and Shen Hong announces to her husband the death of their marriage. She has fallen in love with another man and wants a divorce in order to marry him.

Further, in a take almost four minutes long towards the end of *Still Life*, Sanming bids farewell to his fellow demolition workers. The gathering, despite its informal atmosphere and the camera's proximity to the characters, brings to mind the reunions and partings of more privileged men in Ozu's films. "I'm going home tomorrow", Sanming softly declares amid the convivial eating, drinking and smoking. "Don't forget us", replies one of the seven or eight men seated around him. But a moment later they learn that Sanming anticipates earning far higher wages in coal mining back home than they earn wrecking buildings in Fengjie; hence they pledge to join him as soon as their present assignment ends. When he reminds them, though, of the perils of coal mining, of the many miners who have died near his home in the last year alone, the enthusiasm subsides and his companions fall almost silent. Jia's camera pans ever more slowly over the body of a man reclining and smoking outside the circle of friends; finally the pan becomes almost imperceptible, and in the wake of Sanming's warning about human fatality, the exceptionally long take ends in stillness and silence.

Considerably less quiet, but more suggestive of the divide in *Still Life* between slow and fast action, of the time lag between "fast and furious economic transformations and … slower-moving changes in people's behavior and mentality", is a bifurcated exterior shot that shortly follows Shen Hong's declaration to Buo Ding under the bridge. The divided shot features, on the right, an immense video screen with wide black borders, while on the left appear a few young men and women partially hidden by the video screen. The young people and the video screen are at the front of the Yangtze Jetfoil, a vessel bound for Shanghai, where Shen Hong is to be married. An image of her inside the boat – seated alone, drinking bottled water – succeeds the divided shot. The latter lasts twenty-two seconds, during which the young passengers, possibly Chinese tourists, step in and out of the limited area that is neither occupied nor obscured by the video screen. During the same period, ten images – two still photographs followed by eight motion-picture excerpts – fill the video screen. While the still photographs conjure an era prior to motion pictures, the excerpts depict more recent history. Together, the still and moving images encapsulate the history of the Three Gorges dam, with three excerpts focused on Mao Tse-tung surveying the region from a boat on the Yangtze river and another showing Deng Xiaoping, who ruled from 1978 to 1992, heading an entourage visiting a construction site. Condensed into just twenty-two seconds on the video screen, then, is probably more than a half century of epic striving. By contrast, the continuous, "real-time" activity of the passengers in the marginalised area outside the screen (or the frame within the frame) seems minimal as well as random and slow. Virtually nothing happens in this bifurcated shot apart from the synoptic heroism on the video screen.

Throughout these twenty-two seconds, an amplified female voice, which has commenced in the preceding high-angle long shot of the Jetfoil, narrates the historical footage in a way that imagines a community greatly enhanced by the Three Gorges project. The unseen narrator represents Chinese government interests, much as the historical footage does – the Yangtze Jetfoil thus becomes a veritable ship of state. As the Jetfoil advances in the river in the aerial shot preceding the bifurcated image, the female voice quotes eighth-century poet Li Bai in praise of the region's grandeur. Then the narrator leaps to the present renaissance: "Today the world's eyes", she says, and the film cuts from the overhead shot of the boat, the passengers, the river and the river's banks to the divided shot in which the historical images appear on the video screen. She continues: "look toward the region again, thanks to the Three Gorges Project. The Three Gorges Dam has been a dream of our leaders for several generations." Now the historical footage cuts from Mao to Deng. "The people of this region have made great sacrifices for it", continues the voice. "On May 1, 2006 the water level here will rise to 156.30 meters." *Still Life* here cuts to Shen Hong, seated inside the boat, drinking bottled water. "The houses on the river banks will all be submerged", the narrator concludes both casually and proudly, as Shen Hong looks offscreen, her face resigned to irreversible loss.

There is no evidence that Shen Hong sees from her seat the propaganda on the immense video screen; nor is it certain she listens to the voice-over narration. Similarly, the passengers on deck by the video screen neither face its images nor evince interest in its totemic presence; these passengers seem heedless as well of the voice-over. Kevin B. Lee writes that "what may elevate Jia Zhangke above his peers is his acute sense of how the local occurrences that appear onscreen [in his films] are shaped by immense, unfathomable global forces emanating from sources well off-screen".[64] Though this may be the case, particularly in a film like *The World*, the divided shot featuring the huge video screen suggests something else. Here powerful dictators propelled by nationalism and industrialisation advance onscreen, while "local" or ordinary individuals are positioned *off*screen. Moreover, fast action on the video screen contradicts slow inaction off the screen. Thus the divided shot encapsulates the displacement of local and ordinary occurrences by immense if not unfathomable forces. The shot also indicates that those who have been displaced and harmed may turn away or turn off, even as epic actions on the video screen are dramatically accelerated via cinematic ellipsis. Hence the slow and the fast are disconnected and estranged in this shot, as elsewhere in this film of disruption.

The dichotomy of slow and fast in contemporary life prompts Jia's insertion of surreal special effects in *Still Life*. In one instance, a mysterious tower within view of Shen Hong as she hangs a shirt to dry on an apartment balcony ascends suddenly like a missile or interplanetary probe and passes out of frame. Another surreal effect marks *Still Life*'s shift of narrative focus from Sanming to Shen Hong: a small object J. Hoberman has described as "a neon-limned flying saucer transversing the Yangtze"[65] soars past Sanming in one shot, rivets Shen Hong's gaze in the next, then burns out over a misty bank of the river. Jia adjudges these surreal moments consistent with – as Manohla Dargis writes – the film's "overriding realism".[66] The director emphasises that while Fengjie, "a town with a very long history in the Tang Dynasty ... was gradually established over the past two thousand years ... the space, the buildings, the culture, the interpersonal relations ... all has been taken apart in two years."[67] He stresses that "the contrast between the number 2,000 and the number 2 ... is very surrealistic ... beyond human logic ... [and that] this kind of absurd ... feeling appears very often in China's reality ... the surrealistic atmosphere is a part of China's reality."

Of course, not just the rapidity but also the magnitude of Fengjie's destruction strikes Jia as surrealistic, beyond human logic. His references to "nuclear war", "alien attack" and "disappearance of substance" suggest that he views the sweeping devastation as virtually unprecedented, as beyond the pale of both reason and imagination – especially since the perpetrators are countrymen rather than foreign or alien powers. Already troubled by how many Chinese are "unable to keep up" (as Jiwei says) in modern China, Jia is sickened by the destruction of Fengjie and other Three Gorges towns. He grows more alienated from the Chinese government he deems responsible for the equivalent of an alien invasion. His account of the ascending tower in *Still Life* reflects his anger and disaffection: "The tower ... was built as a memorial tower, dedicated to the immigrants", he explains. But since the government ran out of money, the tower was not finished – it was just "left there ... unaccomplished, naked, sitting on the most beautiful shore along the Yangtze River." "The first time I saw it," he continues, "it felt like it didn't belong to the human world; it's more like an alien object." Consequently he sent the memorial tower in his movie "back to where it belongs – flying to outer space",[68] and thereby took a small, symbolic step towards reclaiming his country.

Without insisting that *only* slow movies like his address real-life problems of good people in China who are "unable to keep up", Jia denounces big-budget Chinese action films for neglecting the country's pressing social needs. "In this era of worshipping gold," he asks, "who is still interested in good people?"[69] "When faced with the complexity of real society," Jia writes of the creators of big, fast motion pictures that distract good people from confronting reality, "their hands and feet quiver, and they deliriously shoot a bunch of childish fairy tales."[70] Jia singles out Zhang Yimou, nineteen years his senior, as one such quivering artist. Acclaimed internationally for masterworks including *Red Sorghum* (1983), *Ju*

Dou (1990) and *Raise the Red Lantern* (1991), Zhang twice won the Golden Lion at Venice well before Jia did. But Jia claims that Zhang has recently descended to making "childish fairy tales" like *Curse of the Golden Flower* (2006), a film Evan Osnos has described in the *New Yorker* as "a forty-five-million-dollar palace drama" and possibly "China's priciest production to date".[71]

Curse of the Golden Flower premiered in China the same day as *Still Life*, and swamped the more frugal, meditative and socially conscious film at the box office. Two years later, Zhang directed the opening and closing ceremonies at the 2008 Summer Olympics in Beijing. Both *Curse of the Golden Flower* and Zhang's designs for the China-hosted Olympics have provoked what may be Jia's most severe charge against Zhang and other creators of blockbuster action cinema: besides sidestepping truth and pre-empting more honest filmmakers like Jia at the box office, they align themselves with China's authoritarian rulers. Rather than criticising the government responsible for the "alien attack" on Fengjie, for example, a film like *Curse of the Golden Flower* (along with complicity in the Olympics) "underscores power", says Jia, "that we should 'bow down' before power!" He adds caustically, "For 'harmony in the world', we should give up individual fights and efforts" against "the authority of power".[72]

Upholding the individual is in fact crucial to Jia. In his view, a major distinction between his filmmaking generation and Zhang's is that his more ardently respects "the personal experience".[73] Having matured during "the reform and opening up" following the Tiananmen Square massacre, says Jia, he and his classmates at the Beijing Film Academy "escaped from the collective life" and the "collective sense in Communist Party arts" and came to regard "the individual reaction" and "individual freedom" as paramount. Perhaps reflecting this emphasis, *Still Life*'s final scene highlights the individual more than the group. The scene begins with Sanming leading his co-workers outdoors following the farewell get-together recounted above. Sanming then stops and stands apart from his cohorts as they move on. His back to the camera and quite still, he observes in the sky a distant human silhouette taking small, slow steps on a tightrope stretched from the roof of one building about six stories high to another. Demolition workers atop one of the buildings ignore the tightrope walker. Only Sanming attends this imperilled individual who appears as a tenuous vertical line in empty space.

In a sense, individuality emerges where life and death converge in *Still Life*. The fixed expressions of sorrow and grief on the faces of Sanming and Shen Hong register their experience of something like Morrison's "death-in-life" and Dabashi's "being-unto-death". Both the miner and the nurse have suffered the loss or disappearance of loved ones and observed the hardships of their countrymen. Both have witnessed the horrifying demolition of Fengjie and grown estranged from vast social and economic forces careless of their needs and beyond their control. Further, both Sanming and Shen Hong perhaps reflect that timeless "profound sorrow intrinsic to all humanity or symptomatic of society" cited by the artist Liu Xiaodong in *Dong*. Liu also avers, however, that "even in a deeply tragic environment or a condition of utter despair, you discover that life itself is truly moving". Despite Sanming and Shen Hong's irrevocable sorrows and losses, they move on, he by reuniting with his wife, she by undertaking a new marriage. As Freud might say, these individuals make detours from death.[74]

Rebellion's Limits

The Turin Horse, Werckmeister Harmonies and 12:08 East of Bucharest

"Even among the masters of slow films, Tarr is unique in making the passage of time or its painfully slow-paced movement the essence of his work: this is the existence of human beings deprived of action and events in their allotted time."

– Yvette Bíro, *Turbulence and Flow in Film: The Rhythmic Design*[1]

Although Tarr's films are unique, Bíro's notion of "human beings deprived of action and events in their allotted time" applies to many slow-movie characters. Both the personality and circumstances of these characters curtail their capacity for action, whether as individuals or in concert with others. Confronted by misfortune and injustice, passive and naive characters such as Sanming in *Still Life* and William Blake in *Dead Man* respond, for the most part, minimally and slowly; rarely, moreover, does a slow-movie character – other than Blake's rescuer, Nobody, and the celebrities in *A Talking Picture* – articulate strong political and social views. Yet another reason that rebellion seems limited in slow movies is the extreme indeterminacy of these films. Such works as *Ossos*, *Elephant*, *Werckmeister Harmonies* and *The Turin Horse* depict mysterious and illogical events with a minimum of explanation and resolution. The silence and inarticulateness of key characters obviously contribute to the indeterminacy. Both what is happening and why it is happening prove difficult to know. Yet though indeterminacy obscures conduct and limits prospects of rebellion in slow movies, it ensures that these films are rebellious in their form or style. For the resistance to explanation and accessibility flaunted by Pedro Costa and other slow-movie makers violates most mainstream film conventions (Susan Sontag called Tarr's films "heroic violations of the norms"[2]), even as it conveys the mystery and entrapment of slow-movie characters and their alienation from the world they inhabit. These characters deprived of action, movement, expressiveness and dialogue receive no more sympathy or illumination from the filmmakers who bring them into being than from the silent, unwelcoming universe they enter.

James Wood has written that *The Melancholy of Resistance*, László Krasznahorkai's novel on which Tarr's *Werckmeister Harmonies* is based, "seems to take repeated ironic shots at the possibility of revolution".[3] *Werckmeister Harmonies* does so as well. It features a variety of characters disposed to overthrow the existing order, though what constitutes that order and what will replace it remain unclear. One such character is a viperous circus freak called "the Prince" who arrives in a circus van that also contains a gigantic and ominous dead whale. The Prince appears only as a diminutive shadow on an interior wall of the van; but rumoured to hold sway over grim, idle men gathered outside in the public square, he threatens to wreak havoc. Meanwhile, a music theorist's estranged wife pledges to restore order and cleanliness in the town; and an inebriated police chief, her ally, vows to deploy tanks and to show "no mercy" towards an unidentified enemy. Corneliu Porumboiu's *12:08 East of Bucharest*, winner of the Caméra d'Or for best first feature film at Cannes in 2006, satirises the possibility of revolution yet more bluntly and persistently than *Werckmeister Harmonies*. Porumboiu's film repeatedly casts doubt that the Romanian revolution of 1989 changed people's lives enough to be called a revolution. The film also asks whether any revolution that may have occurred in 1989 extended to Vaslui, the small town where Porumboiu was born and where the film's present action (or lack thereof) takes place. A prominent TV talk-show host sets the droll terms for arriving at an answer: the town will have participated in the revolution if proof can be found that some of its citizens protested against Ceausescu's brutish regime in the public square adjoining the town hall prior to 12.08 in the afternoon on 22 December 1989 – the moment Ceausescu fled Bucharest by helicopter.

The Turin Horse also "takes shots" at revolution, but in a less sustained and amusing fashion than *Werckmeister Harmonies* or *12:08 East of Bucharest*. Rebellion figures in an unseen narrator's report at the start of *The Turin Horse* while the screen remains black. The voice-over explains that Friedrich Nietzsche emerged on a Turin street in 1889 to embrace an old horse which was being flogged for ignoring its cabman's order to pull his carriage. The narrator adds that Nietzsche collapsed and never recovered from the ordeal, and that the rebellious horse's fate remains unknown. Next, in a four-and-a-half-minute long take, a horse caked in mud and sweat hauls a driver and wagon on a country road through a powerful windstorm that will persist for most of the film. Various accounts of the film identify the bearded driver as Ohlsdorfer (János Derzsi) and the struggling horse as Ricsi. During *The Turin Horse*'s remaining two hours after the long take on the country road, rebellion of a sort arises when Ricsi refuses to pull Ohlsdorfer's wagon and then stops eating and drinking. The film stresses not Ricsi's plight, however, but that of Ohlsdorfer and his daughter (Erika Bók), who dwell in a primitive one-room stone house in a remote, stormy wasteland. They too rebel, if one can call it that, by moving out of their home when their well goes dry. But within moments they return and lug all the goods they have piled into their handcart back into the house, where they will likely perish for lack of water. Like Ricsi, they do not so much rebel as surrender.

Robert Koehler recalls that he found *The Turin Horse* "funnier" the second time he saw it; he found himself "laughing more" and being reminded of Samuel Beckett's work.[4] In a similar vein, Peter Hames wrote in 2001 that Tarr "alleged that his films are comedies – like Chekhov. They look at reality, and human life must inevitably be regarded as funny."[5] If *The Turin Horse* is funny, one reason may be that the silent protagonists mechanically follow their routine without discussing its incredible physical and emotional stringency or how to change it. The father and daughter make do with just a piping-hot potato at each meal. The only additional sustenance seems to be a gulp or two of brandy (or "palinka"), often in the morning and when Ohlsdorfer prepares to venture outdoors. The ground surrounding the house bears no sign of plant life such as might yield fruit or vegetables to supplement the potato; nor is there a chicken, cow or other animal except Ricsi. Moreover, the place where Ohlsdorfer and his daughter acquire food, drink and supplies for their remote home is not revealed. When a neighbour (Mihály Kormos) visits to buy palinka and Ohlsdorfer asks why he hasn't shopped in town for it, the gruff reply is that the town no longer exists: "the wind's blown it away … it's gone to ruins … everything's in ruins." Comical in itself is that the grieving, swaggering neighbour, a bit like Nietzsche's "madman" though without his emphasis on the killing of God,[6] spews allegations of moral failure, depravity and physical calamity for six minutes before Ohlsdorfer finally dismisses him: "Come off it. That's rubbish!" As I have begun to indicate, though, Ohlsdorfer and his daughter are scarcely less odd and perhaps no less comical than their neighbour. At mealtime they use dishes but no utensils; they just peel, slice, chop and eat each potato with their bare hands. When Ohlsdorfer is very hungry early in the film, he practically scalds himself by repeatedly trying to eat his potato before it cools.

Thus something like comedy, even slapstick, does figure in *The Turin Horse*, though less prominently than in *Werckmeister Harmonies* or *12:08 East of Bucharest*. Arguably *The Turin Horse*'s predominant vision of the near impossibility of rebellion and positive change, its delineation of entrapment, desiccation and deprivation, verges on horror and tragedy more than comedy. Indeed, its vision may be as severe as any in slow movies.

◆

Unlike Sanming and Shen Hong in *Still Life*, *The Turin Horse*'s Ohlsdorfer and his unnamed daughter find no detour from death. Instead, their capacity for action and motion steadily declines, especially after they run gypsy intruders off their property and wake up the next day to find their well dry. Ohlsdorfer, a large, strong man with a disabled arm and chronic cough, decides they must pack and leave. But as indicated above, perhaps due to the windstorm that rages virtually until the film's last scene, father and daughter return almost immediately after dragging their horse and the handcart packed with meagre belongings over the rim of the desiccated hill, surmounted by a leafless tree, rising in the distance opposite their home. Silence reigns between them throughout *The Turin Horse* – twenty minutes of the film elapse before either of them speaks (the daughter speaks first, telling Ohlsdorfer "it's ready", meaning that a boiled potato awaits each of them on the dining table). Now, after the aborted escape, the two individuals grow increasingly immobile as well as silent, not least as one or the other sits rigidly staring through a window at the arid hill with its bare tree.

The impassive daughter sits staring in this manner towards the end of the six-minute long take that depicts their return to the house. When the take begins, cinematographer Fred Kelemen's camera, which remains stationary almost until the shot ends, displays the front of the house in long shot as dust and debris fly across the windswept space. Soon, father and daughter enter the shot. He leads their horse out of frame towards the barn, then returns and helps his daughter unload the cart and convey the contents inside. She remains inside and almost immediately appears at the window (while he draws the wagon out of frame before returning and going into the house himself). The static long shot emphasising her small face affixed to the lower part of the window persists for some time before the camera or the zoom moves slowly but steadily towards her and the image fades out. By this point her sojourn at the window facing the hill has lasted two minutes and twenty seconds.

Three shots later, it is the father who appears fixated in a chair at the window. The new long take begins, Kelemen has noted, as a "long focal length shot"[7] of the distant hill on a foggy day, observed through the window as if from the daughter's vantage in the earlier shot when the camera was located outside. Now the camera withdraws within the house to discover the still mass of the father's back as he sits before the window with his head bowed. Thus he remains as the camera draws back further (Kelemen describes the move as "both a zoom out and reverse moving shot back"[8]), incorporating the daughter, who is sewing an article of clothing – probably for her father, whom she generally helps to dress and undress. Soon she sets their sturdy dishes on the rough-hewn table, where-upon Ohlsdorfer rises at last, some two minutes after the moving camera first revealed his body. As the long take continues, he joins his daughter at the table for a piping-hot potato. The father picks listlessly at his potato with his fingers, and after taking just a bite, returns to his seat at the window, where he remains another minute before the image goes entirely black, deepening the sense of immobility and paralysis.

"What's this darkness?" asks the daughter's voice from within the totally black space. Twelve minutes remain in *The Turin Horse* at the moment she poses this question in response to the unnatural extinction of light and the obliteration of form, action and movement. Assisted by her father in both this long take and the next, the daughter tries to relight the oil lamps with dying flames and embers drawn from the failing wood stove. But the lamps quickly burn out. Darkness seems as irreversible in this pair of takes as the father and daughter's declining mobility – and as intractable as the hill beyond the window. In the subsequent long take, which lasts four minutes to conclude the film, darkness suffuses most of the frame; yet along with a portion of the dining table, the faces and hands of the father and daughter are illuminated, magically one might say, since the characters failed in the previous shots to keep the lamps lit. Furthermore, silence pervades the darkness engulfing the two characters, especially since sounds of the storm ceased during the previous shot. Ohlsdorfer and his daughter, their eerily lit faces and hands afloat in blackness on either side of the table, muster no appetite for the potatoes perched before them. "Eat ... we have to eat", pleads Ohlsdorfer, but both individuals lack the requisite energy and desire. She remains stiff and mute, her lifeless gaze lowered for the duration of the shot. Ohlsdorfer, too, though only after distractedly scraping rind from his potato and taking a bitter bite, grows still and silent. Thus all action except the occasional blinking of the daughter's eyes ceases. The image fades slowly out, restoring complete darkness one last time – for twenty seconds – before the closing credits appear.

◆

Almost certainly the stillness, darkness and silence at *The Turin Horse*'s end signal the death of Ohlsdorfer and his daughter, though not necessarily, as we will see, their death only. While I have suggested that death looms when the well dries up, which occurs before darkness overtakes their world, Jonathan Rosenbaum sees death prefigured yet earlier – in Ricsi's refusal to go on pulling the wagon or eating or drinking. But such questions of timing aside, there is agreement that *The Turin Horse*'s barebones plot proceeds inexorably towards death. "What passes for plot gradually gets even more minimal", writes Rosenbaum, "when [Ohlsdorfer's] horse first refuses to pull the wagon then refuses to eat. Eventually father and daughter also become immobilized, confirming one of Tarr's helpful statements – that this is a film about the inescapable fact of death."[9] Remarking that *The Turin Horse* offers "no escape [from] the conditions of life of which death is surely an integral part",[10] Fred Kelemen, too, considers death central to the film, as does J. Hoberman, who calls *The Turin Horse* "death-haunted".[11] Tarr concurs, but goes a step further regarding the *scope* of death in his film. Addressing journalists at the 2011 Berlin International Film Festival, where *The Turin Horse* premiered and received the Jury Grand Prix, he portrayed death's inescapability in the tale of Ohlsdorfer, his daughter and Ricsi as simply an aspect of universal "transience". "Everything in the world", he said, "passes away. Perhaps the world itself will pass away."[12] On another occasion he added that "the end of the world [in *The Turin Horse*] is very silent, very weak. So the end of the world comes as I see it coming in real life – slowly and quietly."[13]

Characters in Tarr's films often refer to the pervasiveness of emptiness and death in the universe – in contrast, implicitly, to the rarity of human life. Describing the distance between the earth and the sun in a tavern at night at the start of *Werckmeister Harmonies*, János Valuska (Lars Rudolph), a postman or courier, marvels at "the boundlessness where constancy, quietude and peace, infinite emptiness, reign; infinite sonorous silence; everywhere ... an impenetrable darkness". Perhaps even this vast, dark, silent emptiness passes away along with life itself when the world ends. Yet more dire in a sense is the possibility, broached in both *The Turin Horse* and *Werckmeister Harmonies*, that the world already has passed away: "the whole ... is nothing", the Prince says in *Werckmeister Harmonies* – what appears to be life is merely a delusion or mirage. Or as E. M. Cioran once said, "nothing *is* ... things do not even deserve the status of appearances".[14] Tarr's conjecture at Berlin that the world itself may pass away need not be entirely disheartening. For his notion points to an affinity rather than estrangement between humanity and the world, since the two are regarded as similarly fragile, finite and, perhaps, illusory. Yet such affinity may afford small comfort in the context of the Prince and Cioran's "nothing *is*". Their "nothing", after all, belies or nullifies humanity as well as the world and our solar system's vastness as described by Janos. A passage in the *Rigveda* possibly suggests the extreme nullity posited at moments in *Werckmeister Harmonies*, *The Turin Horse* and other minimalist films by Tarr: "The non-existent was not; the existent was not / Darkness was hidden by darkness / That which became was enveloped by the Void."[15]

Prospects of emptiness and death loom in many slow movies, as this book has noted. Indeed, whereas action cinema may be criticised as escapist partly because it is judged to treat dying, non-existence, or suffering casually or superficially, a hallmark of slow movies may be their deeper probing of such conditions. "In the midst of life, we are in death", asserted in *The Book of Common Prayer*'s burial service,[16] sums up a central preoccupation of slow movies. In a similar vein, James Morrison's phrase "death-in-life"[17] bears on slow movies beyond those by Todd Haynes to which Morrison refers; and Alexander Sokurov's belief that art must help humanity prepare for death pertains to slow movies besides his own.[18] Even more than other slow movies, Tarr's films track human misery relentlessly and unsentimentally; as Tarr has claimed, such works as *Damnation* (1988), *Satantango*, *The Turin Horse* and *Werckmeister Harmonies* centre on "the pain of the world", "how miserably we live" and "the unbearable heaviness of life".[19] But in addition, his films are more elegant and persuasive than most in depicting death as unsparing and the Prince's "nothing" as surpassing all that can be observed or imagined.

◆

Commentators have not ignored that Tarr's films often portend "the end of the world"[20] and "a world on the brink of catastrophe";[21] Peter Hames, for example, described the Hungarian's films in 2001 as "never far from the threats of apocalypse and damnation".[22] Observers like Hames echo Tarr's characters, who repeatedly cite such threats and thus alert the film spectator to look out for them. Townspeople offscreen on a street corner in *Werckmeister Harmonies* warn György Eszter (Peter Fitz), an esteemed citizen and music theorist, that the world may be "coming to an end" and that they "can't look on passively while catastrophe swoops down". Shortly after, in the circus van parked in the public square, the Prince promises destruction. As mentioned earlier, through the factotum (Mihály Kormos) who speaks for him a few feet from the dead whale occupying most of the van's dark interior, the Prince both vows that "his followers are going to make ruins of everything" and hints that the world already has ended, even that it never really existed: "The Prince alone sees the whole. And the whole is nothing, completely in ruins. What they build and what they will build, what they do and what they will do, is delusion and lies ... In ruins all is complete."

Not inappropriate is that the factotum who translates the Prince's words in *Werckmeister Harmonies* is played by the same actor (Kormos) who plays the neighbour in *The Turin Horse*. The neighbour's sentiments approximate those of the Prince and his factotum, as when he explains that he did not go to town for palinka because a mysterious "cataclysm" has occurred, "everything's in ruins ... everything, everything is lost forever". Like the Prince and his translator, moreover, the neighbour is not only preoccupied with disaster but attracted to intimations of nonexistence, to notions that "the whole is nothing" and that life's sensations and appearances are illusory: "those many nobles, great and excellent", who were unable to prevent the cataclysm, he says, "all at once ... realised that there is neither God nor gods ... neither good nor bad. Then they saw that ... they themselves did not exist either!"

The neighbour adds in regard to the nobles who saw they did not exist: "I reckon this may have been the moment when we can say that they were extinguished, they burnt out." Thus he recapitulates the opposition in *The Turin Horse* between light and vitality on the one hand, and darkness and death on the other, and reminds us of the key role darkness and the black screen play in the film, which opens and closes in blackness. Indeed, Tarr's films generally, almost all of them in black-and-white, have been lodged in darkness, at least since *Damnation*; and the absence or extinction of light in these films has frequently suggested extreme danger if not life's absence or end. Echoing this theme, *Werckmeister Harmonies*' Janos summons his fellow patrons at the tavern in the opening scene to contemplate not just cosmic space's presumably normal darkness and emptiness, but the perils to life on earth of the "awful, incomprehensible dusk" of an eclipse: "The air suddenly turns cold, the sky darkens, and then goes all dark … dogs howl … rabbits hunch down … deer run in panic … then complete silence." Unlike the darkness enveloping Ohlsdorfer and his daughter towards the end of *The Turin Horse*, though, the "awful … dusk" cited by Janos lifts: "the moon swims away", he explains, "and the sun once again bursts forth … light and warmth again floods the earth. Deep emotion pierces everyone. They have escaped the weight of darkness."

But darkness stays with Janos and weighs him down. It is night when he describes the eclipse, leaves the tavern, walks alone on empty streets, and stops to watch the huge circus van lumber into town. Later, after the van has been parked in the public square, he repeatedly enters its dark interior to view the magnificent whale, and at moments during his final visit only Janos's eyes are visible in the dense darkness of the van as he listens to the Prince and circus director rage at each other. Night persists as Janos flees the square ahead of the grim loiterers who, presumably incited by the Prince, march through the streets and into the hospital, where they seize and pummel the patients, all of whom are bedridden males. The attackers yank them from their beds and overturn tables, cabinets, beds and other objects. Only at the end of this strange rampage against individuals too dormant and infirm to fight back does Tarr's camera reveal Janos standing in a dark recess of a wall, hiding, watching and listening, as in the circus van moments earlier.

Janos never escapes "the weight of darkness" in *Werckmeister Harmonies*, which persists both day and night. As he makes his rounds in the town, he confronts paranoia, violence and finally military rule. And the weight of darkness, which seems little different from what Tarr has called "the unbearable heaviness of life", only increases after the hospital assault – in a series of bleached or overexposed daylight images near the film's end. In one image, Janos discovers his friend, old Lajos Harrer (Alfréd Járai), husband of Gyorgy Eszter's fearful housekeeper (Irén Szajki), lying dead in an alleyway. In another, he furtively observes Tünde (Eszter's estranged wife, played by Hanna Schygulla) take control of a few military officers, troops and tanks on an otherwise deserted road. Next, Janos attempts to escape by running along railroad tracks leading out of town (as Lajos's widow has advised him to do), but finds a helicopter ominously circling and descending towards him. Finally, in the film's penultimate scene, he ends up a mute patient in a hospital gown who sits straitened and traumatised, staring vacantly into white space. Eszter, who has come to visit, promises him a place in his home – or at least in the rear of it, where Eszter himself has had to retire since Tunde and the police chief have commandeered the rest for themselves. Eszter also shares with Janos a sentiment that harks back to the Prince's ravings, though possibly it is meant to ease the weight on Janos of all he has witnessed and endured: "Nothing counts. Nothing counts at all," says the visitor.

Despite Eszter's effort to console him, Janos ends up bereft and immobilised in white space much as Ohlsdorfer and his daughter become transfixed in blackness. His vacant, shocked look testifies to the painful role he has borne as Tarr's Deleuzian seer – in this case the beholder of horrific events who, like Ohlsdorfer and his daughter at the window after their aborted escape, is unable to act. Although Janos's role of passive seer is not unusual in slow movies, it is made unusually explicit during an exchange between him and Tunde in which she defines the role and he unreservedly accepts it: "Go to the main square", she tells him, having begun their conversation by asking what violence was occurring in the square. "Take a look around, observe how many there are, who is talking to who and what about, then come back here and tell us everything." Janos responds with alacrity: "I'll go and take a look around. I'll gladly observe and tell everything."

◆

Like *Werckmeister Harmonies* and other films by Tarr, *The Turin Horse* depicts human beings whose personality and circumstances limit their ability to act. Both Ohlsdorfer and his daughter are dour, silent people inured to poverty and to a brutish existence devoid of joy. Physical circumstances such as the relentless windstorm, the inert horse, Ohlsdorfer's lame arm and the isolation of the stone house make it all the more difficult for the father and daughter to get out and about. Moreover, their inclination is to remain apart from any larger community. They take no pleasure, for instance, when their zany neighbour visits, ostensibly to buy palinka but also in quest of companionship. Even before the man starts to rant, Ohlsdorfer coldly asks why he has come to them for palinka rather than going into town. When the wagonload of gypsy strangers appears on the rim of the hill opposite their home, Ohlsdorfer and his daughter evince alarm and dismay long before the strangers get close enough to be identified as jaunty gypsies in quest of water. Further, *The Turin Horse*'s two main characters seem no more inclined to speak to each other than to communicate with neighbours and strangers. Ohlsdorfer often looks both defiantly and imperiously at his daughter, particularly when he expects her to help him dress or undress. But he does not say a word. Nor does she. Their life together includes moments of marvellously synchronised motion as they collaborate on routine tasks like harnessing Ricsi to the wagon, washing and drying underwear or sheets, and getting Ohlsdorfer's attire on or off. But the absence of extended dialogue between father and daughter scarcely nurtures dreams of a better life. Sparse remarks ventured by either character stress immediate physical needs: the potato is ready, the horse is not eating, strangers are approaching, lamps will not stay lit. No talk of the past or future, or of affection or caring, interrupts the silence between parent and child. Perhaps the closest either of them comes to evincing empathy or tenderness is when the daughter addresses the horse; looking as impassive as ever, she poignantly entreats the animal to eat – "Do it for me!" – and to drink – "For my sake!" For the most part, though, not action or warm emotion, but restriction and repression distinguish the lives of the daughter and her father.

One might say their existence is as arid, bleak and ungiving as the landscape that surrounds them. Not just darkness and silence erode their physical and spiritual well being, but also climate and the natural environment. Indeed, as commentators have noted, Tarr's films more than most are set in locations inimical to life. One has only to compare the tracking shot of cows slogging through mud and pools of rainwater under a dark, dreary sky at the start of *Satantango* to the crisp, effulgent white clouds and sheep in the panning shot introducing Dreyer's *Ordet* (1955) to know that at least some of Dreyer's characters will be better off than any of Tarr's. The importance Tarr attaches to climate and environment as well as the notion that these factors simultaneously oppress and mirror his human characters has been asserted by Tarr himself as well as by commentators. Asked by Vladan Petkovic how he starts to make a film, Tarr replied, "When you're doing a movie, you don't do theories. I just look for locations. A location has a face. It's one of the main characters. So I found this little valley in Hungary and the lonely tree."[23] Since he dislikes artificial sets, Tarr and his crew built the house, stable and well. Then, during filming, they simulated the all-important windstorm by activating a wind machine, much as a rain machine had been deployed in *Satantango*.

Regarding Tarr's belief in the near equivalence of location, face and character, Susan Doll has noted that besides saying "a location has a face", Tarr has stressed – to David Bordwell, among others – that "the face is the landscape". "So", concludes Doll, "we have the faces being places, and the places being faces."[24] Tony McKibbin also observes that places in Tarr's cinema are faces and characters, each of which Tarr chooses most carefully. McKibbin stresses, moreover, Tarr's repeated "interest in finding a malignant environment. He's talked about how he needs 'a special impression from the locations'. Any hint of optimism implied in location must be quickly vanquished."[25] Slow-movie locations generally tend to be austere, but those in Tarr's films are particularly severe. Further, the human face holds no more hint of optimism than the location. Places and faces conspire, like the darkness and silence in *The Turin Horse*, to diminish hope, vitality, movement and action, until nothing seems to be happening and life comes to a halt.

The Turin Horse's rendering of the slow dying of Ohlsdorfer and his daughter repeatedly brings to mind what André Bazin termed "duration"[26] – the natural continuity of time passing. No doubt Tarr respects time or duration at least as much as he does location, character and the human face. Moreover, he clearly considers time more important than story. "I despise stories," he has said, "as they mislead people into believing that something has happened. In fact, nothing really happens as we flee from one condition to another ... All that remains is time. This is probably the only thing that's still genuine – time itself; the years, days, hours, minutes and seconds."[27] Like *The Death of Mr. Lazarescu* and other slow movies, *The Turin Horse* emphasises a particular time, described by Sylviane Agacinski as "the time of waiting, of coming death, of death that is going to come [which] the cinema has made into one of its principal domains".[28] Yet Tarr's remark about time's importance privileges no one interval, not even that in which we await death. Instead he regards time as a singular continuum more genuine and significant than any specific action or condition.

Not surprisingly, Tarr's films (starting with his 1982 television adaptation of *Macbeth*) make prominent use of long takes, which Bazin and others have considered a major technique for conveying duration or the natural continuity of time in the cinema. Cristi Puiu has said he used long takes in *The Death of Mr. Lazarescu* to convey "truth" and the "feeling of time passing".[29] And when Tarr was asked at Cannes in 2000 why he used long takes as his "main narrative instrument", he replied: "You know I like the continuity."[30] As is consistent with Tarr's emphasis on temporal truth and continuity, long takes prevail in *The Turin Horse* and *Werckmeister Harmonies* more than in most slow movies. Although each of these two films lasts 145 minutes, just thirty shots occur in *The Turin Horse* and merely thirty-nine in *Werckmeister Harmonies*.

In these long takes comprising each film, the camera often moves slowly and mysteriously, virtually carving out multiple shots that flow into one another without a cut. Yet the stationary camera is just as central to Tarr's cinema as the moving one. He rivals masters of camera mobility such as Miklós Jancsó and F. W. Murnau, but also emulates the respectful stillness of Yasujiro Ozu. In whatever way Tarr employs the camera in *The Turin Horse*, moreover, he tends to heighten rather than diminish the sense of time passing slowly and of characters losing mobility and strength. Two of the film's most riveting images, hailed by J. Hoberman as "moments of startling beauty when Tarr fills the entire screen with a weathered wooden gate [and] a wrinkled, just-washed sheet",[31] are of still objects recorded with a perfectly still camera. Tarr's motionless camera also holds on other stationary subjects for extended intervals: the back of Ohlsdorfer's bowed head; the daughter's face at the window; the horse in the barn unwilling to eat or drink. The camera remains stationary as well before subjects in motion, as when the daughter dons her clothes in the dark, cold morning of the saga's third day. In the two-and-a-half-minute medium-long shot of her getting dressed, *The Turin Horse* emphasises, as it does when the father dresses or undresses, the immense time and effort its characters expend on mundane tasks. The camera also remains stationary during most of the six-minute-long take in which Ohlsdorfer and his daughter, moments after departing with their horse and handcart of belongings, re-enter the space in front of their home and carry their cumbersome possessions into the house and barn. As they move in and out of frame, no camera movement or cut to a new shot occurs. There is no hint of involvement by the film apparatus in their strenuous efforts in the storm. Instead, the apparatus seems as inert as the weighty objects transported by the characters. Rarely does *The Turin Horse* convey a stronger sense of what Tarr has referred to as the slow, inexorable heaviness of being.

Even when the camera moves and space opens up in *The Turin Horse*, the pace of the film rarely quickens and the sense of weightiness and confinement persists. One reason is that the camera usually moves slowly. And when it proceeds more rapidly, the main subjects framed by it often remain stationary, in which case the contrasting camera movement underscores their immobility. Such is the case when the camera moves towards or away from Ohlsdorfer or his daughter as each remains stationary at the window. Another form of stasis or fixity appears, in *The Turin Horse* as in other slow movies, when the camera and its subject (whether a character, animal or thing) move in tandem so that the subject's position in the frame remains largely unchanged. Such is the case in Sokurov's *The Second Circle*, as indicated in the first chapter, when the son remains fixed in the right half of the frame for the entire long take of his ride to the outpatient clinic. The recurring image in *A Talking Picture* of the ship's prow moving through the sea is another instance of stillness in motion. Similar, though compositionally more flexible, is the long take early in Van Sant's *Elephant* of Nathan striding off the playing field and through the school's corridors. *Werckmeister Harmonies*, too, presents images in which the position of one or more characters remains fixed in the frame while the characters advance through space. Examples include long takes of Janos walking briskly alone on empty streets at night and of him walking beside Eszter in the afternoon after relaying Tunde's demand that Eszter back her effort to take over the town. Instances early in *The Turin Horse* of such relatively static motion include portions of the opening four-and-a-half-minute-long take of Ohlsdorfer, his horse, or both as the old man drives his wagon on a rural dirt road. Static motion persists early in the following shot, too, as Ohlsdorfer, now pulling the horse and wagon, approaches his home on foot. Although the fixity achieved through deliberate pacing and framing in these long takes arises also in action films, the effect seems especially well-suited to slow movies because they generally emphasise stasis and confinement.

Yet the movements of Tarr's camera and characters do not always converge to yield long takes of static motion. Rather, the camera and characters often pursue separate paths. At a symposium devoted to Tarr's cinema in 2007, Scott Foundas addressed the relation of both Tarr's camera and his long takes to his characters:

> You rarely ever feel in one of his films ... that the movement of the camera or the length of the shot is being dictated by anything other than the characters and the physical presences on the screen. The camera is moving with them, is dancing with them, not just when it's a dancing scene. He is really sort of immersing you in this world.[32]

The assertion that Tarr's camera dances with the characters serves to highlight that every movement in Tarr's cinema feels utterly choreographed and rehearsed. As Tarr has said: "Everything is controlled from the sky to the ground."[33] Moreover, the interweaving of the camera's movements and those of human characters, horses, dogs, cats, cows, rain and wind is mesmerising. But to say that characters dictate "the movement of the camera or the length of the shot" overlooks that both the camera's trajectory and the length of the shot often seem relatively independent of the doings of persons, animals and things. Further, the implication that Tarr's characters dictate either camera movement or shot length exaggerates their power and freedom.

Indeed, if the camera dances with the characters, which in a way it does, it seems just as likely to dictate to them as not. When *The Turin Horse*'s camera stares at Ohlsdorfer's empty bed or the empty space in front of his house, for instance, it seems to both foretell his entrance into the frame and summon him to fill the void. And rather than pursue a character such as Ohlsdorfer or *Werckmeister Harmonies*' Janos as he moves out of view, the camera may simply pause or take a divergent path (after which the character may re-enter the frame, as if catching up to the camera). Moreover, while the camera's viewpoint seems at times conjoined to a character's, it turns out not to be. In *The Turin Horse*, for instance, a view of the outdoors through a window turns out in a long take to belong to the camera rather than to Ohlsdorfer as he sits looking out. The divergence grows evident as the camera pulls back, passes Ohlsdorfer, and veers away until he is well out of frame and the camera's line of sight clearly ceases to correspond to his. At such moments the camera appears both disengaged from *The Turin Horse*'s characters and possibly in greater command of their world than they are. Even Tarr's images of static motion mentioned above, in which the camera engages with characters, but in a way that fixes them in place or pins them down, display the commanding force of his camera.

Hardly subservient to Tarr's characters, the camera in *The Turin Horse* often seems in step with impersonal, perhaps ominous forces such as the darkness, the silence, the windstorm and the desiccation that leave the characters – as Bíro would say – "deprived of action". Tony McKibbin alludes to this camera more than to Scott Foundas's benign one when he writes that Tarr's "complicatedly blocked sequence shots seem to take away from his characters any sense of self-imposition. The characters don't act in the world so much as seem to be acted upon by the world; a decision made is secondary to the forces compelling them."[34] McKibbin regards the camera in these celebrated sequence shots as being in league with the "malignant environment" oppressing Tarr's characters. In any case, the camera in such shots attracts spectatorial attention in its own right, apart from the characters. Even though "practically nothing happens" in *The Turin Horse*,[35] as Jonathan Rosenbaum has said, the camera's long-take journeys, here as in other films by Tarr, yield not dead time but keen tension and suspense. What the camera is up to is often more riveting and unpredictable than the actions of the characters.

The influence on Tarr's characters of the long take (or "the length of the shot") may be as open to debate as the impact of his camera. Tarr has indicated he favours the long take because its continuity matches that of real life – and "it's very important to make the film a real psychological process".[36] Rosenbaum believes that Tarr "has this existential idea that if you impose a long take on the characters, you're really getting at who they are".[37] Probably the "real psychological process" cited by Tarr pertains not only to his characters but also to spectators of his films, since long takes afford them sustained access to the characters, who are difficult to know.[38] A question remains as to whether long takes enhance or diminish the characters' stature. Perhaps responding to Tarr's remark that "All of my films are about the dignity of people",[39] Rosenbaum and Bordwell comment that Tarr's long takes elevate and demonstrate respect for Tarr's characters. Rosenbaum also stresses the long take's provision of time and space to think: "You could interpret the long takes as both respect for the actors and respect for the audience ... It is about giving them both space to arrive at certain ideas." Bordwell states: "The long take is ... a token of respect for the integrity of the person ... I think there is something about this idea of the long take either on a face, or even on an entire city street, that it is a kind of token of respect for their dignity, even if the drama that they're in is about their indignity, their loss of dignity."[40]

Yet Bordwell also mentions the "overall confine" of the long take.[41] Perhaps he has in mind that the long take, in postponing the exit or escape afforded by a cut, conveys a feeling of confinement rather than freedom. In addition, the tendency of the long-take style to forgo or limit point-of-view shots and shot/reverse-shots perhaps reduces the sense that characters possess narrative agency – or distinctive visions and perspectives conducive to effective action. The characters instead become passive victims of "forces compelling them", or captives of the overall design of the film.

Tarr's evolution as a filmmaker perhaps bears on this question of human agency in relation to the length of the shot. For his embrace of the long take, in conjunction with slow, intricate camera movement, seems to have coincided with his growing perception of human frailty and limitation. He has remarked that when he began making films he "wanted to change the world",[42] but found his fellow citizens incapable of solving social problems such as those addressed in his early realistic works like *Family Nest* (1977) and *The Outsider* (1981). More generally, human attempts to improve existence, to change the world, to evolve or rebel, were in Tarr's view proving futile. Yet he concluded that people alone were not to blame. As Fergus Daly has noted, the director grew convinced that the universe itself, not just humanity, was "wayward" and "out of joint".[43] In Tarr's words, "a whole pile of shit [was] coming from the cosmos".[44] Or as a woman informs Janos in the printing plant in *Werckmeister Harmonies*: "The world has gone completely mad. Now it's not down here but up there that something's gone wrong." Without entirely abandoning the realism of his early work ("film is always something definite – it can only record real things",[45] Tarr has said), his films took on what Tarr, who had briefly aspired to become a philosopher, called a more "cosmic perspective".[46] They evinced greater metaphysical wonder and dread about the universe and humanity's place in it. Their spatiotemporal environment grew more abstract. Tarr's early films, Scott Foundas has noted, "have a kind of fixed urban, contemporary reality to them", but the "later films, starting with *Damnation*, really seem to be taking place in some kind of suspended reality. You can't really identify the time period or the location; it is going into this more cosmic or macrocosmic or allegorical realm."[47] In this new or more cosmic realm, which is rendered in longer takes and camera movements than occur in most of Tarr's early films, human limitation is ever more obvious. As Tarr said after completing *Werckmeister Harmonies*, "Everything is much bigger than us. I think the human is just a little part of the cosmos."[48]

◆

The abundant talk of "apocalypse", "damnation", "catastrophe" and "ruins" in Tarr's cinema suggests more action, motion, spectacle and noise than his slow, dark, often silent movies deliver. Probably one reason for the discrepancy is Tarr's belief that "nothing really happens". Or as he has said regarding *The Turin Horse*, "The apocalypse is a huge event. But reality is not like that ... death is always the most terrible scene, and when you watch someone dying – an animal or a human – it's always terrible, and the most terrible thing is that it looks like nothing happened."[49] A further reason less action occurs in his cinema than one might expect is that disastrous happenings, while ever imminent, remain offscreen. Further, the disasters often seem imagined rather than real – at which point Tarr's cinema seems to render the mental, spiritual and emotional life of his characters rather than external reality. In these circumstances, what is real or imagined, true or false, remains unresolved; as a character says amid *Werckmeister Harmonies'* mists of indeterminacy, "You can never know anything for sure."

Prompting such uncertainty is the neighbour in *The Turin Horse* who rages about loss, cataclysm and moral debasement though no physical, social or political details back up his story. He says the town has been blown away by the wind – a wind J. Hoberman describes as "apocalyptic"[50] – but no images or sounds of the town's destruction appear. By the end of the neighbour's explosive but vague and unsubstantiated six-minute rant, the destruction he cites seems more imaginary or metaphorical than real. Something similar occurs in *Werckmeister Harmonies*. While the ostensible causes of its characters' distress are more specific than in *The Turin Horse*, and though some violence eventually occurs on screen, sparse evidence appears of the devastation to which people refer. A female character in *Werckmeister Harmonies*, observed in extreme long shot in the printing plant where Janos goes to pick up newspapers he will distribute in town, raves that "mysterious unknown plagues are here [and] great frozen mountains of refuse are everywhere". But as Janos strode through town on his way to the printing plant, such problems were nowhere evident; he and others at the plant pay the overwrought woman no heed. Later, Eszter's housekeeper tells Janos she fears to go home because of "talk that they're breaking the shop windows and setting fire to the hotel ... and the butcher got his head cracked open". Again, no such calamity has transpired on screen, or been witnessed by someone who appears on screen. Hence Janos seems perfectly correct to assure the rattled housekeeper, "There's no problem. You can go home easily."

During much of *Werckmeister Harmonies*, the public square (which Janos calls "market square") is the focus of the townspeople's dread. The common concern is that roughnecks gathering around the circus van in the square are being incited by the Prince's fury and the dead whale's presence to commit looting and violence and perhaps to launch a reign of terror. But when Tarr's camera finally accompanies Janos into the square after thirty-five minutes of the film have elapsed, this large space appears free of violence as well as quiet except for a faint collective murmur. The sombre working-class men well past their youth who stand idly within view of the van evince little interest in it, even when the back of the van opens to admit the public. Only Janos enters the van's extreme darkness and proceeds slowly along the body of the whale, which he estimates to be twenty metres in length, all the way to its large, open eye and supine head. In keeping with the notion that external reality in Tarr's film proves less eventful and exciting than advertised, "this great sensation of the century", as Janos later refers to the whale, is but a drab, hokey construct of pitch and wood. Despite the awe it evokes in Janos, it merits not wonder or dread but a response more like Robert Koehler's laughter as he watched *The Turin Horse*.

Although disorder and violence are not evident in the van, the public square or elsewhere, Tunde arrives at Janos's apartment soon after his visit to the square to tell him of "a movement which will restore order, create cleanliness". As already indicated, she then commands Janos to engage Eszter, whereupon the latter's reluctance to join any endeavour of his wife's is overcome by townspeople's complaints about failures of electricity, telephones and other public services. Again, though, no such failures have been observed by Tarr's camera, Janos or Eszter. Eszter nonetheless declares that they "must take action", a decision followed by

Janos's second visit to the square, with less than an hour remaining in the film. This time small fires blaze there, apparently to warm the assembled men, and one of the idlers frightens Janos by forcing him to take a swig of whiskey. But no other sign of violence or disorder appears.

When Janos arrives at Tunde's home, however, she immediately asks whether "they [are] ripping [the square] apart, or setting it on fire". Unable to say truthfully that they are, Janos praises "the wonderful whale", which continues to enthral him. Threats of violence then emerge from a room in Tunde's home, where the inebriated police chief, her romantic and political ally, shouts with revolver in hand, "Show no mercy!" – a sentiment echoed later by the Prince – and adds, "Shoot right into them ... I've called for the tanks." Hence the loiterers in the square, the ludicrous Prince, the dead whale and the anxious townspeople are no longer the only threats to peace and order. Now loom as well Tunde and her mad policeman, who flaunts the first lethal weapon visible in the film, now more than half over. While both characters stand ready to fight the absent, anonymous enemy, no violence has yet occurred on screen, and whether any has occurred at all remains unclear.

A half hour before the film ends, images of violence finally appear: loiterers from the square, after marching through dark streets for more than four minutes, invade the hospital and attack patients, tables and other objects. This attack may represent one of those "repeated ironic shots at the possibility of revolution" encountered by James Wood in Krasznahorkai's novel on which *Werckmeister Harmonies* is based. For this violence targets no unjust authority and advances no moral cause or programme. Authority of any kind, by the way, is conspicuously absent in the bleak, nearly empty hospital: no doctors, nurses, guards or administrators are present to obstruct the attackers. Only abandoned patients appear, too feeble to repel thugs whose discontents and purposes remain mute and indeterminate. If rebellion occurs in any sense, it resides in the rejection of norms of decency, in the inhumanity of injuring the weak and infirm without cause.

The lack of good reason for what happens in the hospital is suggested in a report, presumably composed by one of the attackers, that Janos reads aloud afterwards: "We didn't find the real object of our abhorrence and despair, so we rushed at everything we came across with wilder and wilder fury." Janos then reads of additional barbarous acts, for which, as with other disasters in the film, no clear evidence appears on screen: "We destroyed the shops, threw out and trampled everything ... turned over cars in the streets ... destroyed the telephone centre because we saw the lights inside, and we had the two post-office girls, and we left only when they had fainted and like two used rags, lifeless, hands clasped between knees, hunched over, they slipped off the bloody table." The hospital and its patients, which go unmentioned in Janos's reading, hardly seem more deserving of the attackers' "abhorrence and despair" than the shops, cars, telephone centre or post-office girls. Moreover, the hospital attack, though it is the only onscreen violence in *Werckmeister Harmonies*, feels no more real, immediate or convincing than the unseen acts of violence reported throughout the film. One reason is that most of the long take of the hospital destruction is a long shot of the backs of attackers and victims. Hence we see mostly anonymous shapes, rather than individuals with distinct faces, expressions or identities. Another reason that the patients in particular remain abstract and unknown is that the attackers usually stand between them and the camera, blocking them from view. Yet more distancing and unreal is that the patients make no sound – not a cry, word or thud is audible. The attackers, too, are surprisingly silent, except for their muffled footsteps. Finally, in no more than four minutes – about the same amount of time the aggressors have spent marching to the hospital – they exhaust their fury and energy. The sight of a naked old man too pitiful to be abhorred, standing still and alone in white space beyond a shower curtain, halts them. With glimmers of shame on their faces, they turn and leave the hospital slowly and silently.

Much of the hospital scene suggests an ungainly, dystopian dance that is imaginary rather than real. The scene brings to mind Jarmusch's characterisation of *Werckmeister Harmonies* as dreamlike,[51] Bordwell's reference to Tarr's films as "trance movies"[52] and Foundas's comment that Tarr's later cinema occurs in a "suspended reality".[53] Relevant as well is James Wood's reflection about revolution in the novel on which *Werckmeister Harmonies* is based. Yet the events in *Werckmeister Harmonies'* hospital suggest an ironic view of all action, not just revolution. Years after seeing the film, Gus Van Sant remembered the "angry crowd" as marching "to burn down the hospital".[54] But despite the ominous atmosphere, the structure does not burn; and while the minimal action within the hospital is horrifying, it betokens nightmare rather than actuality. Not human agency is depicted here, but a painful flailing in the night that speaks to Bíro's notion of "human beings deprived of action" and Tarr's view that "nothing really happens as we flee from one condition to another".

◆

As indicated earlier in this chapter, ironic shots at the possibility of revolution proliferate in *12:08 East of Budapest*. Various characters contribute to the fusillade, since few if any are inclined in 2005, the year in which the film's events occur, to take the 1989 revolution seriously. Tiberiu Manescu (Ion Sapdaru), a school teacher recruited for a television talk-show devoted to the revolutionary "events which changed the course of our lives", sceptically tells Virgil Jderescu (Teodor Corban), the TV entrepreneur who is also the show's host, "You think people will watch. No one gives a shit." When Manescu mentions his upcoming TV role to a bartender – a friend and former student to whom he owes money – the young man laughs and mockingly asks, "What revolution?" Jderescu's mistress, a star reporter on another of his TV shows, complains, "I don't get it. What's all the fuss about the revolution? No one could care less any more." Emanoil Piscoci (Mircea Andreescu), the white-haired pensioner enlisted to join Manescu and Jderescu on the show, implies that not everyone should be expected to care – or to agree on what constitutes revolution. It's all up to the individual rather than the collective: "One makes whatever revolution one can, each in their own way", he says late in the televised conversation, which takes up more than half the film.

Jderescu is less flexible and philosophical than Piscoci. Though he invokes Plato for cultural panache at the top of the show, his main interest is to attract large audiences, who presumably prefer firmer guidelines than Piscoci's. Jderescu sets an unequivocal standard: revolution will have occurred on 22 December 1989 in Vaslui – described by Piscoci as "our town in the middle of nowhere" – if it can be shown that townspeople protested against Ceausescu in the central square prior to Ceausescu's departure at 12.08 from Bucharest. Again Piscoci quibbles, noting that the big clock in the square has always been slow. In any case, Manescu, a debt-ridden alcoholic, declares that he protested on time in the square, and thus helped to shape history. Viewers phone in to dispute his claim, though. One says that she saw him and his cronies in the square before 12.08, but that they were not protesting. "They're drunks", she exclaims. "Some revolutionaries! ... Stop playing the hero, for Christ's sake!" Others call in to affirm that the square was empty before 12.08, or that there was no revolution. Meanwhile, as Stuart Klawans has observed,[55] Jderescu staves off minor rebellions in the studio. He stops Manescu drinking liquor on camera, for instance, and restrains both guests from fiddling with bits of paper and a paper boat. Jderescu also admonishes the show's young videographer to calm his jittery camera and to stop darting pointlessly between close and long shots of Jderescu and his guests. Unsurprisingly, the TV show ends without determining what, if anything, happened in the square before 12.08 and whether or not a revolution took place in Vaslui.

Along with obvious differences, points of resemblance exist between *12:08 East of Bucharest*, *Werckmeister Harmonies* and *The Turin Horse*. Of consequence in both Porumboiu's film and *Werckmeister Harmonies*, for instance, are matters of regime change and revolution. In both films, too, a public square becomes a central site of anxiety and indeterminate action, though in *12:08 East of Bucharest* the square appears only as a flat photomural mounted behind the panellists and devoid of action and people. In *The Turin Horse* and *Werckmeister Harmonies*, as in *12:08 East of Bucharest*, the camera is palpably present. The suspense of its slow, assured movements, as of its lengthy pauses, pervades Tarr's films, while disagreements over how the camera is to be used – for instance, on the tripod or off, for long shots or close-ups – augment the comedy in *12:08 East of Bucharest*'s TV studio. The constant interplay of light and darkness in *The Turin Horse* and *Werckmeister Harmonies* devolves into a naturalistic framing device in *12:08 East of Bucharest*: the film starts with a seven-shot sequence in which street lights go off near daybreak and ends in a similar series of images as the lights come back on at night. In Tarr's cinema, time and space – especially the dark spaces in *The Turin Horse* – seem boundless. Yet in both *The Turin Horse* and *12:08 East of Bucharest*, the plot is minimal and characters are few; moreover, each film is largely confined to a single location: the stone house in *The Turin Horse*, the TV studio in the second half of *12:08 East of Bucharest*. Further, the duration of events is limited in each film – to one day in *12:08 East of Bucharest* and six in *The Turin Horse* (*Werckmeister Harmonies'* plot spans a short time, too, but the duration is unclear). Finally, both Tarr's characters and Porumboiu's are physically limited or hemmed in – whether by a windstorm, lack of water, fear of violence, or a TV camera pinning them against a wall-size photomural. In other ways as well, these characters lack agency.

Their limitations may reflect the human condition everywhere, but perhaps with a Central European twist. When asked in 2000 what he wanted the audience to derive from *Werckmeister Harmonies*, Tarr said he hoped the film would increase understanding of "our life … in middle Europe, how we are living there, in a kind of edge of the world".[56] Milan Kundera's 1984 essay, "The Tragedy of Central Europe", which appeared the same year as his novel, *The Unbearable Lightness of Being*, anticipated Tarr's reference to life at the "edge of the world". The Czech author's essay describes Middle or Central Europe as "an uncertain zone of small nations between Russia and Germany", and defines a small nation thus: "One whose very existence may be put in question at any moment; a small nation can disappear and it knows it."[57] Whatever the small nation's former stature, it exists in Kundera's view on the edge of extinction or absorption by larger powers. "A French, a Russian, or an English man is not used to asking questions about the very survival of his nation", wrote Kundera. "His anthems speak only of grandeur and eternity. The Polish anthem, however, starts with the verse: "Poland has not yet perished."[58] Kundera added that a Czech, Romanian or Hungarian seeking to celebrate his nation evinces wariness comparable to the Pole's.

Tarr was born in 1955, a year before Soviet tanks suppressed the Hungarian uprising, and he grew up in Soviet-dominated Budapest. The extreme injury to Hungarian political and cultural identity, as to that of other nations in the "uncertain zone" under Soviet rule, could not have been lost on him. Clearly rebellion often failed, depleting the hope and dignity of the oppressed, leaving them bereaved for generations. Further, in crushing the Hungarian revolt, Soviet power had laid bare the failure of the Soviet communist revolution, which, despite its early utopian promise, was no ally of freedom and equality by 1956. The weight of such past failures seems implicit in Tarr's remark that Central Europe remained on the edge of the world in 2000. More than a decade after the Iron Curtain fell, the uncertain zone still faced rebellion's limits and oppression's aftermath.

Notes

Introduction

1   *Talking About Tarr: A Symposium at Facets*, with film critics Jonathan Rosenbaum and Scott Foundas as well as David Bordwell (Chicago: Facets Cine-Notes, 2008), p. 16. The printed transcript cited here accompanies the Facets DVD of Tarr's *Satantango* (1994). The symposium, attended by Tarr and moderated by Susan Doll, was conducted on 16 September 2007.

2   Karen Beckman and Jean Ma (eds), *Still Moving: Between Cinema and Photography* (Durham: Duke University Press, 2008), p. 10.

3   Further examples of this use of "flat" or "depthless" to describe a cultural situation, if not a particular person, appear in Fredric Jameson, *Postmodernism, or, The Cultural Logic of Late Capitalism* (Durham: Duke University Press, 1992), p. 9.

4   Agnès Varda, "On Photography and Cinema, 1984", trans. Ian Farr, in David Campany (ed.), *The Cinematic* (London & Cambridge: Whitechapel and MIT Press, 2007), p. 63.

5   Gilles Deleuze, *Cinema 2: The Time Image*, trans. Hugh Tomlinson and Robert Galeta (Minneapolis: University of Minnesota Press, 1989), pp. 9, 100.

6   "Nothing happens", a phrase that occurs frequently in descriptions of slow movies, plays and other narrative works, forms part of the title of Ivone Margulies's splendid account of Akerman's films: *Nothing Happens: Chantal Akerman's Hyperrealist Everyday* (Durham: Duke University Press, 1996).

7   Raymond Bellour, "The Pensive Spectator" (1984), trans. Lynne Kirby, in Campany (ed.), *The Cinematic*, p. 123.

8   Peter Baker and Jim Rutenberg, "The Long Road to a Clinton Exit", *New York Times*, 8 June 2008.

9   Manohla Dargis, "Cannes Journal: Box-Office Beasties", *New York Times*, 19 May 2008.

10 Laura Mulvey, "Stillness in the Moving Image" (2003), in Campany (ed.), *The Cinematic*, p. 135.

11 Sylviane Agacinski, *Time Passing: Modernity and Nostalgia*, trans. Jody Gladding (New York: Columbia University Press, 2003), p. 101.

12 Stanley Cavell, *The World Viewed*, enlarged edition (Cambridge: Harvard University Press, 1979), p. 42.

13 Agacinski, *Time Passing*, p. 96.

14 D. N. Rodowick, *Gilles Deleuze's Time Machine* (Durham: Duke University Press, 1997), pp. 109–10.

15 Stephen Holden, "Cultures and Sexes Clash in the Aftermath of a Rape in Turkey", *New York Times*, 7 August 2009.

16 Jarmusch made this remark to Geoff Andrew in an interview appearing in *The Guardian*, 15 November 1999.

17 Teshome Gabriel, "Towards a Critical Theory of Third World Films", in Jim Pines and Paul Willemen (eds), *Questions of Third Cinema* (London: British Film Institute, 1989), pp. 30–53. The phrase "sense of time and rhythm of life" occurs on p. 45.

18 Agacinski, *Time Passing*, p. 169.

19 Agacinski, *Time Passing*, p. 113. Actually, Agacinski makes this point about art historian Aby Warburg, but she makes clear it applies to Benjamin as well.

20 Nicolai Ouroussoff, "Modernist Master's Deceptively Simple World", *New York Times*, 5 August 2007.

21 Quoted in Ouroussoff, "Modernist Master's Deceptively Simple World".

22 Jessica L. Israel, M.D., "Slowing Down to Let the Moment Sink In", *New York Times*, 22 July 2008.

23 Steven Kurutz, "Slow, Easy, Cheap and Green", *New York Times*, 25 March 2009. See also Kim Severson, "Slow Food Savors Big Moment", *New York Times*, 23 July 2008; Penelope Green, "The Slow Life Picks Up Speed", *New York Times*, 31 January 2008.

24 Patricia Leigh Brown and Carol Pogash, "The Pleasure Principle", *New York Times*, 15 March 2009.

25 Agacinski, *Time Passing*, p. 173.

26 Agacinski, *Time Passing*, p. 168.

27 Agacinski, *Time Passing*, p. 162.

28 Agacinski, *Time Passing*, front jacket.

29 Mehrnaz Saeed-Vafa and Jonathan Rosenbaum, *Abbas Kiarostami* (Urbana & Chicago: University of Illinois Press, 2003), p. 32. Rosenbaum's comment appears in a section of this book written exclusively by him.

30 Quoted in Saeed-Vafa and Rosenbaum, *Abbas Kiarostami*, pp. 28–9.

31 A. O. Scott, "The Whole World Is Watching, Why Aren't Americans?", *New York Times*, 21 January 2007.

32 The full title of this satirical film about NASCAR racing is *Talladega Nights: The Ballad of Ricky Bobby*.

33 Manohla Dargis, "Defending Goliath: Hollywood and the Art of the Blockbuster", *New York Times*, 6 May 2007.

34   Robert Warshow, "The Gangster as Tragic Hero", in Warshow, *The Immediate Experience* (New York: Atheneum, 1979), p. 127.

35   Henry David Thoreau, *Walden*, in *The Portable Thoreau*, ed. Carl Bode (New York: Viking Press, 1976), p. 263.

36   Warshow, "The Gangster as Tragic Hero", in Warshow, *The Immediate Experience*, p. 128.

37   Robert Bresson, *Notes on Cinematography*, trans. Jonathan Griffin (New York: Urizen, 1977), p. 28.

38   Bresson, *Notes on Cinematography*, p. 64.

39   J. Hoberman, "Being and Nothingness" (review of *Elephant*), *Village Voice*, 21 October 2003.

40   Lauren Sedofsky, "Plane Songs: Lauren Sedofsky Talks with Alexander Sokurov – Interview", *Artforum*, November 2001.

41   Andrew Sarris, "*Mother and Son*, a Still Life", *New York Observer*, 8 February 1998.

42   Roland Barthes, *Camera Lucida: Reflections on Photography*, trans. Richard Howard (New York: Hill and Wang, 1981), p. 6.

43   Asuman Suner, *New Turkish Cinema: Belonging, Identity and Memory* (London: I. B. Tauris, 2010), p. 96.

44   Gilles Deleuze, *Cinema 2: The Time Image*, trans. Hugh Tomlinson and Robert Galeta (Minneapolis: University of Minnesota Press, 1989), p. 9.

45   Martin Esslin, *The Theatre of the Absurd* (New York: Anchor Books, 1969), p. 29.

46   Peter Bradshaw, "Pedro Costa, the Samuel Beckett of Cinema", *The Guardian*, 17 September 2009.

47   Jean-Francois Lyotard, "The Sublime and the Avant-Garde" (1988), in Simon Morley (ed.), *The Sublime: Documents in Contemporary Art* (London: Whitechapel Gallery & Cambridge: MIT Press, 2010), p. 37.

48   Quoted in Gerald Peary, "Interviews: Gus Van Sant", March 2003 (http://www.geraldpeary. com/interviews/stuv/van-sant.html).

49   Quoted in Dennis West and Joan M. West, "Cinema Beyond Words: An Interview with Lisandro Alonso", *Cineaste*, Vol. 36, No. 2 (2011), p. 37.

50   Jacques Rancière, *The Emancipated Spectator*, trans. Gregory Elliott (London: Verso, 2011), p. 14.

51   Rancière, *The Emancipated Spectator*, p. 15.

52   Pedro Costa, *Home: A Closed Door That Leaves Us Guessing*, pp. 7, 15 of transcript of Costa's lectures at Tokyo Film School, 12–14 March 2004 (available at http://www.rouge. com.au/10/costa_seminar.html). First published in catalogue of Pedro Costa retrospective, Sendai Mediatheque and Rouge Press, 2005. Transcription by Valerie Anne Christen; English translation by Downing Roberts.

53   Kiarostami discusses this decision in *Around Five: Abbas Kiarostami's Reflections on Film and the Making of Five* (2005), included on Kino's DVD of *Five*.

54   Slavoj Zizek, *First as Tragedy, Then as Farce* (London & New York: Verso, 2009), p. 47. Zizek credits Giorgio Agamben for this notion of "homo sacer, the one excluded".

55   Fritz Wittels, quoted in Peter Gay, *Freud: A Life for Our Time* (New York & London: W. W. Norton, 1988), p. 395.

56   Quoted in Roger Ebert, "Werckmeister Harmonies: A Haunted Film about a Haunted Village", 8 September 2007 (http://rogerebert.suntimes.com/apps/pbcs.dll/article?AID=/ 20070908/70909001/1023&template=printart).

57   Samuel Beckett, *Waiting for Godot* (New York: Grove Press, 1954).

58   Quoted in Roger Ebert, "Werckmeister Harmonies: A Haunted Film about a Haunted Village", 8 September 2007 (http://rogerebert.suntimes.com/apps/pbcs.dll/article?AID=/20070908/70909001/1023&template=printart).

Chapter 1

1   Quoted in Manohla Dargis, "Her Place is in the Home" (review of *The Maid*, directed by Sebastian Silva), *New York Times*, 16 October 2009. According to Robert Ray in *The ABCs of Classic Hollywood* (New York: Oxford University Press, 2008), p. 34, Garbo asked Mamoulian on the set of *Queen Christina*, "What do I express in this last shot?", to which he replied, "Nothing, absolutely nothing. You must make your mind and heart a complete blank."

2   Sokurov makes this statement in an interview that is included on the Facets Video DVD (2005) of his *Elegy of a Voyage (Hubert Robert: A Fortunate Life)*.

3   Ludvig Hertzberg (ed.), *Jim Jarmusch Interviews* (Jackson: University Press of Mississippi, 2001), p. 92. From "Mystery Man", interview with Jarmusch by Luc Sante.

4   Hertzberg, *Jim Jarmusch Interviews*, p. 76. From "In Between Things", interview with Jarmusch by Peter Von Bagh and Mika Kaurismaki.

5   Quoted in David Thomson, *The New Biographical Dictionary of Film* (New York: Alfred A. Knopf, 2004), p. 843; and in Nancy Ramsey, "Outsider at Home with the Inner Life", *New York Times*, 1 February 1998.

6   These words attributed to Sterritt appear on Kino Video's case containing its 2006 DVD of *The Second Circle*.

7   Hertzberg, *Jim Jarmusch Interviews*, p. 34. From "Jim Jarmusch", interview conducted by Peter Belsito.

8   Juan A. Suárez, *Jim Jarmusch* (Urbana & Chicago: University of Illinois Press, 2007), p. 31.

9   Hertzberg, *Jim Jarmusch Interviews*, p. 87. From "Mystery Man", interview with Jarmusch conducted by Sante.

10   J. J. Murphy, *Me and You and Memento and Fargo: How Independent Screenplays Work* (London: Continuum, 2007), p. 37.

11   Dennis Lim, "A Director Content to Wander On", *New York Times*, 26 April 2009.

12   Hertzberg, *Jim Jarmusch Interviews*, p. 178. From "Jim Jarmusch Interview" by Geoff Andrew.

13   Kirill Galetski, "The Foundations of Film Arts: An Interview with Alexander Sokurov" by Galetski, *Cineaste*, Vol. 26, No. 3 (2001).

14   Robert Bresson, *Notes on Cinematography*, trans. Jonathan Griffin (New York: Urizen, 1977), p. 64.

15   Bresson, *Notes on Cinematography*, p. 28.

16   Bresson, *Notes on Cinematography*, p. 11.

17   Bresson, *Notes on Cinematography*, p. 71.

18   Bresson, *Notes on Cinematography*, p. 46.

19   Bresson, *Notes on Cinematography*, p. 11.

20   Bresson, *Notes on Cinematography*, p. 26.

21 Bresson, *Notes on Cinematography*, p. 18.

22 Bresson, *Notes on Cinematography*, p. 55.

23 Bresson, *Notes on Cinematography*, p. 51.

24 Bresson, *Notes on Cinematography*, p. 27.

25 Bresson, *Notes on Cinematography*, p. 49.

26 Bresson, *Notes on Cinematography*, p. 44.

27 Bresson, *Notes on Cinematography*, p. 64.

28 Cited by Martin La Salle in *The Models of Pickpocket* (2003), a documentary directed by Babette Mangolte, who was Chantal Akerman's cinematographer on *Jeanne Dielman...* (1975). Mangolte's documentary is included in the 2005 Criterion Collection DVD of *Pickpocket* (1959).

29 La Salle reminiscing in *The Models of Pickpocket*.

30 Hertzberg, *Jim Jarmusch Interviews*, p. 125. From "Regis Filmmaker's Dialogue: Jim Jarmusch", interview by Jonathan Rosenbaum.

31 Bresson, *Notes on Cinematography*, p. 64.

32 Bresson, *Notes on Cinematography*, p. 48.

33 Bresson, *Notes on Cinematography*, p. 35.

34 Murphy, *Me and You and Memento and Fargo: How Independent Screenplays Work*, p. 32.

35 Quoted by Jane Shapiro in her interview with Jarmusch, "Stranger in Paradise", in Hertzberg, *Jim Jarmusch Interviews*, p. 59.

36 Thomas Elsaesser and Malte Hagener, *Film Theory: An Introduction Through the Senses* (New York & London: Routledge, 2010), p. 132.

37 Quoted in Richard Linnett, "As American as You Are: Jim Jarmusch and *Stranger Than Paradise*", *Cineaste*, Vol. 14, No. 1 (1985), p. 27.

38 Luc Sante, "Mystery Man", his interview with Jarmusch in Hertzberg, *Jim Jarmusch Interviews*, p. 87.

39 Cathleen McGuigan, "Shot by Shot: *Mystery Train*", her interview with Jarmusch in Hertzberg, *Jim Jarmusch Interviews*, p. 99.

40 Quoted in Lim, "A Director Content to Wander On", *New York Times*, 26 April 2009.

41 Suárez, *Jim Jarmusch*, p. 24.

42 Suárez, *Jim Jarmusch*, p. 20.

43 Suárez, *Jim Jarmusch*, p. 32.

44 Suárez, *Jim Jarmusch*, p. 32.

45 Suárez, *Jim Jarmusch*, p. 31.

46 Suárez, *Jim Jarmusch*, p. 24.

47 Suárez, *Jim Jarmusch*, p. 27.

48 Suárez, *Jim Jarmusch*, p. 29.

49 Stuart Klawans, "Deepening Spiritually Over Time", *New York Times*, 20 January 2002.

50 Quoted in Manohla Dargis, "Her Place is in the Home" (review of *The Maid*, directed by Sebastian Silva), *New York Times*, 16 October 2009.

51 Ian Johnston, "Review of *The Second Circle*", *Not Coming to a Theater Near You*, 6 July 2006 (http://www.notcoming.com/reviews/secondcircle).

52 Ramsey, "Outsider at Home with the Inner Life", *New York Times*, 1 February 1998.

53 See José Alaniz, "Vision and Blindness in Sokurov's *Father and Son*", in Helena Goscilo and Yana Hashamova (eds), *Cinepaternity: Fathers and Sons in Soviet and Post-Soviet Film*

(Bloomington: Indiana University Press), p. 285.

54 Michael Sicinski, "Spiritual Voice, Material World: The Trouble with Sokurov's *Alexandra*", *cinemascope* (http:/www.cinema-scope.com/cs34/feat_sicinski_sokurov.html#top).

55 Quoted in Ramsey, "Outsider at Home with the Inner Life", *New York Times*, 1 February 1998.

56 Ramsey, "Outsider at Home with the Inner Life", *New York Times*, 1 February 1998.

57 Fernando F. Croce, "The Second Circle", *SLANT*, 3 April 2006 (http://www.slantmagazine.com/dvd/dvd_review.asp?ID=903).

58 Interview with Sokurov in 2005 included in the Facets Video DVD of Sokurov's *Elegy of a Voyage* (*Hubert Robert: A Fortunate Life*).

59 Quoted in Lauren Sedofsky, "Plane Songs: Lauren Sedofsky Talks with Alexander Sokurov – Interview", *Artforum*, November 2001.

60 Quoted in Sedofsky, "Plane Songs".

61 Quoted in Sedofsky, "Plane Songs".

62 Quoted in Sedofsky, "Plane Songs".

63 Quoted in Jonathan Rosenbaum, *Dead Man* (London: British Film Institute, 2000), pp. 68–70.

64 Quoted in Gregg Rickman, "The Western Under Erasure", in Jim Kitses and Gregg Rickman (eds), *The Western Reader* (New York: Limelight Editions, 1999), p. 399.

65 Jonathan Rosenbaum, "Acid Western: *Dead Man*", *Chicago Reader*, 6 December 2006, p. 9.

66 Murray Pomerance, *Johnny Depp Starts Here* (New Brunswick: Rutgers University Press, 2005), p. 85.

67 Stephen Holden, "Film Review: *Dead Man*", *New York Times*, 10 May 1996.

68 Jonathan Rosenbaum writes that Cole "crushes [the head] like a rotten cantaloupe under his heel". In Rosenbaum, *Dead Man*, p. 40.

69 Quoted in Rosenbaum, *Dead Man*, p. 40.

70 Rosenbaum, *Dead Man*, p. 61.

71 Rosenbaum, *Dead Man*, p. 27.

72 Rosenbaum, *Dead Man*, p. 8.

73 Holden, "Film Review: *Dead Man*", *New York Times*, 10 May 1996.

74 Rosenbaum, *Dead Man*, p. 11.

75 Rickman, "The Western Under Erasure", in *The Western Reader*, p. 390.

76 Holden, "Film Review: *Dead Man*", *New York Times*, 10 May 1996.

77 Rosenbaum, *Dead Man*, p. 67.

78 Rickman, "The Western Under Erasure", in *The Western Reader*, p. 399.

79 Rickman, "The Western Under Erasure", in *The Western Reader*, p. 397.

80 Rickman, "The Western Under Erasure", in *The Western Reader*, p. 401.

81 Rickman, "The Western Under Erasure", in *The Western Reader*, p. 399.

82 Suárez, *Jim Jarmusch*, p. 106.

83 Suárez, *Jim Jarmusch*, p. 115.

84 Suárez, *Jim Jarmusch*, p. 116.

85 Roger Ebert, "Dead Man", 28 June 1996 (rogerebert.com).

86 Jean-Francois Lyotard, "The Sublime and the Avant-Garde" (1988), in Simon Morley (ed.), *The Sublime: Documents of Contemporary Art* (London & Cambridge: MIT Press, 2010), pp. 33–4.

Chapter 2

1   J. Hoberman, "Being and Nothingness" (*review of Elephant*), *Village Voice*, 21 October 2003.

2   Quoted in Gerald Peary, "Interviews: Gus Van Sant", March 2003 (http://www.geraldpeary.com/interviews/stuv/van-sant.html).

3   Jean-Francois Lyotard, "The Sublime and the Avant-Garde" (1988), in Simon Morley (ed.), *The Sublime: Documents in Contemporary Art* (London: Whitechapel Gallery and Cambridge: MIT Press, 2010), p. 37.

4   Quoted in Matthew Hays, "Down with the Kids", *The Guardian*, 21 December 2007.

5   Quoted in Simon Hattenstone, "All the World's an Art School", *The Guardian*, 24 January 2004.

6   Thomas Elsaesser and Malte Hagener, *Film Theory: An Introduction Through the Senses* (New York & London: Routledge, 2010), p. 45.

7   Quoted in Gerald Peary, "Interviews: Gus Van Sant – Elephant", November 2003 (http://www.geraldpeary.com/interviews/stuv/van-sant-elephant.html).

8   Dennis Lim, "Film", *Village Voice*, 31 August 2004 (http://www.villagevoice.com/content/printVersion/185859).

9   Quoted in Peary, "Interviews: Gus Van Sant – Elephant", November 2003.

10 Erwin Panofsky, "Style and Medium in the Motion Pictures", in Leo Braudy and Marshall Cohen (eds), *Film Theory and Criticism: Introductory Readings*, fifth edition (Oxford: Oxford University Press, 1999), p. 281.

11 Panofsky, "Style and Medium in the Motion Pictures", in *Film Theory and Criticism: Introductory Readings*, p. 279.

12 However, in the replay of this scene from another camera angle later in the film, it is another member of the trio who appears to say "He's so cute".

13 See Jorge Luis Borges, *Labyrinths: Selected Stories and Other Writings*, trans. and ed. Donald A. Yates and James E. Irby (New York: New Directions, 2007).

14 Gerald Peary, "Interviews: Gus Van Sant – Elephant", November 2003.

15 Alain Robbe-Grillet, *Last Year at Marienbad* (New York: Grove Press, 1962), pp. 17–18.

16 Carl Plantinga, *Moving Viewers: American Film and the Spectator's Experience* (Berkeley, Los Angeles: University of California Press), p. 7.

17 Quoted in Nancy Ramsey, "Outsider at Home with the Inner Life", *New York Times*, 1 February 1998.

18 Andrew Sarris, "Mother and Son, a Still Life", *New York Observer*, 8 February 1998.

19 Edward Guthmann, "'Mother and Son' Celebrates Intimate Family Relationships", *San Francisco Chronicle*, 20 February 1998.

20 Lauren Sedofsky, "Plane Songs: Lauren Sedofsky Talks with Alexander Sokurov – Interview", *Artforum*, November 2001.

21 Guthmann, "Mother and Son".

22 See Laura U. Marks, *The Skin of the Film: Intercultural Cinema, Embodiment, and the Senses* (Durham: Duke University Press, 2000).

23 Guthmann, "Mother and Son".

24 Quoted in Sedofsky, "Plane Songs".

25 Guthmann, "Mother and Son".

26 Interview with Sokurov in 2005 included in Facets Video DVD of Sokurov's *Elegy of a Voyage*.

27 Sedofsky, "Plane Songs".

28 Quoted in Sedofsky, "Plane Songs".

29 Quoted in Sedofsky, "Plane Songs".

30 Stan Brakhage, "From Metaphors on Vision", in Leo Braudy and Marshall Cohen (eds), *Film Theory and Criticism: Introductory Readings*, fifth edition (Oxford: Oxford University Press, 1999), p. 228.

31 Brakhage, "From Metaphors on Vision", p. 230.

32 Brakhage, "From Metaphors on Vision", p. 230.

33 Brakhage, "From Metaphors on Vision", pp. 230–1.

34 He speaks of "old masters" and cites El Greco and Turner in his interview on the *Elegy of a Voyage* DVD.

35 Quoted in Sedofsky, "Plane Songs".

36 Quoted in Sedofsky, "Plane Songs".

37 Quoted in Joan Dupont, "A Russian Director Films the Flow of Time", *International Herald Tribune*, 25 May 2002.

38 Quoted in Dupont, "A Russian Director Films the Flow of Time", *International Herald Tribune*, 25 May 2002.

39 Guthmann, "Mother and Son".

40 Henceforth I'll refer to the look resulting from Sokurov's use of glass panes, mirrors and anamorphic-like lenses simply as "anamorphic".

41 Quoted in Sedofsy, "Plane Songs".

42 Michael Sicinski, "Spiritual Voice, Material World: The Trouble with Sokurov's *Alexandra*", *Cinema Scope Magazine*, 31 December 2008 (http://cinema-scope.com/cinema-scope-magazine/features-spiritual-voice-material-world-the-trouble-with-sokurov%E2%80%99s-alexandra/).

43 Sicinski, "Spiritual Voice, Material World".

44 Sicinski, "Spiritual Voice, Material World".

45 Lyotard, "The Sublime and the Avant-Garde", in *The Sublime: Documents in Contemporary Art*, p. 38.

Chapter 3

1 Roger Ebert, "Distant" (review), rogerebert.suntimes.com, 9 April 2004.

2 Seymour Chatman, *Antonioni, or, The Surface of the World* (Berkeley: University of California Press, 1985), p. 55. Chatman addresses here what he calls Antonioni's "great tetralogy": *L'Avventura*, *La notte*, *Eclipse* and *Red Desert*.

3 Seymour Chatman, *Antonioni*, p. 79.

4 See, for example, J. Hoberman, "Only Disconnect" (review of *Distant*), *Village Voice*, 2 March 2004; Philip French, "Where Did Our Love Go?" (review of *Climates*), *The Observer*, 11 February 2007; Manohla Dargis, "The Spaces Between People, Even Lovers, in Images of Deceptive Simplicity" (review of *Climates*), *New York Times*, 27 October 2006; A. O. Scott, "Provocation in Cannes from a Wily Provocateur", *New York Times*, 21 May 2003.

5   Dargis, "The Spaces Between People".

6   French, "Where Did Our Love Go?".

7   Hoberman, "Only Disconnect".

8   French, "Where Did Our Love Go?".

9   Asuman Suner, *New Turkish Cinema: Belonging, Identity and Memory* (London: I. B. Tauris, 2010), p. 96.

10 Gilles Deleuze, *Cinema 2: The Time Image*, trans. Hugh Tomlinson and Robert Galeta (Minneapolis: University of Minnesota Press, 1989), p. 9.

11 Deleuze, *Cinema 2: The Time Image*, p. 9.

12 Asuman Suner, *New Turkish Cinema: Belonging, Identity and Memory*, p. 90.

13 Jonas Mekas, "*Eclipse*: Silence Is Content" (excerpted from the *Village Voice*, 13 December 1962), in Pierre Leprohon, *Michelangelo Antonioni: An Introduction*, trans. Scott Sullivan (New York: Simon & Schuster, 1963), pp. 174–5.

14 Gönül Dönmez-Colin, *Turkish Cinema: Identity, Distance and Belonging* (London: Reaktion Books, 2008), p. 196.

15 See Ian Cameron, *Antonioni* (New York: Praeger, 1969), p. 105.

16 *Screenplays of Michelangelo Antonioni: Il Grido, L'Avventura, La Notte, L'Eclisse*, trans. Louis Brigante (New York: Orion Press, 1963), p. 344.

17 Chatman, *Antonioni*, p. 117.

18 Chatman, *Antonioni*, p. 110.

19 Leonardo Autera and Ettore Mo, "*The Eclipse*" (interview), trans. Dana Renga (from *Corriere della Sera*, 15 October 1975), in *Michelangelo Antonioni, The Architecture of Vision: Writings and Interviews on Cinema*, eds Carlo di Carlo, Giorgio Tinazzi and Marga Cottino-Jones (Chicago: University of Chicago Press, 2007), p. 276.

20 "Graphic sonority" is a phrase I draw from Jacques Aumont, *Montage Eisenstein*, trans. Lee Hildreth, Constance Penley and Andrew Ross (London: BFI Publishing, and Bloomington & Indianapolis: Indiana University Press, 1987), p. 31.

21 *Screenplays of Michelangelo Antonioni*, p. 361.

22 Chatman, *Antonioni*, p. 72.

23 "The banality of the streetlamp", writes Chatman, "makes it an icon of that ultimate banality, push-button atomic war". See Chatman, *Antonioni*, p. 112.

24 Chatman, *Antonioni*, p. 108.

25 Chatman, *Antonioni*, p. 110.

26 Michelangelo Antonioni, in Leonardo Autera and Ettore Mo "*The Eclipse*" (interview), in *The Architecture of Vision*, p. 281.

27 Michelangelo Antonioni, *The Architecture of Vision: Writings and Interviews on Cinema*, eds Carlo di Carlo, Giorgio Tinazzi and Marga Cottino-Jones, p. 199. From Aldo Tassone, "The History of Cinema Is Made on Film [La storia del cinema la fanno i film]" (interview), trans. Dana Renga, in *Parla il cinema italiano*, ed. Aldo Tassone, trans. Dana Renga, Milan: Il formichiere, 1979.

28 Michelangelo Antonioni, in Leonardo Autera and Ettore Mo "*The Eclipse*" (interview), in *The Architecture of Vision*, p. 277.

29 Quoted in Chatman, *Antonioni*, p. 73.

30 See Dönmez-Colin, *Turkish Cinema*, p. 198.

31 Chatman, *Antonioni*, p. 89.

32 *Screenplays of Michelangelo Antonioni*, p. 98.

33 *Screenplays of Michelangelo Antonioni*, p. 154.

34 *Screenplays of Michelangelo Antonioni*, p. 185.

35 Michelangelo Antonioni, in Leonardo Autera and Ettore Mo, *"The Eclipse"* (interview), in *The Architecture of Vision*, p. 280.

36 Chatman, *Antonioni*, p. 116. While *Cronaca*'s running time was 69% of *L'Avventura*'s, it had but 34% as many shots as the later film.

37 See Bela Balazs, *Theory of the Film: Character and Growth of a New Art*, trans. Edith Bone (New York: Dover, 1970), especially "The Face of Man", pp. 60–89.

38 Hoberman, "Only Disconnect".

39 Richard Kuhns, *Tragedy: Contradiction and Repression* (Chicago & London: University of Chicago Press, 1991), p. 111.

40 Kuhns, *Tragedy*, p. 97.

41 Quoted in Walter Addiego, "Climates' Drama" (review of *Climates*), *San Francisco Chronicle*, 26 January 2007.

42 Philip Rieff, *Freud: The Mind of the Moralist* (Chicago: University of Chicago Press, 1979), p. 317.

43 Dargis, "The Spaces Between People".

44 Dargis, "The Spaces Between People".

45 J. Hoberman, "Heavy Weather: Intimate Turkish Drama Chronicles a Rocky Relationship" (review of *Climates*), *Village Voice*, 17 October 2006.

Chapter 4

1 Stanley Cavell, *The World Viewed*, enlarged edition (Cambridge: Harvard University Press, 1979), pp. 150–1.

2 Vivian Sobchack, *Carnal Thoughts: Embodiment and Moving Image Culture* (Berkeley: University of California Press, 2004), p. 84.

3 Haynes's commentary on *Safe* DVD from Sony Classics.

4 J. Hoberman, "The Art of Dying: A Romanian Unknown's Ode to Mortality is the Most Remarkable Film of the Year so Far" (review of *The Death of Mr. Lazarescu*), *Village Voice*, 18 April 2006.

5 Christoph Huber, "A Tale from the Bucharest Hospitals: Cristi Puiu on *The Death of Mister Lazarescu*", *Cinema Scope*, spring 2006. This interview appears in "Articles", a publication from Tartan Video accompanying Tartan's DVD of *The Death of Mr. Lazarescu*. Puiu's remarks are found on page 9 of "Articles".

6 J. Hoberman, "The Art of Dying".

7 A. O. Scott, "New Wave on the Black Sea", *New York Times Magazine*, 20 January 2008, p. 32.

8 Scott, "New Wave on the Black Sea", p. 32.

9 Scott, "New Wave on the Black Sea", p. 30.

10 Scott, "New Wave on the Black Sea", p. 35.

11 J. Hoberman, "The Art of Dying".

12 Quoted in "Articles", p. 8.

13 Quoted in "Articles", p. 9.

14 Quoted in "Articles", p. 11.

15 Quoted in "Articles", p. 10.

16 Quoted in Alan Riding, "*Death of Mr. Lazarescu* Comes After a Bout of Hypochondria", *New York Times*, 23 April 2006.

17 See Siegfried Kracauer, *From Caligari to Hitler: A Psychological History of the German Film* (Princeton: Princeton University Press, 1947).

18 Quoted in "Articles", p. 9.

19 Quoted in "Articles", p. 12.

20 Quoted in "Articles", p. 12.

21 Quoted in "Articles", p. 12.

22 Quoted in "Articles", p. 9.

23 Quoted in "Articles", p. 14.

24 Quoted in Tony Judt, *Reappraisals: Reflections on the Forgotten Twentieth Century* (London: Penguin Books, 2008), p. 264. Cioran's statement originally appeared in his book, *The Temptation to Exist* (1956).

25 Judt, *Reappraisals*, pp. 251–2.

26 Judt, *Reappraisals*, p. 255.

27 Judt, *Reappraisals*, p. 250.

28 Puiu has evinced interest in Murnau's cinema, contrasting his own film *Aurora* (2010) to Murnau's *Sunrise* (1927). See Manohla Dargis, "Following in the Shadows of a Very Shadowy Man" (review of *Aurora*), *New York Times*, 29 June 2011.

29 Kracauer, *From Caligari to Hitler*, p. 100.

30 Quoted in "Articles", p. 10.

31 Quoted in "Articles", p. 10.

32 Quoted in "Articles", p. 9.

33 Quoted in "Articles", p. 9.

34 Cited here is the late Ben Sonnenberg. See "Cool Devastation", Stuart Klawans's review of *4 Months, 3 Weeks and 2 Days*, in *The Nation*, 25 February 2008, p. 44.

35 Sobchack, *Carnal Thoughts*, p. 1.

36 Sobchack, *Carnal Thoughts*, p. 4.

37 Manohla Dargis, "Friend Indeed Who Doesn't Judge or Flinch" (review of *4 Months, 3 Weeks and 2 Days*), *New York Times*, 25 January 2008.

38 Dargis, "Friend Indeed Who Doesn't Judge".

39 James Naremore, "Films of the Year, 2009: James Naremore Makes His Selection of the Year's Best U.S. Releases", *Film Quarterly*, Vol. 63, No. 4 (summer 2010), p. 19.

40 Quoted in Randy Kennedy, "For Carl Andre, Less Is Still Less", *New York Times*, 17 July 2011.

41 Naremore, "Films of the Year, 2009", p. 19.

42 Richard Porton, "Not Just an Abortion Film: An Interview with Cristian Mungiu", *Cineaste* (http://www.cineaste.com/articles/not-just-an-abortion-film.htm).

43 Ben Walters, "Heartbreak Hotel: Film of the Month: *4 Months, 3 Weeks and 2 Days*", *Sight & Sound*, January 2008.

44 Anthony Lane, "The Current Cinema: Monstrous Times", *New Yorker*, 28 January 2008 (http://www.newyorker.com/arts/critics/cinema/2008/01/28/080128crci_cinema_lane?printable=true#ixzz1SIR7uAsS).

45 IFC Films DVD of *4 Months, 3 Weeks and 2 Days*.

46 Richard Porton, "Not Just an Abortion Film".

47 Dargis, "Friend Indeed Who Doesn't Judge".

48 Roger Ebert, "*4 Months, 3 Weeks and 2 Days*: The Price of an Abortion", 7 February 2008 (http://rogerebert.suntimes.com/apps/pbcs.dll/article?AID=/20080207/REVIEWS/802070 302&template=preprint).

49 J. Hoberman, "Gone Baby Gone: The Heroines of *4 Months, 3 Weeks and 2 Days* Don't Get to Play Pregnancy Indie-cute", *Village Voice*, 15 January 2008 (http://www.villagevoice. com/content/printVersion/296737/).

50 Porton, "Not Just an Abortion Film".

51 Walters, "Heartbreak Hotel".

52 Porton, "Not Just an Abortion Film".

53 Manohla Dargis praises the film for averting sentimentality in Dargis, "Friend Indeed Who Doesn't Judge".

54 Porton, "Not Just an Abortion Film".

55 Stuart Klawans, "Film: Cool Devastation" (review of *4 Months, 3 Weeks and 2 Days*), *The Nation*, 25 February 2008, p. 42.

56 Klawans, "Film: Cool Devastation" (review of *4 Months, 3 Weeks and 2 Days*), *The Nation*, 25 February 2008, p. 44.

57 Peter Travers, review of *4 Months, 3 Weeks and 2 Days*, *Rolling Stone*, 25 January 2008.

58 Lane, "The Current Cinema: Monstrous Times", *New Yorker*, 28 January 2008 (http://www. newyorker.com/arts/critics/cinema/2008/01/28/080128crci_cinema_lane?printable=true #ixzz1SIR7uAsS).

59 Barbara Ehrenreich, *Bright-Sided: How the Relentless Promotion of Positive Thinking Has Undermined America* (New York: Metropolitan Books Henry Holt, 2009).

60 Murray Pomerance, "Safe in Lotosland", in James Morrison (ed.), *The Cinema of Todd Haynes: All That Heaven Allows* (London: Wallflower Press, 2007), p. 83.

61 Todd Haynes, *Far from Heaven, Safe, Superstar: The Karen Carpenter Story. Three Screenplays* (New York: Grove Press, 2003), p. 180.

62 Roger Ebert, review of *Safe*, 28 July 1995 (http://rogerebert.suntimes.com).

63 Janet Maslin, "Life of a Hollow Woman", *New York Times*, 23 June 1995.

64 *Safe* DVD from Sony Pictures Classics.

65 Janet Maslin, "Life of a Hollow Woman", *New York Times*, 23 June 1995.

66 Roger Ebert, review of *Safe*, 28 July 1995.

67 Edward Guthmann, "Even in Suburbia, No One Is 'Safe.' Unsettling Film About Environmental Illness", *San Francisco Chronicle*, 28 July 1995.

68 Gilles Deleuze, *Cinema 2: The Time Image*, trans. Hugh Tomlinson and Robert Galeta (Minneapolis: University of Minnesota Press, 1989), p. 9.

69 *Safe* DVD from Sony Pictures Classics.

70 James Morrison, "Todd Haynes in Theory and Practice", in James Morrison (ed.), *The Cinema of Todd Haynes: All That Heaven Allows* (London: Wallflower Press, 2007), p. 134.

71 Morrison, "Todd Haynes in Theory and Practice", in Morrison (ed.), *The Cinema of Todd Haynes: All That Heaven Allows*, p. 141.

72 Morrison, "Todd Haynes in Theory and Practice", in Morrison (ed.), *The Cinema of Todd Haynes: All That Heaven Allows*, p. 141.

73 Todd Haynes, *Far from Heaven, Safe, Superstar: The Karen Carpenter Story. Three Screenplays*, p. 162.

74 Roger Ebert, review of *Safe*, 28 July 1995.

75 Edward Guthmann, "Even in Suburbia, No One Is 'Safe.' Unsettling Film About Environmental Illness", *San Francisco Chronicle*, 28 July 1995.

76 Gilles Deleuze, *Cinema 2: The Time Image*, trans. Hugh Tomlinson and Robert Galeta (Minneapolis: University of Minnesota Press, 1989), p. 7.

77 *Safe* DVD from Sony Pictures Classics.

78 Quoted in Richard Linnett, "As American as You Are: Jim Jarmusch and *Stranger Than Paradise*", *Cineaste*, Vol. 14, No. 1 (1985), p. 27.

79 Interview with Sokurov in 2005 included in the Facets Video DVD of Sokurov's *Elegy of a Voyage* (*Hubert Robert: A Fortunate Life*).

80 Francois Lyotard, "The Sublime and the Avant-Garde" (1988), in Simon Morley (ed.), *The Sublime: Documents in Contemporary Art* (London: Whitechapel Gallery & Cambridge: MIT Press, 2010), p. 37.

81 *Safe* DVD from Sony Pictures Classics.

82 Edward Guthmann, "Even in Suburbia, No One Is 'Safe.' Unsettling Film About Environmental Illness", *San Francisco Chronicle*, 28 July 1995.

83 Desson Howe, review of *Safe*, *Washington Post*, 4 August 1995.

84 Jonathan Rosenbaum, short review of *Safe*, *Chicago Reader*, 21 July 2010.

85 Roger Ebert, review of *Safe*, 28 July 1995.

86 Edward Guthmann, "Even in Suburbia, No One Is 'Safe.' Unsettling Film About Environmental Illness", *San Francisco Chronicle*, 28 July 1995.

87 *Safe* DVD from Sony Pictures Classics.

88 Haynes' commentary on *Safe* DVD from Sony Pictures Classics.

Chapter 5

1 Quoted in Dennis West and Joan M. West, "Cinema Beyond Words: An Interview with Lisandro Alonso", *Cineaste*, Vol. 36, No. 2 (spring 2011), p. 37.

2 Costa made these remarks during his filmmaking course on 12–14 March 2004 at the Tokyo Film School under the auspices of Athenee Francais Cultural Center and Cinematrix. The statements appear on pages 7 and 15 of a transcript of the lectures, *Home: A Closed Door That Leaves Us Guessing*, available on the Internet. The transcript was first published in the catalogue of the Pedro Costa retrospective, Sendai Mediatheque and Rouge Press, 2005. Transcription by Valerie Anne Christen; English translation by Downing Roberts.

3 Quoted in Dennis West and Joan M. West, "Cinema Beyond Words: An Interview with Lisandro Alonso", p. 30.

4 Dennis West and Joan M. West, "Cinema Beyond Words: An Interview with Lisandro Alonso", p. 30.

5 Quoted in Dennis West and Joan M. West, "Cinema Beyond Words: An Interview with Lisandro Alonso", p. 34.

6 J. Hoberman, "Jobber Adrift at Sea Takes Leave in *Liverpool*", *Village Voice*, 1 September 2009.

7 Bela Balazs, *Theory of the Film: Character and Growth of a New Art*, trans. Edith Bone (New York: Dover, 1970), pp. 64, 62.

8   R. Emmet Sweeney, "Interview with Lisandro Alonso, Director of *Liverpool*", transcript accompanying Kino's DVD of *Liverpool*.

9   Quoted in Dennis West and Joan M. West, "Cinema Beyond Words: An Interview with Lisandro Alonso", p. 37.

10 Shigehiko Hasumi, "Adventure: An Essay on Pedro Costa", 2005 (http://www.rouge.com.au/10/costa_hasumi.html).

11 For more on Sokurov's views, please see the second chapter here.

12 Pedro Costa, *Home: A Closed Door That Leaves Us Guessing*, pp. 7, 15 of transcript of Costa's lectures at Tokyo Film School, 12–14 March 2004, available on Internet. First published in catalogue of Pedro Costa retrospective, Sendai Mediatheque and Rouge Press, 2005. Transcription by Valerie Anne Christen; English translation by Downing Roberts.

13 James Quandt, "Ride Lonesome: James Quandt on the Films of Lisandro Alonso", *Artforum International*, 1 November 2008 (http://www.thefreelibrary.com/_/print/PrintArticle.aspx?id=188962460).

14 Quandt, "Ride lonesome: James Quandt on the Films of Lisandro Alonso".

15 Hoberman, "Jobber Adrift at Sea Takes Leave in *Liverpool*", 1 September 2009.

16 Quoted in Dennis West and Joan M. West, "Cinema Beyond Words: An Interview with Lisandro Alonso", p. 37.

17 Quoted in Dennis West and Joan M. West, "Cinema Beyond Words: An Interview with Lisandro Alonso", p. 37.

18 Manohla Dargis, "A Bleak Journey Through a Snowy Tierra del Fuego", *New York Times*, 2 September 2009.

19 Nancy Condee, *The Imperial Trace: Recent Russian Cinema* (Oxford: Oxford University Press, 2009), p. 166. In perceiving "a useful working opposition in Sokurov's work", Condee credits Edwin Carels for characterising one pole of the work as "baroque" and "kaleidoscopic". "Minimalist" and "ascetic" are among Condee's terms for describing the opposite pole.

20 Quoted in Matthew Hays, "Down with the Kids", *The Guardian*, 21 December 2007.

21 Quoted in Hays, "Down with the Kids", *The Guardian*, 21 December 2007.

22 Quoted in Lauren Sedofsky, "Plane Songs: Lauren Sedofsky Talks with Alexander Sokurov – Interview", *Artforum*, November 2001.

23 Quoted in Sedofsky, "Plane Songs: Lauren Sedofsky Talks with Alexander Sokurov – Interview", *Artforum*, November 2001.

24 Quoted in Dennis West and Joan M. West, "Cinema Beyond Words: An Interview with Lisandro Alonso", p. 37.

25 Quoted in Simon Hattenstone, "All the World's an Art School", *The Guardian*, 24 January 2004.

26 Quoted in Dennis West and Joan M. West, "Cinema Beyond Words: An Interview with Lisandro Alonso", p. 37.

27 Quoted in Gerald Peary, "Interviews: Gus Van Sant", March 2003 (http://www.geraldpeary.com/interviews/stuv/van-sant.html).

28 Quandt, "Ride Lonesome: James Quandt on the Films of Lisandro Alonso".

29 Quoted in Gonzalo Aguilar, *New Argentine Film: Other Worlds*, trans. Sarah Ann Wells (New York: Palgrave Macmillan, 2008), p. 60.

30 Quoted in Dennis West and Joan M. West, "Cinema Beyond Words: An Interview with Lisandro Alonso", p. 37.

31 Quoted in Dennis West and Joan M. West, "Cinema Beyond Words: An Interview with Lisandro Alonso", p. 37.

32 James Morrison, "Todd Haynes in Theory and Practice", in James Morrison (ed.), *The Cinema of Todd Haynes: All That Heaven Allows* (London: Wallflower Press, 2007), p. 134.

33 Quandt, "Ride Lonesome: James Quandt on the Films of Lisandro Alonso".

34 Susan Neiman, *Evil in Modern Thought: An Alternative History of Philosophy* (Princeton: Princeton University Press, 2002), p. 304.

35 Neiman, *Evil in Modern Thought: An Alternative History of Philosophy*, p. 305.

36 Neiman, *Evil in Modern Thought: An Alternative History of Philosophy*, p. 305.

37 Neiman, *Evil in Modern Thought: An Alternative History of Philosophy*, p. 305.

38 Sweeney, "Interview with Lisandro Alonso, Director of *Liverpool*", transcript accompanying Kino's DVD of *Liverpool*.

39 Dennis West and Joan M. West, "Cinema Beyond Words: An Interview with Lisandro Alonso", p. 37.

40 Aguilar, *New Argentine Film: Other Worlds*, pp. 60–1.

41 Dargis, "A Bleak Journey Through a Snowy Tierra del Fuego".

42 See the interviews (cited above) conducted by R. Emmet Sweeney and Dennis and Joan West.

43 Hoberman, "Jobber Adrift at Sea Takes Leave in *Liverpool*".

44 Quandt, "Ride Lonesome: James Quandt on the Films of Lisandro Alonso".

45 Dargis, "A Bleak Journey Through a Snowy Tierra del Fuego".

46 Hoberman, "Jobber Adrift at Sea Takes Leave in *Liverpool*".

47 Hoberman, "Jobber Adrift at Sea Takes Leave in *Liverpool*".

48 Quandt, "Ride Lonesome: James Quandt on the Films of Lisandro Alonso".

49 Jeff Wall offers the comments cited here in his video essay on the DVD of *Ossos* in the Criterion Collection, *Letters from Fontainhas: Three Films by Pedro Costa*.

50 Tag Gallagher, "Straub Anti-Straub", *Senses of Cinema*, No. 43.

51 Cyril Neyrat, "Rooms for the Living and the Dead", in the booklet accompanying the Criterion Collection's three DVDs jointly titled *Letters from Fontainhas: Three Films by Pedro Costa*, p. 12.

52 Hasumi, "Adventure: An Essay on Pedro Costa", 2005 (http://www.rouge.comau/10/costa_hasumi.html).

53 Costa, *Home: A Closed Door That Leaves Us Guessing*, p. 7 of Internet transcript.

54 Costa, *Home: A Closed Door That Leaves Us Guessing*, p. 10 of Internet transcript.

55 Costa, *Home: A Closed Door That Leaves Us Guessing*, p. 7 of Internet transcript.

56 Costa, *Home: A Closed Door That Leaves Us Guessing*, p. 27 of Internet transcript.

57 Hasumi, "Adventure: An Essay on Pedro Costa", 2005 (http://www.rouge.com.au/10/costa_hasumi.html).

58 Luc Sante, "The Space Between", in the booklet accompanying the Criterion Collection's *Letters from Fontainhas: Three Films by Pedro Costa*, p. 24.

59 Neyrat, "Rooms for the Living and the Dead", p. 12.

60 Sante, "The Space Between", p. 22.

61 Sante, "The Space Between", p. 23.

62 Gallagher, "Straub Anti-Straub", p. 3.

63 Barbara Barroso, "Ossos/Bones", *Senses of Cinema*, No. 49 (http://www.sensesofcinema.com/2009/cteq/ossos/).

64 Hasumi, "Adventure: An Essay on Pedro Costa".

65 Wall, video essay on *Ossos* DVD.

66 Wall, video essay on *Ossos* DVD.

67 Hasumi, "Adventure: An Essay on Pedro Costa".

68 Hasumi, "Adventure: An Essay on Pedro Costa".

69 Hasumi, "Adventure: An Essay on Pedro Costa".

70 Sante, "The Space Between", p. 25.

71 "Pedro Costa, the Samuel Beckett of Cinema", *Guardian Film Blog*, 17 September 2009 (http://www.guardian.co.uk/film/filmblog/2009/sep/17/pedro-costa-tate-retrospective/print).

72 Gallagher, "Straub Anti-Straub".

73 Costa cites their zombie-like aspect in his conversation with Jean-Pierre Gorin, one of the supplements on the *Ossos* DVD. "Suffused with death" are the words of Joao Benard da Costa, whose commentary appears as another supplement on the *Ossos* DVD.

74 Thom Anderson, "A Band of Outsiders", in the booklet accompanying the Criterion Collection's *Letters from Fontainhas: Three Films by Pedro Costa*, p. 27.

75 Hasumi, "Adventure: An Essay on Pedro Costa".

76 Robert Bresson, *Notes on Cinematography*, trans. Jonathan Griffin (New York: Urizen, 1977), p. 64.

77 Costa, *Home: A Closed Door That Leaves Us Guessing*, p. 14 of Internet transcript.

78 Bresson, *Notes on Cinematography*, p. 11.

79 See Wall's commentary, a supplement on the *Ossos* DVD.

80 Costa, *Home: A Closed Door That Leaves Us Guessing*, p. 5 of Internet transcript.

81 Costa, *Home: A Closed Door That Leaves Us Guessing*, p. 6 of Internet transcript.

82 Quoted in Dennis West and Joan M. West, "Cinema Beyond Words: An Interview with Lisandro Alonso", p. 36.

83 Quoted in Dennis West and Joan M. West, "Cinema Beyond Words: An Interview with Lisandro Alonso", p. 38.

Chapter 6

1 Quoted in Jared Rapfogel, "An Ethical Cinema: An Interview with Manoel de Oliveira", *Cineaste*, Vol. 33, No. 3 (summer 2008), p. 19.

2 Laura Mulvey, *Death 24x a Second: Stillness and the Moving Image* (London: Reaktion Books, 2007), p. 52.

3 Quoted in Peter Gay, *Freud: A Life for Our Time* (New York: W. W. Norton, 1988), p. 395.

4 Quoted in Jared Rapfogel, "An Ethical Cinema: An Interview with Manoel de Oliveira", p. 19.

5 Randal Johnson, *Manoel de Oliveira* (Urbana: University of Illinois Press, 2007), p. 4.

6 Quoted in Jared Rapfogel, "An Ethical Cinema: An Interview with Manoel de Oliveira", p. 18.

7 Quoted in Jared Rapfogel, "An Ethical Cinema: An Interview with Manoel de Oliveira", p. 20.

8 Thomas Elsaesser, "A Bazinian Half-Century", in Dudley Andrew with Herve Joubert-

Laurencin (eds), *Opening Bazin: Postwar Film Theory and Its Afterlife* (Oxford: Oxford University Press, 2011), p. 3.

9   Scott Bukatman, *The Poetics of Slumberland: Animated Spirits and the Animating Spirit* (Berkeley: University of California Press, 2012), p. 166.

10   Michael Wood, *Film: A Very Short Introduction* (Oxford: Oxford University Press, 2012), p. 16.

11   Terrence Rafferty, "Directing at the Speed of an Aircraft", *New York Times*, 12 February 2012.

12   Quoted in Jared Rapfogel, "An Ethical Cinema: An Interview with Manoel de Oliveira", p. 21. "The filmmaker I like the most is Dreyer", remarks Oliveira, "and the film I like the most is *Gertrud*."

13   Quoted in Evan Osnos, "A Reporter at Large: The Long Shot", *New Yorker*, 11 May 2009, p. 91. "Bresson took plot, photography, and performance, and one by one he negated them, leaving only the purity of the film", said Jia Zhang-ke, quoted in the *New Yorker*, after he saw *A Man Escaped* (1956). "It was the first time that I ever felt the charm of time itself, and understood a kind of transcendent amusement with the spirit of film."

14   Laura Mulvey, "Stillness in the Moving Image", in David Campany (ed.), *The Cinematic: Documents of Contemporary Art* (London & Cambridge: Whitechapel & MIT Press, 2007), p. 136.

15   Laura Mulvey, "Stillness in the Moving Image", p. 135.

16   Quoted in Michael Wood, *Film: A Very Short Introduction*, p. 3.

17   Laura Mulvey, *Death 24x a Second: Stillness and the Moving Image*, p. 79.

18   Michael Wood, *Film: A Very Short Introduction*, p. 16.

19   Michael Wood, *Film: A Very Short Introduction*, p. 4.

20   Laura Mulvey, *Death 24x a Second: Stillness and the Moving Image*, p. 52.

21   Quoted in Peter Gay, *Freud: A Life for Our Time*, p. 395.

22   James Morrison, "Todd Haynes in Theory and Practice", in James Morrison (ed.), *The Cinema of Todd Haynes: All That Heaven Allows* (London: Wallflower Press, 2007), p. 134.

23   Oliveira makes this statement in the course of *Absoluto*, an interview with him accompanying the Cinema Guild DVD of *The Strange Case of Angelica* issued in 2011.

24   Dennis Lim, "Ship of Fools: The Life Aquatic with Captain John Malkovich" (review of *A Talking Picture*), *Village Voice*, 30 November 2004.

25   See Steven Pinker, *The Better Angels of Our Nature: Why Violence Has Declined* (New York: Viking, 2011).

26   Gilles Deleuze, *Cinema 2: The Time Image*, trans. Hugh Tomlinson and Robert Galeta (Minneapolis: University of Minnesota Press, 1989), p. xi.

27   Bukatman attributes this phrase to Deleuze in *The Poetics of Slumberland: Animated Spirits and the Animating Spirit*, p. 128.

28   Gilberto Perez, "It's a Playground" (review of *Close-up: Iranian Cinema, Past, Present and Future* by Hamid Dabashi), *London Review of Books*, 27 June 2002, p. 28.

29   Quoted in Jared Rapfogel, "An Ethical Cinema: An Interview with Manoel de Oliveira", p. 20.

30   Quoted in Khatereh Khodaei, "*Shirin* as Described by Kiarostami", *Offscreen.com*, 31 January 2009. See also *Taste of Shirin* (2008), a documentary on the making of *Shirin* by Hamideh Razavi, included in the Cinema Guild DVD (2010) of *Shirin*.

31   Quoted in Mehrnaz Saeed-Vafa and Jonathan Rosenbaum, *Abbas Kiarostami* (Urbana:

University of Illinois Press, 2003), p. 124.

32 Jean Ma discusses "the conjuncture of the real and the fantastic" in Tsai Ming-Liang's *Goodbye, Dragon Inn*, for example, in Jean Ma, *Melancholy Drift: Marking Time in Chinese Cinema* (Hong Kong: Hong Kong University Press, 2010), p. 101.

33 Dennis West and Joan M. West, "Cinema Beyond Words: An Interview with Lisandro Alonso", *Cineaste*, Vol. 36, No. 2 (spring 2011), p. 37.

34 Dennis West and Joan M. West, "Cinema Beyond Words: An Interview with Lisandro Alonso", p. 37.

35 Jared Rapfogel, "A Steady Gaze: The Films of Manoel de Oliveira", *Cineaste*, Vol. 33, No. 3 (summer 2008), p. 14.

36 Quoted in Jared Rapfogel, "An Ethical Cinema: An Interview with Manoel de Oliveira", p. 19.

37 See Tom Dawson, review of *Five*, "Movies", BBC Homepage, 12 May 2005.

38 Dawson, review of *Five*, "Movies", BBC Homepage, 12 May 2005.

39 Jean-Francois Lyotard, "The Sublime and the Avant-Garde" (1988), in *The Sublime: Documents of Contemporary Art* (London & Cambridge: MIT Press, 2010), pp. 33–4.

40 See the film *Around Five: Abbas Kiarostami's Reflections on Film and the Making of Five* (2005), included in Kino's DVD of *Five*. Statements about *Five* attributed to Kiarostami over the next four paragraphs derive from *Around Five*.

41 Quoted in "Alfred Hitchcock", in Andrew Sarris (ed.), *Interviews with Film Directors* (New York: Bobbs-Merrill, 1967), p. 202. This interview with Hitchcock was conducted by Ian Cameron and V. F. Perkins; it originally appeared in *Movie*, No. 6 (January 1963).

42 Quoted in Matthew Hays, "Down with the Kids", *The Guardian*, 21 December 2007.

43 Quoted in Lauren Sedofsky, "Plane Songs: Lauren Sedofsky Talks with Alexander Sokurov – Interview", *Artforum*, November 2001.

44 Hamid Dabashi, *Close Up: Iranian Cinema, Past, Present and Future* (London: Verso, 2001), p. 73.

45 Quoted in Mehrnaz Saeed-Vafa and Jonathan Rosenbaum, *Abbas Kiarostami* (Urbana: University of Illinois Press, 2003), p. 108.

46 Quoted in Saeed-Vafa and Rosenbaum, *Abbas Kiarostami*, p. 108.

47 Kiarostami makes this statement in the film *Around Five: Abbas Kiarostami's Reflections on Film and the Making of Five* (2005), included in Kino's DVD of *Five*.

48 A. O. Scott, "'Platform': When 1980's China Went Pop, Discovering Pink Polyester and Spandex", *New York Times*, 7 October 2000.

49 Roger Ebert, review of *The World*, 29 July 2005 (http://rogerebert.suntimes.com/apps/pbcs.dll/article?AID=/20050728/REVIEWS/5071300).

50 Manohla Dargis, "Politics Arch and Subtle at Toronto Film Festival", *New York Times*, 14 September 2006.

51 The phrase "world of any-space-whatevers" comes from Scott Bukatman, *The Poetics of Slumberland: Animated Spirits and the Animating Spirit*, p. 128.

52 Unless otherwise indicated, these and subsequent statements by Jia are found in *Interview with the Director*, a short film included in the New Yorker DVD of *Still Life* issued in 2008.

53 *Interview with the Director*, included in the New Yorker DVD of *Still Life*.

54 See Evan Osnos, "A Reporter at Large: The Long Shot", *New Yorker*, 11 May 2009, p. 90.

55 André Bazin, "The Ontology of the Photographic Image", in *What Is Cinema?*, trans. Hugh Gray (Berkeley: University of California Press, 1967), p. 15.

56 See Dennis Lim, "Blurring Reality's Edge in Fluid China", *New York Times*, 20 January 2008.

57 *Interview with the Director*, New Yorker DVD of *Still Life*.

58 *Interview with the Director*, New Yorker DVD of *Still Life*.

59 Jiwei Xiao, "The Quest for Memory: Documentary and Fiction in Jia Zhangke's Films", *Senses of Cinema*, No. 59 (2011) (http://www.sensesofcinema.com/2011/feature-articles/the-quest-for-memory-documentary-and-fiction-injia-zhangke's-films/).

60 Jiwei, "The Quest for Memory: Documentary and Fiction in Jia Zhangke's Films."

61 Jiwei, "The Quest for Memory: Documentary and Fiction in Jia Zhangke's Films."

62 Jiwei, "The Quest for Memory: Documentary and Fiction in Jia Zhangke's Films."

63 Kevin B. Lee, "Great Directors: Jia Zhangke", *Senses of Cinema*, No. 29 (2003) (http://www.sensesofcinema.com/2003/great-directors/jia/).

64 Lee, "Great Directors: Jia Zhangke".

65 J. Hoberman, "Drowning in Progress: Contemporary China, Fluid yet Unstable, in *Still Life*", *Village Voice*, 8 January 2008.

66 Manohla Dargis, "An Upscale Leap Forward That Leaves Many Behind", *New York Times*, 5 June 2009.

67 See *Interview with the Director*, included in the New Yorker DVD of *Still Life*.

68 Jia's statements quoted here are from *Interview with the Director*, included in the New Yorker DVD of *Still Life*.

69 Quoted in Osnos, "A Reporter at Large: The Long Shot", *New Yorker*, 11 May 2009, p. 94.

70 Quoted in Osnos, "A Reporter at Large: The Long Shot", p. 94.

71 Osnos, "A Reporter at Large: The Long Shot", p. 94.

72 Quoted in Osnos, "A Reporter at Large: The Long Shot", p. 94.

73 Jia's words in this paragraph come from *Interview with the Director*, included in the New Yorker DVD of *Still Life*.

74 See Sigmund Freud, *Beyond the Pleasure Principle*, trans. and ed. James Strachey (New York: W. W. Norton, 1961), p. 33.

Chapter 7

1 Yvette Bíro, *Turbulence and Flow in Film: The Rhythmic Design*, trans. Paul Salamon (Bloomington: Indiana University Press, 2008), p. 69.

2 Quoted in Jonathan Romney, "Out of the Shadows", *The Guardian*, 23 March 2001 (http://www.guardian.co.uk/film/2001/mar/24/books.guardianreview/print).

3 James Wood, "Madness and Civilization: The Very Strange Fictions of Laszlo Krasznahorkai", *New Yorker*, 4 July 2011, p. 75.

4 Robert Koehler, "Interview/The Thinking Image: Fred Kelemen on Béla Tarr and *The Turin Horse*", *Cinema Scope*, November 2012, p. 6 (http://cinema-scope.com/cinema-scope-magazine/interview-the-thinking-image-fred-kelemen-on-bela-tarr-and-the-turin-horse/).

5 Peter Hames, "The Melancholy of Resistance: The Films of Béla Tarr", *Kinoeye: New Perspectives on European Film*, Vol. 1, No. 1 (September 2001), p. 8 (http://www.kinoeye.org/01/01/hames01.php).

6 Walter Kaufmann cites words of the madman in his study *Nietzsche: Philosopher*,

Psychologist, Antichrist, fourth edition (Princeton: Princeton University Press, 1974), pp. 96–7.

7   Quoted in Koehler, "Interview/The Thinking Image: Fred Kelemen on Béla Tarr and *The Turin Horse*", p. 4.

8   Quoted in Koehler, "Interview/The Thinking Image: Fred Kelemen on Béla Tarr and *The Turin Horse*", p. 4.

9   Jonathan Rosenbaum, "Voluptuous Misery", *Film Comment*, Vol. 47, No. 5 (September–October 2011), p. 48.

10 Quoted in Koehler, "Interview/The Thinking Image: Fred Kelemen on Béla Tarr and *The Turin Horse*", p. 9.

11 J. Hoberman, "Brute Existence: *The Turin Horse*", a printed essay included with *The Turin Horse* DVD (2011) from Cinema Guild.

12 Press conference (2011, 49 minutes) at Berlin Film Festival in which Tarr and his collaborators discussed *The Turin Horse*. The discussion appears as a special feature on Cinema Guild's DVD (2011) of the film.

13 Tarr makes this statement in Vladan Petkovic, "Simple and Pure: Béla Tarr, Director", *Cineuropa*, 3 April 2011.

14 Quoted in Jim Holt, *Why Does the World Exist? An Existential Detective Story* (New York: Liveright Publishing Corporation, 2012), p. 31.

15 Quoted in Frank Close, *Nothing: A Very Short Introduction* (New York: Oxford University Press, 2009), p. 145.

16 Quoted by James Wood, "God Talk: The Book of Common Prayer at Three Hundred and Fifty", *New Yorker*, 22 October 2012, p. 73.

17 James Morrison, "Todd Haynes in Theory and Practice", in James Morrison (ed.), *The Cinema of Todd Haynes: All That Heaven Allows* (London: Wallflower Press, 2007), p. 134.

18 See Nancy Ramsey, "Outsider at Home with the Inner Life", *New York Times*, 1 February 1998.

19 Berlin Film Festival press conference (2011, 49 minutes).

20 This phrase was used by an unidentified journalist who questioned Tarr at the Berlin Film Festival press conference. Also, the phrase appears in Fabien Lemercier, "Tarr Inspired by Nietzsche for *The Turin Horse*", *Cineuropa*, 21 October 2008. See also J. Hoberman's comment that *The Turin Horse* is a "great poem on the end of the world" in "Brute Existence: *The Turin Horse*".

21 Fergus Daly, "Waiting for the Prince: An Interview with Béla Tarr", *Senses of Cinema*, 13 February 2001, p. 1 (http://sensesofcinema.com/2001/feature-articles/tarr-2/).

22 Hames, "The Melancholy of Resistance: The Films of Béla Tarr", p. 10.

23 Vladan Petkovic, "Simple and Pure: Béla Tarr, Director", *Cineuropa*, 3 April 2011 (http://cineuropa.org/2011/it.aspx?t=interview&lang=en&documentID=198131).

24 Doll's remarks were made at the symposium "Talking About Tarr", conducted in September 2007 at Facets Multi-Media in Chicago. She moderated the discussion, which featured David Bordwell, Scott Foundas and Jonathan Rosenblum. See *Talking About Tarr: A Symposium at Facets* (Chicago: Facets Multi-Media, 2008), p. 11.

25 McKibbin, "Cinema of Damnation: Negative Capabilities in Contemporary Central and Eastern European Film", *Senses of Cinema*, 8 February 2005, p. 3.

26 André Bazin, "The Ontology of the Photographic Image", in *What Is Cinema?*, trans. Hugh Gray (Berkeley: University of California Press, 1967), p. 15.

27 Quoted in Roger Ebert, "*Werckmeister Harmonies*: A Haunted Film About a Haunted Village", 8 September 2007 (http://rogerebert.suntimes.com/apps/pbcs.dll/article?AID=/20070908/70909001/1023&template=printart).

28 Sylviane Agacinski, *Time Passing: Modernity and Nostalgia*, trans. Jody Gladding (New York: Columbia University Press, 2003), p. 96.

29 Christoph Huber, "A Tale from the Bucharest Hospitals: Cristi Puiu on *The Death of Mister Lazarescu*", *Cinema Scope*, spring 2006. This interview appears in "Articles", a publication from Tartan Video accompanying Tartan's DVD of *The Death of Mr. Lazarescu*. Puiu's remarks are found on page 9 of "Articles".

30 Quoted in Eric Schlosser, "Interview with Béla Tarr", *Bright Lights Film Journal*, No. 30 (October 2000), p. 2 (http://www.brightlightsfilm.com/30/belatarr1.html).

31 J. Hoberman, "Brute Existence: *The Turin Horse*".

32 *Talking About Tarr: A Symposium at Facets* (Chicago: Facets Multi-Media, 2008), p. 11.

33 Quoted in Schlosser, "Interview with Béla Tarr", *Bright Lights Film Journal*, No. 30 (October 2000), p. 2 (http://www.brightlightsfilm.com/30/belatarr1.html).

34 McKibbin, "Cinema of Damnation: Negative Capabilities in Contemporary Central and Eastern European Film", *Senses of Cinema*, 8 February 2005, p. 1.

35 Jonathan Rosenbaum, "Voluptuous Misery", *Film Comment*, Vol. 47, No. 5 (September–October 2011), p. 50.

36 Quoted in Schlosser, "Interview with Béla Tarr", *Bright Lights Film Journal*, No. 30 (October 2000), p. 2 (http://www.brightlightsfilm.com/30/belatarr1.html).

37 *Talking About Tarr: A Symposium at Facets* (Chicago: Facets Multi-Media, 2008), p. 9.

38 On this question of closeness to people, see Hames, "The Melancholy of Resistance: The Films of Béla Tarr", *Kinoeye: New Perspectives on European Film*, p. 6.

39 Quoted by Jonathan Rosenbaum in *Talking About Tarr: A Symposium at Facets* (Chicago: Facets Multi-Media, 2008), p. 9.

40 *Talking About Tarr: A Symposium at Facets* (Chicago: Facets Multi-Media, 2008), p. 10.

41 *Talking About Tarr: A Symposium at Facets* (Chicago: Facets Multi-Media, 2008), p. 6.

42 Quoted in Petkovic, "Simple and Pure: Béla Tarr, Director", *Cineuropa*, 3 April 2011, p. 1.

43 Daly, "Waiting for the Prince: An Interview with Béla Tarr", *Senses of Cinema*, 13 February 2001, p. 1.

44 Quoted in Daly, "Waiting for the Prince: An Interview with Béla Tarr", *Senses of Cinema*, 13 February 2001, p. 2.

45 Quoted in Hames, "The Melancholy of Resistance: The Films of Béla Tarr", *Kinoeye: New Perspectives on European Film*, p. 10.

46 Quoted by David Bordwell in *Talking About Tarr: A Symposium at Facets* (Chicago: Facets Multi-Media, 2008), p. 8.

47 *Talking About Tarr: A Symposium at Facets* (Chicago: Facets Multi-Media, 2008), p. 9.

48 Quoted in Daly, "Waiting for the Prince: An Interview with Béla Tarr", *Senses of Cinema*, 13 February 2001, p. 2.

49 Tarr makes this statement in Vladan Petkovic, "Simple and Pure: Béla Tarr, Director", *Cineuropa*, 3 April 2011.

50 Hoberman, "Brute Existence: *The Turin Horse*".

51 Quoted in Roger Ebert, "*Werckmeister Harmonies*: A Haunting Film About a Haunted Village", 8 September 2007 (http://rogerebert.suntimes.com/apps/pbcs.dll/article?AID=/20070908/REVIEWS08/70909001/1023&template=printart).

52 *Talking About Tarr: A Symposium at Facets* (Chicago: Facets Multi-Media, 2008), p. 19.

53 *Talking About Tarr: A Symposium at Facets* (Chicago: Facets Multi-Media, 2008), p. 9.

54 "Gus Van Sant in the Light of Béla Tarr", Walker Art Center, 17 March 2008 (http://blogs. walkerart.org/filmvideo/2008/03/17gus-van-sant-light-bela-tarr/).

55 Stuart Klawans, "Good News from Romania? *12:08 East of Bucharest*", *The Nation*, 25 June 2007, p. 35.

56 Schlosser, "Interview with Béla Tarr", *Bright Lights Film Journal*, No. 30 (October 2000), p. 5 (http://www.brightlightsfilm.com/30/belatarr1.html).

57 Milan Kundera, "The Tragedy of Central Europe", trans. Edmund White, *New York Review of Books*, Vol. 31, No. 7 (26 April 1984).

58 Kundera, "The Tragedy of Central Europe", p. 8.

Index